Getting Spe

Getting Specific

Postmodern Lesbian Politics

Shane Phelan

University of Minnesota Press
Minneapolis
London

An earlier version of chapter 1 was previously published in *differences* 3, no. 1 (Spring 1991): 128–43. An earlier version of chapter 3 was previously published in *Signs* 18, no. 4 (Summer 1993): 765–90. Copyright 1993 by the University of Chicago. All rights reserved. Reprinted with permission.

Published by the University of Minnesota Press
111 Third Avenue South, Suite 290, Minneapolis, MN 55401
Printed in the United States of America on acid-free paper

Library of Congress Cataloging-in-Publication Data

Phelan, Shane.
  Getting specific : postmodern Lesbian politics / Shane Phelan.
    p.   cm.
  Includes bibliographical references (p.   ) and index.
  1. Lesbianism—Philosophy.   2. Lesbianism—Political aspects.
3. Feminist theory.   I. Title.
ISBN 0-8166-2109-8 (hc; acid-free paper)
ISBN 0-8166-2110-1 (pbk; acid-free paper)
HQ75.5.P47   1994
305.48'9664—dc20   94-17529

Contents

Acknowledgments

Many people contributed to this book. Christine Di Stefano, Ann Ferguson, Dennis Fischman, Nancy Love, and Diana Robin read and commented on the entire manuscript, and their critical effort and support are more important to me than I can ever say. Dennis read everything, wrote long letters, and nourished me. I would also like to thank Mark Blasius, Bill Chaloupka, Tom Dumm, Kathy Ferguson, Minrose Gwin, Kirstie McClure, Bill Norris, Ruth Salvaggio, Jana Sawicki, Christine Sierra, Vicky Spelman, Carolyn Woodward, and Iris Young for reading and critiquing chapters. Dorrie Mazzone, John Sharpe, and Edmundo Urrutia provided excellent research assistance and enthusiastic discussion. Sandi Gonzalez and Mary Morell helped me to think through some of the arguments presented here. Janaki Bakhle, my editor at the University of Minnesota Press, pushed me to think and calmed me when I panicked. This book is much better because of her efforts. Paul Schwankl and Laura Westlund did a fine job of copyediting, and I appreciate their help. Kaile Goodman read the manuscript with great care, saving me from embarrassment and misunderstanding.

Both the Political Science Department and the Women Studies Program at the University of New Mexico have been tremendously supportive over the years. I wish to thank the Women Studies Program for the semester I spent as research scholar; without that time to think, this book would be more jumbled than it is.

An earlier version of chapter 1 appeared in *differences: A Journal of Feminist Cultural Studies*. An earlier version of chapter 3 appeared in *Signs: Journal of Women in Culture and Society*. I would like to thank these journals for permission to reprint.

I dedicate this book to the lesbians of Albuquerque, New Mexico, who have shown me the pain and the possibilities of coalition politics. Without their work the storytelling that is political theory would have no life. To the extent that I know what I am talking about, it is because they have given me a chance to learn.

Preface

My first book, *Identity Politics: Lesbian Feminism and the Limits of Community*, was written five years ago. In it, I explored the way that themes of identity and community were developed and deployed within the loose collection of thinkers known as lesbian feminists. I concluded that lesbian feminist theorists had been mistaken in their construction of a too-monolithic, often essentialist "lesbian," and that lesbian feminist understandings of subjectivity and authenticity propelled the battles of the 1980s between "sex radicals" and "lesbian feminists." I concluded that community was a dangerous ideal in modernity, though one that moderns find inescapable. I thought then that I had had my say on the topic, and I expected to move on.

Identity Politics was published, as it happened, in the midst of a wave of critiques of lesbian feminism and of identity politics in general. These critiques eventually led me back to the question of lesbian identity and the politics that might foster different, more resilient, and potentially coalitional identities. I am a political theorist; as such I am driven by a love of theory and philosophy simply for their beauty, as well as by the desire to foster justice in the world. It became clear to me that my first book honored the first love above the second, and that more than critique was needed. In short, I needed to attempt an answer to the classic question of politics: What is to be done?

This awareness grew simultaneously with the conviction that the problem of global theory was not a problem just for some feminists, or some theorists, but in fact shadowed all our contemporary efforts to think through a democratic politics. The thread of specificity emerged as I sat listening to a debate on whether women should press legal and political strategies based on equality (understood roughly as sameness) or on difference from men. I knew then that neither was sufficient, that progressive strategies have to focus on specifics of differences and commonalities. This knowledge and this argument have been developed over the last several years among legal theorists but have been slower to develop in political theory. I realized that one of the problems that I had been describing in early lesbian feminism was the construction of a "lesbian" who was different from all nonlesbians but not significantly different from any other "lesbian." This was not a politics of alliance or coalition but of identity as homogeneity. Such a politics will always be brittle and nondemocratic, even as its participants try to treat one another well.

Identity politics began its life as a concept that distinguished newer social movements such as civil rights and feminism from earlier Left, class-centered, analyses. Identity politics was challenged from the Left as being too narrow, as unable to provide the basis for coalitions in the way they imagined class analysis could do. The point, however, was simple; as the Combahee River Collective put it, they needed to put their own identities and the oppressions that flowed from them at the center of their analysis. Identity politics was not "narrower" than class politics but broader: the refusal to subsume one movement into another offered greater possibilities for common action than an imperialist agenda resting on a binary opposition. To women of all sorts, as to gay men and men of color, class analysis did not fully address the specifics of their lives. Thus the lines were drawn: class analysis versus identity politics.

In the years since the term was coined, "identity politics" has come to signify a range of nonaligned movements and analyses (including non-Marxist class ones). These movements have, indeed, not coalesced very well. However, that failure is due not to their loss of a comprehensive theory but to a confluence of factors. First is the essentialism, whether of race, ethnicity, gender, or sexuality, that assures people that they are "really" one thing or another, so that identities become reified into solid chunks rather than fluid and negotiable locations. Second is the seductive power of American political thought and institutions, which reward interest-group activity and ignore or punish broader progressive agendas. These beliefs and institutions reinforce essentialist divisions even as they tug at those whose identities cut across the categories. Lacking a nonessentialist language of identity, persons must negotiate frontiers that theories cannot describe without seeming to destroy the identities as well. It is my intention to begin developing that language and thereby to restore to identity politics its original broader capacity for vision.

The past few years have witnessed the rise of ferocious attacks on identity politics. These attacks moved from legitimate concerns with the narrowness of earlier identity politics to a wholesale rejection of identity politics per se. As the mainstream media and American political processes began to distort new social movements into interest-group liberalism, identity politics indeed seemed unable to provide a basis for wholesale political transformation. Academic treatments of identity politics have often played unwittingly into this distortion, leaving us with movements that many academics participate in only with a sense of irony. As this trend rises, it is crucially important for those whose oppression is not adequately explained by earlier, Marxist accounts (that is, for all oppressed peoples) to make their oppression the first business of public debate and policy. This does not require essentialism, nor does it require wholesale separatism; both of these moves in fact weaken that public business. It does require acknowledgment of significant cultural differences and power differentials when they exist. If the lesbian feminists of the 1970s and 1980s were excessively narrow in their quest for community, the 1990s paradigm of "lesbian and gay" too often heralds a return to male-dominated politics. In this context, it is crucial that the insights of lesbian feminists into patriarchy and power not be abandoned. When lesbian and gay studies conferences have no preparation for or publicity of feminist caucuses, when "lesbian feminist" is a simple code for outdated theory in a way that "gay liberation" is not, there is a need for strong feminist voices.

As one commentator remarked, *Identity Politics* was the story of how not to do lesbian feminism, how not to think about identity and community. It is my hope that this book will contribute to a new dialogue about the place of lesbian identities and issues in a broader, feminist democratic politics, one that does not abandon identity politics or hopes for community, but that transforms them from sources of pain and division into resources for a just polity.

Introduction

What do lesbians want?

Feminists have debated for years over the nature of women's oppression and the aims of feminism. Should our aims be conceived in terms of equality with men, or should they be understood as the valorization of our differences from them? Are these mutually exclusive aims? Further, what should we do with differences among women? Are differences obstacles to solidarity, or are they resources? Is there a sort of equality we need, and another that must be rejected?

Among lesbians, these debates have a certain inflection. Do we want equality with heterosexual women? Or do we want to transform the social landscape, changing the nature of heterosexuality as well as getting "equal rights"? Should we work with straight women? With gay men? With straight men? When, and for what?

These are not questions that admit of simple answers. As stated, they may admit of no adequate answers at all. To address them, we need to ask other questions: Who are lesbians? What is lesbianism? What is/are the political location/locations of lesbians? How does movement for lesbians intersect with other movements—feminism, gay rights, antiracist work, nationalisms, socialism, democracy? Asking does not guarantee answers. What is guaranteed, in the United States of the 1990s, is that formulations such as "equality" versus "difference" will never get us anywhere.

This book centers on the notion of specificity and its importance for lesbian identity politics. I want to argue for an "identity politics" that is not based on "identitarian" theory. "Identity theory," in Theodor Adorno's terminology, is that which seeks to reduce diverse elements to a single point, either by subsuming differences or by interpreting the different in terms of a single one, "the same," which serves as an inviolable Archimedean point. One example of the first identitarian strategy is Hegel's attempt to understand everything as part of a

xiii

world spirit, a *Geist*, with a unity "beneath" the appearance of diversity; an example of the second strategy is Freud's psychology, based on the experience of the male, in which the female exists either as the inverse or, when not the inverse, as anomalous or mysterious, somehow lacking in humanity.

The problem of identitarianism has emerged in feminist theory at several points. The first point concerns the differences and similarities between men and women, and the basis for sexist domination. Feminists have been plagued by the question of the root(s) of sexist domination and its relation to other structures of inequality or oppression. They have also been divided on the goal of feminism: what would a just, free order be like? In this they share the concerns of all political theory.

In socialist feminist theory the question of the roots of domination led to lively debates between those advocating "single-system theories," those advancing "dual-systems theories," and those proposing "unified-systems theories." These theories all attempted universal explanations of the relations among sexism, capitalism, and, in some cases, racism and heterosexism. Biddy Martin's 1982 essay "Feminism, Criticism, and Foucault" advocated the abandonment of systems theory in favor of a more "local" analysis.[1] Since that time, there has been tremendous debate about the advantages or disadvantages of systemic theories based on universalizations or generalizations. I want to follow Martin, among others, by arguing that the rejection of totality and identitarian theory—the theoretical effort to incorporate and subsume all the diverse elements in a culture or system under a guiding principle—provides new avenues for theorists. The suggestion that "grand theory" may hinder freedom leads us to ask what other sort of theory there may be, what our aims are as theorists, and how that different theory would look.

The second front of controversy has concerned differences among women. Generally, when white bourgeois women have tried to understand nonwhite or non-middle-class women, either they have denied difference, celebrating the unity of feminine personality or the universality of male oppression of women, or, though acknowledging that not every woman is white and middle class, they have left mysterious the consequences of that difference. A similar phenomenon occurs when lesbianism is under discussion. Too often, feminists have written and acted as though "difference" was something that they experienced only as women, or as lesbians; heterosexuality and whiteness remain the unspoken norm, so that lesbians and women of color are encouraged to discuss their specific histories, but it is assumed that white heterosexual women need not. We can analogize this treatment to the differential exploration of heterosexuality and homosexuality; although both are specific experiences with particular etiologies and patterns, most study is given to the development that is seen as "problematic" or different, so that one gets the impression that heterosexuals just are, just grow, and that only deviation from heterosexuality requires explanation. Similarly, too many white women suppose that whiteness just "is," rather than being a specific experience that calls for interpretation. Or we assume that there is a unity called "men" and that all men have the same history, the same psychology, the same position regarding women, so we need not study their lives. The 1980s witnessed an exciting growth in controversy concerning these seeming nonquestions, but much remains to be done. Most specifically, white women need to inquire into their own histories, asking themselves about their own racism, classism, sexism, and heterosexism, rather than engaging in amateur anthropology toward people of color. This work has been done most visibly by Minnie Bruce Pratt, Elizabeth Spelman, and Adrienne Rich, and is now entering the social sciences through Ruth Frankenberg's work on "the construction of whiteness."[2]

Running on a bias to these debates is the controversy in both political theory and feminist theory concerning the cluster of ideas and thinkers labeled poststructuralist or postmodern. Included in this group are thinkers as diverse as Michel Foucault, Richard Rorty, Jacques Derrida, and Jean-François Lyotard. These writers can be spoken of as a group because of their shared focus on language and their rejection of traditional epistemological and ontological foundations for theory, including the interrogation of the modern subject, but they do not share a single, clear conception of the political implications of their work. Instead, they range from Rorty's "postmodern bourgeois pluralism" to Lyotard's more activist pluralism to Foucault's quasi-anarchist focus on opposition and resistance. The political implications of these various theorists' work have been the site of a great deal of controversy across and within disciplines and orientations. Debates have revolved around whether postmodern or poststructuralist thought gives us a new field for theory or simply removes the ground for any claims we have made about justice and equality. To opponents, the postmodern project appears dangerous. Linda Alcoff, for example, has argued that "post-structuralism undercuts our ability to oppose the dominant trend (and, one might argue, the dominant danger) in mainstream Western intellectual thought, that is, the insistence on a universal, neutral, perspectiveless epistemology, metaphysics, and ethics." For others, the new thought provides precisely the basis for such opposition. Most recently, Nancie Caraway's fine book *Segregated Sisterhood* presents a strong effort to ground her thinking as a white political theorist in the paradigms of Black feminism while also using the resources of poststructuralist theory.[3]

Although the postmodern project has become identified in theoretical jargon with the problematic of "difference," there is another, crucial thematic at work. This thematic centers around the replacement of grand narratives not with new narratives of eternal difference or Rorty's pluralist equivalent, but with what Foucault has labeled "subjugated knowledges." The emergence of these subjugated knowledges entails the rejection of grand, total theory in favor of local, specific theories—theories that do not aim at tying all the strands of life and history into one knot but rather try to locate each of us as the concrete embodiment of overlapping networks of power.

In the United States, feminist theorizing about lesbianism began with the premise that the personal is political. This framework was used to legitimate lesbianism as "feminist theory in action, as visible, integrated love of women and, therefore, of oneself."[4] This view has been manifested in the idea that lesbians are "better feminists" than heterosexual, bisexual, or asexual women;[5] in the belief that men, nonfeminist women, or nonlesbian feminists cannot be trusted as allies; in the argument that problems of racism, classism, and other systems of discrimination are the result of sexism, and therefore a lesser problem among "woman-identified women"; and in various other ways. Such theories have also served as the basis for codes of authentic lesbian existence and identity. Though not mandating these uses, the early recognition of the connection between the personal and the political was often transformed into overarching explanations of every aspect of lesbian lives. Whether explicitly separatist or not, these theories have worked to turn our communities inward rather than to propel us toward alliances and coalitions with others.[6]

Recognizing these difficulties, more recent lesbian theorists such as Gloria Anzaldúa, Diana Fuss, Judith Butler, and Teresa de Lauretis have begun to develop theoretical bases for new interpretations of lesbian identity and sexuality. While retaining "lesbian" as a meaningful category, they have each worked against reification of lesbians and toward views of lesbianism as a critical site of gender deconstruction rather than as a unitary experience with a singular political meaning. Anzaldúa's revolutionary discussions of "mestiza consciousness," a consciousness that arises from living within multiple cultures, have provided new ground for understandings of lesbian subjectivity and politics.[7] Fuss's treatment of "identity as difference," containing "the specter of non-identity within it," links lesbian identity and politics to philosophical issues of identity and difference.[8] Butler's argument that sexual identity is better seen as socially constructed, "neither fatally determined nor fully artificial and arbitrary," leads us to view lesbianism not as an essence or a thing outside of time and place but as a critical space within social structures.[9] De Lauretis's notion of "eccentric subjectivity" attempts to locate a position for lesbians "at once inside and outside" hegemonic institutions and discourses.[10] All these theorists share in the process of feminist discourse on lesbianism but focus on the differences, the gaps and shifts, among women. Those differences and gaps do not preclude alliances and shared interests, but they make these alliances something to produce rather than a given; "being lesbian" provides a basis for mutual recognition but does not guarantee it.

The theories of Anzaldúa, Fuss, Butler, and de Lauretis, though highly academic in presentation, seem to me not only more "faithful" to the texture of lesbian lives than are earlier theories of lesbian identity, but also stronger as supports for political change. My argument rests on the belief that widespread social and political change requires interaction with and intervention in what Nancy Miller calls "the dominant social text."[11] This change is necessarily a local operation, one involving political action at particular locations in our lives independent of global or universal theories. Miller argues that such operations will be ineffective without global theories behind them, but I believe that these local operations are positive, fruitful avenues for our politics, and that more limited theories help us to recognize that as power is diffuse, resistance must be as well.

This book is not, however, oriented around the question of "to be" (postmodern) or "not to be." Rather than sharpen the taxonomy of contemporary theory, I hope to use the insights generated through recent debates to develop a better theoretical perspective on lesbian identity and politics. Specificity enables us to focus on all the issues currently dividing the camps without prematurely closing debate.

Some will read my call for specificity as a return to liberal individualism. Within the confines of theory and politics in the United States, we are pressed to choose: individual or collective? liberal or communitarian (of whatever stripe)? These choices are as false as those of modern/postmodern and same/different. Getting specific enables us to examine and value individual lives, and to celebrate individuality, without the detour of individualism. As Tocqueville recognized, individualism endangers the individuality it claims to protect. Individuals are not abstractions; there is no such being as "the individual." Atomistic liberalism destroys the social supports needed to foster individuals, and individualism simply hides that destruction. Liberalism cannot account either for the systematic nature of social oppressions or for the true uniqueness of human personality. Thus although some will collapse individuals into "individualism" or "the individual," I hope readers will search instead for a fuller understanding of individuality as something that occurs within societies, amid other persons.

Many of the best discussions of the problems of diversity and overlapping networks of domination have occurred within feminist theory. Although political theorists have made allusions to difference, the concrete work of elaborating differences and the way they play out in our lives has been done by feminists. This book draws together the worlds of "high theory," predominantly male, and feminist theory and practice. Writers such as Elizabeth Spelman, Gayatri Spivak, bell hooks, Gloria Anzaldúa, and Audre Lorde have drawn from the conjunction of theory and experience to produce rich accounts of the interweave of oppression and power in individual lives. To political theorists their work offers direction and inspiration. A dialogue between these groups is long overdue and will be supplied in this book. I will argue that a practice of specificity enables us to further that conversation and to transform both theory and practice.

Feminist theory has consistently challenged the divisions between public and private, and the practice of identity politics is an interrogation of power and responsibility in areas of life overlooked by other theories and practices. In the past twenty years many women have written about their experiences of sexism, heterosexism, racism, classism, and all the other barriers and lines of hierarchy in contemporary societies. Their writing has challenged the division between theory and literature, and in so doing it calls into question the idea of theory itself. The distinction between philosophy and literature has been a gendered line of power; although women's capacity to write "great literature" has been questioned, many more women are acknowledged as "writers" than as "thinkers," that is, philosophers. This imbalance is not simply due to the prejudicial rejection of women. It also rests on the fact that many women of all races and classes (and many men as well) have seen modern philosophy as sterile and inherently false in form and intent, and therefore not worth doing. "Doing philosophy" or "doing theory" must mean something other than "abstract" analysis if it is to be meaningful.

This challenge has not been unitary and simple, however. Controversies over the nature and status of theory in general have been replicated within feminism. The modern idea of theory as something basically ahistorical (even when dealing with history), as schematic rather than narrative, participates in a hierarchy. In this mode, theory is the universalization of which individual narratives are instantiations. The unspoken assumptions that theory is opposed to literature and is somehow more comprehensive than literature, combined with the implicit belief that comprehensiveness is a primary virtue, have contributed to a two-tier system of citizenship in feminist theory. On the top tier are the largely white, middle-class literary and social theorists, who rely heavily on the work of male thinkers. On the lower tier are the writers and activists who draw from their lives and remain in those lives in their work. It is not historically accidental that most feminists of color are in the second group. Barbara Christian has noted that the "new emphasis on literary critical theory" emerged "just when the literature of peoples of color, black women, Latin Americans, and Africans began to move to 'the center.' "[12] She argues that "people of color have always theorized," but they have done so in forms "quite different from the Western form of abstract logic," and so have not been heard.[13] So we find that debates over epistemology are also political debates, arguments over who shall be heard and in what voice they must speak to be heard.

Feminists have been more ambiguous in critiquing the relation between philosophy and politics. Politics has often had within feminism the same connotations of interest or power versus philosophy's right as it does within white middle-class America at large, but this has not always been the case. The very idea of "identity politics" challenges the older pluralist landscape of public/private, and more recent explorations by theorists such as Bonnie Honig and Chantal Mouffe have reminded us of the older sense of politics as collective action for a common good.[14] This reminds us that a "truth" that divides interest from justice is inevitably given to oscillations between idealism and cynicism, satisfying neither our need for wholeness and decency nor the realities of an imperfect world.

Getting specific means challenging the lines between philosophy, politics, and literature. It means acknowledging that the public/private split has prevented all of us from seeing the lines of power in our lives and addressing them as matters of common concern. It means more than simple acknowledgment of such general statements; it means examining our own individual lives for these lines and effects of power. A theory that retains in practice the splits between public and private, or among literature, philosophy, and politics, will replicate those divisions no matter how thoroughly they are discussed in the abstract. Thus, this work must begin with concrete descriptions of our lives and identities in the specific terms of race, class, gender, sexuality, and ethnicity that structure it. Though discussion will not rest there alone, without these examinations and descriptions we will be left with our good will and our abstractions. These are a good start, but they break down under the daily pressure of political activity and challenges to one's identity and privilege. Getting specific can transform these challenges from threats to openings, by revealing potential linkages and possibilities for immediate action in our individual lives. Such revelation must occur if lesbians are to avoid either simple interest-group assimilation or nationalistic separatism. I hope that this book will provide avenues for understanding new social movements as a renewal of citizenship, and further debate about the practice of democratic politics in a postmodern world.

Chapter 1

Specificity: Beyond Equality and Difference

In *Thus Spake Zarathustra*, Zarathustra replies to a hunchback's demand for a "cure" by suggesting that such a cure would take away his "spirit"—what makes him distinctively him. William Connolly elaborates on the meaning of this passage when he says that the deformity is not to be pitied or to be remedied: both pity and the "insistence that the hunchback must be helped to reach the plateau of normality" are based in "repugnance to difference and the drive to regularize everyone according to some fictive model of normality."[1] Nietzsche's hunchback lives in a world that assumes that salvation takes the form of being like the rest and that there is a homogeneous "rest" to be like. This assumption can produce only resentment, frustration, and self-pity, forces that bleed the real life and power out of the hunchback. Once these are in place, appeals to be proud, to take charge of one's life, sound hollow and uncaring.[2] We would be callous in simply telling people to enjoy their position. And yet, a true friend will neither pity the hunchback nor seek to make him like others. Zarathustra teaches the contingency of all norms, and in so doing he teaches the value of each of our positions and knowledges. Our value does not rest in approaching "the" norm, nor does it rest in our potential for being other than what we are; it rests in being well what we are.

This has been a crucial lesson for feminists. The first burst of white feminism in the postwar West focused on women's right to the prerogatives and options of (white) men. This strand of "equality" thinking was epitomized in Simone de Beauvoir's *Second Sex* and Betty Friedan's *Feminine Mystique*. Though very different in their intellectual roots, both the existentialist de Beauvoir and the liberal Friedan spoke of women's difference from men as a lack. The focus of political action in this phase was toward legislation eliminating sex-based barriers to women's participation in "the public realm," including traditionally masculine jobs.

Neither de Beauvoir nor Friedan took lesbianism seriously as a social position meriting discussion, but feminists have had similar arguments concerning lesbians. These arguments are epitomized in "equal rights" struggles, where the particulars of lesbian sexuality are often minimized in favor of privacy rights, nondiscrimination ordinances, and the like. The position of heterosexuals is never called into question; the claim is simply "Me too, we're not really different."

Proving that we are "really like men" or "potentially like heterosexuals" and therefore fit to share their power or be their equals has been a losing battle, because it perpetuates our self-hatred and fails to challenge (hetero)sexism. We can never be free by trying to be other than what we are; we can never be men as well as men can, and we will never be "women" just as heterosexual women might be. We will always be second-class men and deviant "women."

Equally important is the fact that most men are not "men" either. The "men" of white feminism have too often been white, middle-class, heterosexual men; white women, especially, did not seek equality with nondominant men. This blindness not only splintered the women's movement through racism and heterosexism; it also contributed to inadequate theorizing about the position(s) and problems of women.

In the 1970s many feminists began to argue that they did not want to give up "being women" to achieve equality and dignity. At the same time women of color, working-class women, and lesbians began pointing to the racism, heterosexism, and classism in a movement that seemed designed to give white bourgeois heterosexual women the privileges of their male counterparts at the cost of "other" people. They pointed out, too, that this strategy was not new for white feminists.[3] At the same time, the issue of lesbianism became salient for feminism. The challenges presented by lesbians were not, and could not be, dealt with simply by appeals to equality.[4]

Thus, feminism in the 1970s began to search for positive images of women, to search for "our" own strength rather than trying to legitimate "ourselves" by copying men. This effort is the source of "difference feminism," in which, nevertheless, the temptation remained to find the universal in the particulars, to find "the" difference that all women shared vis-à-vis all men. This tendency manifested a different face of racism and classism in feminism, a "cultural imperialism" that denies differences in the name of the one, true difference.[5]

The gradual realization on the part of white women that the "we" of women is highly problematic has been matched by exciting and challenging theorization of the domination involved in the "logic of the same." What has been lost in the academic rush to difference, though, is the goal of equality. American feminist theory has been articulated as part of a movement for freedom and equality, but white middle-class women have splintered between the "difference feminists" and the "equality feminists," with little sense of how to hold these together.

Women of color and working-class women, both lesbian and non-lesbian, have had different debates. Very little theorizing from non-dominant women argues that men as a group are the oppressors and that sexism is the originary or deepest oppression; instead, there is a more complex, more subtle understanding of the conflictual nature of gender relations. This is so because the position of their male partners and family members has been less enviable than that of men of the dominant race and class. No one seriously argues, for instance, that if black women were treated equally with black men their problems would be over. Instead, the problem for nonprivileged women has been that of defending a complex vision against, on the one hand, charges that feminism divides groups that need unity for struggle, that women's claims for equality or dignity play into the hands of white men or capitalists, and, on the other, that solidarity with men of color or white working-class men is counterfeminist. As many women of color have insisted, the divisive influence is not feminism or men but the resistance to concern for women's needs and voices that alienates them from male partners and from white feminists.

The position of white lesbians qua lesbians is not quite the same as that of women of color or working-class women. Race and class are lines that cut across gender through family networks, thus usually producing whole families of "the same" race or class,[6] but sexuality is not. It is simply wrong to say that the relation of gay men to lesbians is the same as that of Chicanos to Chicanas. In fact, our sexuality usually divides us rather than uniting us. We are united not by sexuality but by oppression based on categories of sexuality. We may thus share a legal and political interest, but this is not a cultural or a familial link.

The answer to the divisions among women, and among lesbians, is not "bigger" theory, drawn more comprehensively so that "everyone" fits. It is, ironically, more modest theory. Bigger theories make sense only if those of whom they speak base understanding and practice on them, and that requirement in turn presents a political problem: how might we acquire these converts? How might we base a democratic politics on theories designed to subsume other voices? We can't. Instead, a democratic politics that fosters social change will work through a theoretical practice that sounds modest but allows for the involvement and creativity of citizens. Rather than build a total theory and proselytize for it, we must converse rather than convert, moving from the bottom up to make connections rather than defining them a priori.

Essentialism and Cultural Imperialism

The complex, careful analysis and action that arise from the experiences of women who are not privileged by race, class, or sexuality have already borne substantial fruit for feminism. White bourgeois women have not always kept up with this development because we have no material reality pressing these facts home. In fact, we have the opposite; we are the bearers of the hegemonic, that which is so privileged that it appears unquestionable. The work of women of color has served to highlight the specificity of race, class, and gender in their lives, but very little comparable work has been done by white women. Minnie Bruce Pratt and Adrienne Rich were among the first, and their work has a power that has not yet been equaled.[7] Too often do we continue to talk as though "difference" in our (white, middle-class) lives does not include race or class.

Further, the academic training that is accessible to most of us teaches us that good social or political theories are those that are simplest, that cover the most data with the fewest qualifications and complications. For this reason, the value of specific analysis is suspect to many of us; such analysis is "descriptive" rather than "theoretical." The idea of specificity can function both as a methodological precept and as a substantive goal for politics, challenging both our theorizing and our practices. Getting specific can bring together many of the currently diverse threads of feminism, and thus it deserves serious consideration and development in the years ahead.

In her book *Inessential Woman*, Elizabeth Spelman explicates the problem of cultural imperialism in white philosophy and feminist theory. She discusses the ways in which philosophers, male and female, ancient and modern, feminist and nonfeminist, have assumed for their analyses that "women" are females of the privileged race/class. For example, Aristotle discusses the difference between men and women in the household in a manner that implies that the woman being discussed is a freewoman. Female slaves do not count as "women" but are subsumed under the category "slave." Much later, Simone de Beauvoir chooses to discuss only the situation of white middle-class women in *The Second Sex* because she is aware that in fact there are multiple possibilities for the social construction of womanhood across races and classes. She understands that the concrete lives of women and men vary across cultures, and that relations across race or class will not be the same as those within a given group. Yet, Spelman argues, de Beauvoir suggests (if only by neglect) that gender relations are the same in any race or class, so that the concrete details are simply variations on a universal theme. De Beauvoir thus leads us to conclude that sexism operates similarly within any given class or race. More importantly, she sets the scene for later white feminist theory when she argues that sexism operates only among those who are not oppressed in other ways, that "sexual oppression is nullified when men and women are subject to other forms of oppression."[8] Thus she can contrast the position of "women" with that of Blacks, Jews, or workers.

In the simplistic construction of and focus upon gender that is the target of Spelman's work, feminism has been about liberating "women." However, it has not been clear what liberation would mean. If liberation is a matter of achieving equality with men, we must ask which men we wish to be equal to or different from.[9] If it amounts to celebration of our unique womanhood, we must ask, whose unique womanhood? The history of feminist politics has too often been one of enforcement of codes of womanhood within communities. Spelman notes that the idea of an "essential womanness" ironically results in "making women inessential in a variety of ways," for "if there is an essential womanness that all women have and have always had, then we needn't know anything about any woman in particular. . . . If all women have the same story 'as women,' we don't need a chorus of voices to tell the story."[10] Such an idea not only serves to minimize the perception of differences among women, but also obscures the debate about the effect of such differences on the similarities, as well as the fact that "not all participants in the debate get equal air time or are invested with equal authority."[11] The effort to construct a singular "woman" will inevitably leave out the lives of those who do not have the hegemonic power of description. This translates not only into bad theory but into bad politics, as white middle-class women set the legal and political agenda for "women."

Thus white middle-class feminist theorists need to integrate other differences into our analyses, not as adjuncts to studies of women's oppression, but into the heart of them. White feminists cannot pretend that we suffer from generic sexism; Spelman makes clear that the "generic" position is a product of power, and that as long as white feminists treat our position as generic, our feminism as "feminism," we will continue to obscure the situations and thoughts of other women, with implications as racist as those of the "first wave" of feminists who tried to buy their rights at the expense of racial and ethnic minorities. Now that women such as Angela Davis and Paula Giddings have documented this racism, there can be no excuse for such cultural imperialism.

So the first front of theorization lies along the description of who "we" are: "We need to unpack what it means to talk about oneself 'as a woman,' not use the phrase to suggest that there is no unpacking to do, or that even after unpacking we'd find that underneath all their cultural differences women are the same."[12] For some, this move raises the specter of the end of feminism: "If we can't isolate gender from race or class, if we can't talk about the oppression women face as women, or about the experience of women as women, isn't feminism left without a foundation, without a specific focus?"[13]

This dilemma is curiously reminiscent of that posed by the various positions and techniques labeled "postmodern." For the modern, postmodern theories pose the danger of the end of theory. Sheldon Wolin, for example, argues that Foucault's work destroys the possibility of theory because it fails to answer the "fundamental political and theoretical question that used to be asked of a radical thinker . . . has he identified the crucial point of vulnerability in the system(s) of power he seems to be opposing?"[14] By this criterion of theory, Foucault's description of and prescriptions for what he calls the "specific intellectual" can only be read as inadequate, and the more general postmodern critique of "grand theory," and of the need for metaphysical or essentialist foundations, draws charges of nihilism, passivity, relativism, and so on.

Among (mostly white, middle-class) feminists, the analogue to these difficulties has been the fear that a feminism that "complicates" the issue of gender—our foundation—will weaken our political position. This fear leads to two different theoretical strategies. In the first, theorists may claim that race and class are important distinctions, but that they are theoretically irrelevant for feminism; that there is a core of common experience or nature among women that transcends the "artificial" barriers erected by men. Here, all women are aligned against men of all sorts, a scenario most clearly (but not exclusively) presented in the antipornography literature.[15] In the second strategy, race and class are structures that feminists must deal with, but by subsuming them under sexist oppression—"Sexism is the root of all other oppressions"—so that *the* job for feminists is to eliminate sexism.[16]

The two strategies share the desire to build *the* theory, find *the* thread, that will link all women "as women." This desire is also at work in the attempt to cross sexualities, to unite women across the split of lesbian/straight by finding a common experience or psychology.[17] Spelman's work is radical in its suggestion that such an approach is fundamentally flawed. Rather than eliminate or "transcend" differences, Spelman argues that we must recognize them, that feminism "must specify which men and women it is talking about" and "must stop using language that suggests that a white middle-class woman's position vis-à-vis her white middle-class husband is no different than her position vis-à-vis men from other groups."[18]

Spelman urges us to drop the word "difference." She argues that "difference" has come to be used in ways that suggest and thereby reinforce the sense that feminist theory and practice is white women's turf; "difference" never seems to mean white or middle-class, but rather signifies that which is not, just as it has come to mean that which is not male. The effect in both cases is to privilege the hegemonic, "generic" group, a privilege that manifests itself as absence, as the unquestionable.

Specificity

Neither "equality" nor "difference" can get at actual women's varying concerns and needs. Both terms privilege the white male as generic. Both locate women in relation to men, and nonwhites in relation to whites. In place of these Spelman advocates the use of "heterogeneity." She aims at dealing with this problem by emphasizing, not the way(s) in which those who are not white middle-class women are different from those who are, but by locating all women on the same plane of otherness toward one another.

Spelman urges feminists to articulate their particular positions in society and economy. Supporting Simone de Beauvoir's declared rejection of the "metaphysical nugget of pure womanhood that defines all women as women," she argues that "we cannot decide prior to actual investigation of women's lives what they do or do not have in common."[19] De Beauvoir betrays her own quest by taking the position of one group of women to be the standard, a move that Spelman links to de Beauvoir's somatophobia.[20] The rejection of the body, of concrete existence, allows those of us in hegemonic positions to imagine that we are "really all the same." As Adrienne Rich points out, "color-blindness" is really "white solipsism," in which whites "would look at a Black woman and see her as white."[21] Spelman suggests that this white solipsism can be overcome by acknowledging in any analysis just which women we are talking about, and just which women we are. A crucial component or manifestation of white hegemony is the failure to identify oneself as white; just as men are not in fact generic humans, so white women are not generic women. There is no generic person; attempts to claim such a ground do not extend a welcoming hand to others, but serve only to identify oneself as privileged.[22]

The concept of heterogeneity calls upon us to be mindful of difference by locating ourselves within networks of differential power and meaning. Heterogeneity thus urges us toward specificity, its crucial element; without specificity, "heterogeneity" becomes just another word for difference. The focus on specifics aims at destroying white bourgeois hegemony by making it manifest, just as feminism has aimed at destroying male hegemony by highlighting and questioning it. An emphasis on specificity in our analyses and practices aims at disrupting hegemonies, calling out differences for question, and rendering all people accountable for their positions and actions.

One of the virtues of such an emphasis is its redefinition of the important categories for recognition and analysis. We need both to specify, through categorical reference, our location in various systems of power, and to insist that there is more to us than the categories, that we have an integrity that cannot be captured in those terms. Specificity is about recognition of differences, but talk of difference has too often left us with little beyond a suspect pluralism. We need structural analyses of particular differences to show us how our various positions within these structures limit and guide our ideas and actions; in this effort, specificity requires the continuing articulation of theories of oppression(s). We cannot and should not, however, hope to build theories that will completely explain each of us; my sister is not me, though our social origins are shared down to many minute descriptors. Specificity demands the simultaneous exploration of categories of social marks and orders and attention to the unique or the individual. Specificity is the methodological guide to finding individuality in community.

Adrienne Rich makes these points clear in her essay on the politics of location. Rather than by means of a distant or abstract theoretical work, Rich explores her position in the world and the possibility of theorizing it through the essay form. She combines meditations on the body with thoughts on the inadequacy of theorizing from a global/ universal "woman," looking to examine the conditions of her creation and self-creation as a woman, a Jew, a lesbian, a feminist. She pauses to consider the possible connections between cold war thinking, "the attribution of all our problems to an external enemy," and "a form of feminism so focused on male evil and female victimization that it, too, allows for no differences among women, men, places, times, cultures, conditions, classes, movements."[23] She seeks to understand her relation to people in the third world through examining patterns of history, coming to know why and how her neighbors are not "like her" but are inescapably part of her life. She makes an almost revolutionary statement of responsibility: "As a woman I have a country; as a woman I cannot divest myself of that country merely by condemning its government or by saying three times 'As a woman my country is the whole world.' "[24]

Rich's "politics of location" is less a politics of "difference" than one of specificity. Although in fact the two are never fully separable (for a specificity of location is possible only through differentiation), a theoretical formulation in terms of "difference" does not force the thinker to remember the ground of difference, the networks of meaning and power within which differences appear. There is nothing wrong with thinking about difference, but without the imperative of specificity it can too easily become a vague pluralism or fastidious deconstruction. Specificity acknowledges political location and the construction of self that a given location fosters, thus countering abstract individualist politics. Rich does not, however, reduce her personality and consciousness to that location. Her specificity includes systemic effects of power and meaning, but it does not collapse individuality by acknowledging these. She thus challenges the terms of debates between "liberals," who are seen as the champions of abstract equality and freedom, and those who may recognize our embeddedness at the expense of transcendence.

Specificity and Bridge Building

Specificity thus has value as a political tool. It may form the basis of a new intellectual coalition among feminists, enabling us to cross some of the boundaries currently dividing "radical" from "socialist" from "postmodern" feminists. The impulse of radical feminism has largely been to insist on the wholeness of women and on a natural bond between them, broken only by patriarchy. The search for authenticity has too often led radical feminists "outside culture," to a place that cannot understand the divisions among women except as tricks of men. As writers such as Audre Lorde and Bernice Johnson Reagon have noted, such an analysis serves to weaken the unity of women rather than promote it.

Socialist feminists have generally rejected as ahistorical and individualist the authenticity described by radical feminists. However, writers such as Heidi Hartmann and Alison Jaggar have continued to develop "systems theories," whether single, dual, or multiple, to account for the relations between sexist oppression and other oppressions. While this has been important and valuable work, we need to consider Biddy Martin's caution that the choice between various systems theories is still doomed to miss the many local and specific centers of social control and power. If thinkers such as Foucault are correct in their belief that power in the contemporary West is different from earlier powers in its microcontrol, its antisystemic nature, then we need theories and methodologies that can recognize this power and provide foci for resistance.

Feminists whose work has been informed by postmodernism and poststructuralism have objected to both the radical feminist idea of the authentic founding subject and the earlier socialist feminist focus on systems theory.[25] Most people accepting the label "postmodern" (and many who would not) would agree that power resides in language (though not exclusively so, contrary to their opponents' characterizations); more distinctively, postmodernists reject "a polemics of patriarchy which conceives of exclusive and exhaustive divisions between oppressor and oppressed, between a dominant or false and a subversive or true discourse."[26] Chris Weedon objects that general laws "render contradictions and differences invisible" and "inevitably set limits to femininity."[27] Sandra Harding's criticisms of feminist-standpoint epistemologies have centered on the simple links between consciousness and location assumed by these theories, as well as the unitary nature of the subject presumed.[28]

More local, specific analysis then offers the possibility of locating the ways in which (some) women are silenced or erased and the roles (some) women play in that. It enables us to intervene at particular points, rather than being swamped with despair at the magnitude of the task before us.[29] It also provides the strongest critique of bureaucratization and the disciplinary dark sides to humanist activities and ideals. In this respect, postmodern theory intersects with the political and theoretical agendas of many women of color, though nonacademic theorists of all races have often professed disdain or lack of concern for academic theory.[30]

How might getting specific conjoin these diverse attitudes and theories?

A specific focus relies on and develops the local analyses and actions promoted by many postmodern thinkers. It suggests that each of us is located at, indeed *is*, the intersection of various specific discourses and structures, and that we each possess knowledges produced in that location. It enables us to evaluate our position in relation to those systems and to make claims based on that position without the need for hyperintellectualized epistemological claims to justify our voices and experiences. At this level, a specific focus functions to open lines of communication between knowledges and knowers that have been held apart by the logic of social theories. As Foucault has argued, although "global" theories have provided "useful tools for local research," they have done so almost in spite of their stated purpose: "the attempt to think in terms of a totality has in fact proved a hindrance to research,"[31] for "global" theories inevitably betray themselves in their desire to cover the world, to produce a totality, because they participate unwittingly in existing regimes. Foucault argues, rather, for a "local criticism" that is attuned to the "insurrection of subjugated knowledges." These knowledges "were concerned with a *historical knowledge of struggles*," of "hostile encounters which even up to this day have been confined to the margins of knowledge."[32]

One of these hostile encounters has been that between white middle-class feminists and other women, whether feminist or not, of whatever class. The history of the American women's movement in the nineteenth and early twentieth centuries was one of racism, classism, and nativism, and the failure of contemporary white women to deal with this history understandably has left nonwhite women suspicious or hostile; continued neglect can only confirm white feminists' unwillingness to part with their privilege. An emphasis on specificity works to counter this situation by mandating that *all* articulate and carefully examine their position in various economies of power.

Although specificity mandates conscious location of the self, it also gestures to that in each of us which is irreducible to categories. It suggests that even after we have practiced a politics that acknowledges certain categories of difference, there will always be more to us than those categories. We are specific individuals as well as members of multiple groups. The demand for specificity thus provides recognition of the individual, even as it refutes the supposition of a unitary subject. This endeavor should be attractive to gynocentric feminists, who write so eloquently of the free female self; it asserts that one of our goals must be to acknowledge the unique mystery of our being(s). A focus on specificity is not meant to remove the person from her context, though. Indeed, it is opposed to classical variants of individualism that aim at abstraction from social context. Specificity as a methodological precept for social theory suggests that we must locate

ourselves; our individuality does not substitute for social and historical position, but resides within it. Specificity can thus be useful to
those who attempt to understand the interlocking or simultaneous
grids of oppressions and hierarchies experienced by members of modern societies. It suggests that the question we must ask is not simply
whether people are "the same" or "different" within a particular
structure, but *how* they are similar or different and what the implications of that are. Getting specific thus continues the socialist feminist
quest to understand the relations between economic systems and
other structures while eliminating the expectation that an adequate
theory will cover every instance, every aspect of life. It also allows for
a multiplicity of levels of systems, from overarching macrostructures
such as capitalism to more local, specific structures such as the organization of a particular barrio school, without simply reducing the latter
to an instance of the former.

Specificity and Antibureaucratic Politics

Many might begin to worry at this point. What sort of specification
are we talking about? Who does the specifying? Does specification not
advance the invasion of modern individualizing power into the self?
Those persuaded by Foucault's analyses of modern power may find
the best strategy one of silence and anonymity, of refusing to specify
anything about oneself. If "representation and discourses are themselves acts of power, acts of division and exclusion, which give themselves as knowledge,"[33] then it may seem that the path to freedom lies
in silence. Foucault's work shows us that discourses of power can operate on us whether we speak or not; more importantly, it suggests
that resistance is always possible. Such resistance may also be
strengthened by women's claims to their own specificities rather than
to our common, cosmic bond. Biddy Martin explains that "what is
crucial is the capacity to shift the terms of the struggle, the ability to
see our position within existing structures but respond from somewhere else." The lack of organization and clarity in the women's
movement "may very well represent fundamentally more radical and
effective responses to the deployment of power in our society than the
centralization and abstraction that continue to plague Leftist thinking
and strategy."[34]

And this, indeed, may be the political edge of specificity: its antibu-
reaucratic, decentralized nature. If we think about institutionalizing
specificity as a norm, this feature becomes immediately apparent.

"Specificity is all well and good," we might say, "but how can we devise a legal system that allows for such a focus? Doesn't the law rest on generalization and abstraction, on categorization of persons and offenses? How can we devise a bureaucracy that recognizes specificity?"

There are two responses to be offered here. First, we might remember that there was a time, before the advent of the modern state, before the ideal of abstract universalization as the model of principled reason, when the law was not as tightly wedded to the ideal of universality as it is today. The notion of the common law, with its focus on precedent, custom, and locality rather than abstract formulations and formal statutes, is one example of this earlier way of thinking. The common law required judges to interpret broad principles and precedents for specific cases much more actively than does modern statute law. Its force and meaning relied directly upon the communal self-understandings of particular communities.[35]

A second, and perhaps more immediately political, response follows from the first: our project should be not to make an ideal that fits our present system but to speak and think in ways that cannot be fit into it so that we must change it. To do so requires that we critically analyze our dialogue and its context even as we engage in it. If courts and bureaucracies cannot do their work in a way that fosters substantive justice, then we need to challenge the legitimacy of the bureaucratic form. This challenge requires the development of active solidarity and citizenship among feminists; bureaucracy and its twin of individualization are both the products and producers of isolation among citizens. Legal theorists such as Patricia Williams and Martha Minow are developing this challenge through more specific examinations of the social contexts in which legal issues arise, moving from bureaucratic individualist identifications of particular people as "the problem" to analyses of systems of relationship.[36]

One of the problems facing those who have fought for equality is that bureaucratically administered equality produces not equality of freedom but equality of domination. As Kathy Ferguson has argued, "the feminist movement is divided internally, as are most major movements for social change, between those who are primarily interested in gaining access to established institutions and those who aim at the transformation of those institutions."[37] Liberal feminism, through its interest in achieving equality with white men, "has appealed to the bureaucratic apparatus of the state and of the corporate world to integrate women into the public sphere."[38] As a result, its critique of the dominant discourse "has now largely become a voice subservient to that discourse."[39] Because it fails to acknowledge the power of bureaucracy in modern life and relies on "juridicolegal discourse," liberal feminism cannot resist this fate. Those women who know that the problem is not simply marginality in relation to this discourse but the existence of the discourse itself will not rally around this sort of feminism.

While the aim of "difference" or "gynocentric" feminism may be, among other things, the end of bureaucratic organization and thought, its development in the United States has too often resulted in withdrawing from the larger world rather than in struggling to change it. To the extent that radical feminists are focused on building a "women's community" at the expense of other forms of political action, they become less effective at real transformation of society. Within these communities women are free to celebrate their "difference" from the world of modern patriarchal bureaucracies, and that celebration is important. Without entering that world and struggling with it, however, we have no opportunity for lasting safety beyond that of the ghetto.

What is required is a rethinking of the grounds of individuality and its location in communities. Many people have been engaged in this rethinking, challenging the ways in which bureaucracies destroy possibilities for citizenship, for common action, and thus for a secure self. Theories and methodologies with a commitment to specificity locate us as individuals, providing us with a context and a history that bureaucracies, and too often we ourselves, would deny. Insisting on thinking "specifically" will help us resist bureaucratization without throwing us into a free-floating space of authentic selves. This is a tremendous challenge, and an essential one if we are to truly transform our lives rather than escape from them.

The drive for equality has served to assimilate, which is to subjugate, those who are not members of hegemonic groups. Ironically, middle-class feminists' theoretical work on "difference" has too often foreclosed appreciation of differences among women, by constructing a story about "our" unified difference. It thus shifts us from one sort of subjugation to another; whereas the first sort simply shuts us out or up, the second incorporates us on its terms. Neither of these is acceptable. The differences become codified and clichéd too easily. The construction of a "woman" who is the opposite of and better than "man" results in, and mirrors, the neglect of differences among women.

The call for specificity is a call for us to recognize our multiple identifications and locations in power. Specific analyses and politics do not simply rest with or celebrate "difference," both because difference alone is not a sufficient guide for our politics and because difference does not lead us to value what we share. We need to hold together structural analyses of inequalities with a recognition of the unique, multiple embodiments of those without expecting that these mesh completely. A worthwhile politics requires both that we recognize differences and that we share a community; that we value both relationality and individuality. This is an ideal worth striving for.

Chapter 2
Building a Specific Theory

Getting specific does not simply mean pointing to details. It means calling into question the field(s) that organize experience and meaning, problematizing the identities and allegiances that we have come to take for granted. It means coming to see the effects of power and the possibilities for democratic negotiations of that power. To do so requires a social ontology or landscape that can see and address contemporary modes of power.

The problems faced by white feminist theorists are the result of being colonized by global theory: the expectations of white feminists for a theory have been set largely by the (white, male) academic institutions in which we have learned what it is to "do theory." The standard for theory presented is that of a comprehensive model capable of explaining all events and positions in a system.[1] Whether liberal/positivist or Marxist or something else, those who do theory in this mode look for the "big picture" that can contain all the "little pictures" as examples or instances of general laws or processes.

The theory I propose here will call this standard into question, challenging both the class analysis of Marxism and the positions of many of its opponents, feminist or not. Between the monolithic politics of some formulations of Marxism and the proliferations of certain depoliticized poststructuralisms there is a large and fertile ground for action and theory. The critique of reason begun by the members of the Frankfurt school and developed by poststructuralist theorists leads us to the recovery of forms of reason that enable us to resist domination and foster reciprocity. As an enterprise involving actual others, theory must be local and specific, thereby providing the possibility of actual democratic decision making rather than submissive endorsement of a "consensual" order. Still, this specificity must not sacrifice all generalizations; without generalizations conceptualization, much less argument, is not possible. Generality without specificity is meaningless in

16

its abstraction, just as specificity without generalization is unintelligible.

In this chapter I will look briefly at some of the sources and concepts that enable us to theorize more specifically. This is not meant to be a comprehensive introduction, but rather a set of pointers and guideposts for the rest of the book.

Genealogy

The influence of the Frankfurt school has been widespread, though the particular forms of its influence have varied from country to country and over time. Beyond its direct effect there is also what Michel Foucault has called the "strange case of nonpenetration between two very similar types of thinking."[2] This similarity, especially between Adorno's version of critical theory in Germany and the United States and the work of the poststructuralists in France, concerns the task of questioning reason, of "isolating the form of rationality presented as dominant, and endowed with the status of the one-and-only reason, in order to show that it is only *one* possible form among others."[3] This effort is not, as critics (most notably Jürgen Habermas) have argued, an abandonment of reason; Foucault refers to such critiques as "blackmail," offering only the options of acceptance/celebration of reason as presently constituted, on the one hand, and "irrationalism" or incoherence, on the other.[4]

The similarity extends beyond this point. Adorno's insistence on "the disconnected and non-binding character of the form, the renunciation of explicit theoretical cohesion"[5] is meant as a balance to the overwhelming totality of scientific thought. It finds its counterpart in Foucault's work, work that has frustrated commentators for two decades.

Foucault calls into question the identification of generalization with totalization or universalization. His aim, he says, is "to substitute differentiated analyses for the themes of a totalizing history ('the progress of reason' or 'the spirit of a century')."[6] Analyses require generalization, but they do not require totalizing ones such as these. They require specific investigation into specific mechanisms.

What should we make, then, of the "episteme," the premier code word of Foucault's early work? The episteme seems a perfect candidate for the charge of totalization. Foucault describes the episteme as "the total set of relations that unite, at a given period, the discursive practices that give rise to epistemological figures, sciences, and possibly formalized systems."[7] This sounds dangerously like a totalizing notion, and many critics of Foucault have taken it in exactly this way. The figure of the episteme stands at the heart of the charges that Foucault is or was a structuralist.

Yet Foucault denies these charges. He states that the episteme is not a centering notion manifesting "the sovereign unity of a subject, a spirit, or a period,"[8] but one that is used to describe a "space of *dispersion*," an "*open field of relationships*," a "*complex relationship of successive displacements*."[9] An episteme is "*not a slice of history common to all the sciences*"; it defines the relations between these sciences, not as identity but as a field of tension.[10] The episteme is not static, furthermore; elements within it shift and change over time. Foucault's failure to elaborate on the precise nature and timing of these shifts and of the shift from one episteme to another should not be taken to mean that he believes that an episteme exists as a stable, intact whole until the moment at which it is superseded by another.

In the figure of the episteme we feel the resonance of the Adornian constellation. The constellation, a tense relationship between elements rather than an element itself, emerges again in the episteme. Foucault was in fact a master constellation builder, shifting conventional elements of our history into new conceptual relationships that enable perception of forms of power often lost by liberal and Marxist theories. The episteme is not a historical totality, but is a conceptual "force field" that gives different meaning to many discrete elements of events, ideas, and practices. The bracketing of causality occurs, likewise, in both cases; this bracketing is not an evasion of any causality, but a problematizing of the question, Why does this particular event occur when it does, and why does it occur as it does? That is, what system does it participate in that makes this event? In the place of such general(izing) causality, Foucault offers "the play of dependencies"[11] within and among discourses as well as in their relations with economic, political, and social structures and events. Foucault does not abandon causality but replaces one model of causality with another, a more historically specific one. This replacement is complementary to, is part of, the questioning of forms of reason.

At this early point in his work Foucault had failed to account for the historical location of his own discourse, maintaining what Hubert Dreyfus and Paul Rabinow have labeled "the illusion of autonomous discourse."[12] He thus falls prey to legitimate questions concerning the specificity of his own work; although he attempts to grasp the specific in discursive formations, his own posture is that of the person he will later call the universal intellectual, a once useful but now obsolescent figure.

Recognizing this difficulty, Foucault in the 1970s began to develop the method he called genealogy. Genealogy is meant as a complement to archaeology, the ahistorical analysis of discursive formations. The genealogical method shows us that things have no essences beyond time; anything with an "essence" has a history to that essence, a history of the practices by which that essence was constructed. This principle applies, most importantly, to the subject: genealogy is "a form of history which can account for the constitution of knowledges, discourses, domains of objects, etc., without having to make reference to a subject which is either transcendental in relation to the field of events or runs in its empty sameness throughout the course of history."[13]

Thus, genealogy does not look for origins, for founding acts or events; it does not inquire into the unity behind the appearance of diversity. Nor does it seek a telos, a purpose behind the practices recorded. We may see a strategizing occurring within the practices, and we may see patterns of occurrences and relations within the practices, but the practices themselves do not develop as a result of a founding intelligence that "uses" them. Further, human subjects do not simply "use" or "learn" these practices; they are defined by them. As Dreyfus and Rabinow put it, "Subjects do not first preexist and later enter into combat or harmony. In genealogy subjects emerge on a field of battle and play their roles, there and there alone."[14] We emerge as subjects within a particular space, a space defined by the networks of power and intelligibility operative at that place/time.

This insistence on the production of subjects "within the interstices" is key to the role of specificity in Foucault's thought. Living in the interstices implies that each of us occupies a space defined by overlapping discourses and practices, and that each of us exists only in that space. A political theory and a history that will do justice to our lives must elaborate upon and take account of these spaces.

Foucault has been read as a simple opponent of Marxism, destroying categories such as class or even social groups.[15] Edward Said charges that the view that "power is everywhere" leads Foucault to "obliterate the role of classes, the role of economics, the role of insurgency and rebellion in the societies he discusses."[16] Yet work such as *Discipline and Punish* belies this view. Foucault does not deny that institutional forms of power exist; rather, he argues that "these are only the terminal forms power takes."[17] For example, *Discipline and Punish* is very usefully read as a discussion with Marxism about forms of class power and subjectivity. The description in part 4 of "illegalities and delinquency" relies centrally on classes as differential sites of interpretation. Foucault documents here, not the erosion or irrelevance of class, but the ways in which class struggles may work at some points to produce unintended consequences that are not liberatory. The *fait divers* and the *counter-fait divers* are moves to establish difference, to exclude and mark in a certain way, those welcomed by neither the bourgeoisie nor the proletariat. His genealogies show, in a manner that Marx would applaud, the ways in which some struggles by the working class may increase their implication in diverse forms of power. Foucault's treatment of power is not a terminal moment, a unified theory on its own terms or in its own right, but is a corrective and critical moment in progressive social theory.[18] The question we should ask is not "Can Foucault 'fit within' Marxism?" (clearly he can't and won't) but rather "What sorts of relations can be constructed and how can we use them?"

Foucault provides us with historical examples that should lead us to question the automatic liberatory power of any struggle and instead to ask for further examination and self-criticism. He does not, however, leave us with any categories or frameworks for understanding historical change. In his zeal to address unique situations in their specificity, he declines to suggest any general processes or means by which current forms of power may be addressed collectively. Although he hints at the possibility of "new forms of right" based on reciprocity and re-creation or evasion of power/knowledge regimes, he does not go far enough to provide a positive vision. For this we must turn elsewhere.

Hegemony and Articulation

In *Hegemony and Socialist Strategy*, Ernesto Laclau and Chantal Mouffe have traced the debates over the assumptions of Second International Marxist theory. They center these debates on the idea of hegemony, moving from Rosa Luxemburg to current disputes in socialist theory. "Hegemony" is the name given to the practices that link, or "suture," the field of the social. In Lacanian psychoanalysis and literary theory, "suture" designates both the absence of unity and its filling-in. Suturing is needed only when something is not seamless; any unity produced is provisional, not essential or organic. Thus, the suture is a metaphor for the uncentered nature of the late capitalist social totality. In fact, Laclau and Mouffe argue, there is no such thing as "society," if by that we mean a stable field or "founding totality." Rather, there is an "openness" or "multiformity" to the social, as "the constitutive ground or 'negative essence' of the existing."[19]

Hegemonic practices link elements of the social through *articulation*. Articulation involves "the construction of nodal points which partially fix meaning"; it is "any practice establishing a relation among elements such that their identity is modified as a result of the articulatory experience."[20] Thus, articulation does not simply stitch together or draw connections between elements or individuals, as in a contract model of society, but transforms those elements or individuals in the process. Articulation is never simply a stating of what is but is itself a construction of self and the world, laying it out as this and not that. There is a totality to the world, but it is not a simple lawlike totality, verifiable through positivist science. There is order, there is reality, but it is not an order or a reality independent of human praxis. Human action produces and moves within the structures that we abstract as "capitalism," "racism," "sexism," and so forth. These structures, then, are not monoliths that we either live within or without, but are amoebas, with an inside that is capable of changing shape, and with a porous membrane through which inside/outside is negotiated.

Identity is a key part of these structures and practices. As Ernesto Laclau puts it, new social movements such as feminism and gay liberation have made clear in practice what poststructuralist theory suggests: "Strategies create identities, not the opposite."[21] For example, Radicalesbians in 1970 articulated lesbianism as a political identity, as "woman-identification" rather than "simply" a sexual identity. This founding gesture of lesbian feminism in some sense made lesbianism into something it had not previously been and located lesbians as political radicals regardless of their particular individual political consciousnesses. Adrienne Rich's 1980 essay "Compulsory Heterosexuality and Lesbian Existence" furthered this articulation; in contrast with other discourses that located lesbianism as "homosexuality"—an identity shared with gay men—Radicalesbians, Rich, and other lesbian feminists insisted on lesbianism as female experience, as ultimately removed from any men. The consequences of these articulations of lesbian identity were an alignment with feminist women, lesbian and (sometimes) heterosexual, rather than alliance with gay men.[22]

This example helps to make clear that articulation is never simply a verbal game but is a profoundly political act. An articulation, as Laclau and Mouffe put it, produces *discourse*, a "structured totality" that locates and identifies its members, and in so doing points them toward particular political actions and strategies. By focusing on "discourse" Laclau and Mouffe do not mean to suggest that "reality is all in our heads"; discourses are profoundly material, running throughout "the entire material density of the multifarious institutions, rituals, and practices through which a discursive formation is structured." They reject the "assumption of the mental character of discourse" that grounds so many objections to poststructuralism, arguing that this dualism is precisely the problem to be overcome, not the field upon which claims are to be adjudicated.[23]

The process of articulation has been beautifully described, though not in those terms, by Nancy Fraser. In her essay "Struggle over Needs," Fraser shifts the ground for a feminist critical theory from discussion of needs to examination of "discourses about needs, from the distribution of need satisfactions to 'the politics of need interpretation.' "[24] Defending this move, she argues that theories that take needs as given cannot account for the power relations behind a given interpretation. Analysis of these relations is particularly important for studying contemporary welfare-state societies, as the lines of power there are more plural and less official than in other societies. For Fraser, the "struggle over needs" is always also a struggle over the "sociocultural means of interpretation and communication (MIC)."[25] She gives as examples the contesting discourses about AIDS and persons with AIDS, where gay and lesbian interpretations are silenced at the level of official discussion and policy making.[26]

Fraser's discussion is ambiguous concerning the more radical implication of "articulation," the suggestion that social groups are formed through this process rather than prior to it. Her analysis suggests that "groups" exist prior to the articulation (as voicing) of needs, and that the struggle for the MIC is separable from identity formation. However, she notes that interpretations are not "simply 'representations,' " but are "acts and interventions";[27] these interventions are internal to the groups, and to the members of the groups, as well as part of the struggle with other groups. Articulation is never simply giving voice, but is performative description; it is the construction of experience and self.

To see this point, we can use Fraser's example of wife battering. As she notes, "wife battering" is a very recent term, the result of feminist intervention in the dominant social text:

> Feminist activists renamed the practice with a term drawn from criminal law and created a new kind of public discourse. They claimed that battery was not a personal, domestic problem but a systemic, political

one; its etiology was not to be traced to individual women's or men's emotional problems but, rather, to the ways these problems refracted pervasive social relations of male dominance and female subordination.[28]

Fraser notes that "these women came to adopt new self-descriptions"[29] and with them different affinities and affiliations, but this point is not treated theoretically. The lack of theoretical treatment may seem inconsequential to some—after all, doesn't she "really mean" what I want her to argue?—but it is not. The extent to which we acknowledge and develop the relation between political articulation and personal identity is one of the lines dividing older Marxisms such as Gramsci's from newer, poststructurally inflected ones.

Now we must consider the relation of poststructuralism to Marxism. There are many ways to envision or theorize this linkage, ranging from some sort of "deeper harmony" to an overcoming or supplanting. I want to reject both of these neat solutions in favor of another, more "critical" conception of their relation. In this sense, "critical" pertains to being in or bringing to crisis, which Gayatri Spivak describes as "the moment at which you feel that your presuppositions of any enterprise are disproved by the enterprise itself."[30] Such a notion privileges neither Marxism nor poststructuralism but instead looks for the terrain upon which they meet.[31]

If we reenvision poststructuralisms as theories of specificities rather than as theories of difference, we can see poststructuralism not as destroying Marxism but as recovering from it the materialist impulse. The work of "post-Marxists" such as Laclau and Mouffe is crucial for precisely this recovery; analysis of discourses is analysis of relations of hegemonic power and resistance to them. Challenge to dominant discourses is an essential part of social change and cannot be divorced from "material struggle."

Multiple Jeopardy

The decentering of class theory in Marxism, as well as the decentering of sex as class in feminism, is not the decentering of the subjects of theory and practice. The decentering of class theory allows for the recognition of centered, specifically located subjects in the fullness of their locations. Now we need the ability to "recognize" those subjects, that is to say, we need to articulate the specificities of their/our lives. This is perhaps where mainstream (that is, white) feminist theory has been weakest. As the most fully hegemonized group of women, white educated women have been most susceptible to the demand for global theory. In contrast, women of color in the United States have been a major source of "specific theory." This theory is specific not simply because these women mention race and class as important variables, as many white academics also do, but because they elaborate the ways in which race, class, gender, and sexuality are lived as fragmented wholes. Writers such as Patricia Williams, Norma Alarcón, Gloria Anzaldúa, Trinh T. Minh-ha, and Aida Hurtado have worked to challenge the unitary subject without dispensing with consciousness, to build new forms of theory that work from the inside out rather than the reverse, and that consequently provide a stronger basis for alliances than a theory that tries to unite by overlooking differences or simply celebrating them in the name of "diversity."

Women of color—Black, Chicana, Asian, Native American, Middle Eastern—have been writing about sexism and feminism as long as white women. In 1970, the year of the publication of Shulamith Firestone's *Dialectic of Sex*, Toni Cade edited a collection of essays on Black women and feminism.[32] Five years later, Pauli Murray wrote about the sexism of Black men, arguing that "racism and sexism in the United States have shared some common origins, reinforced one another, and are so deeply intertwined in the country's institutions that the successful outcome of the struggle against racism will depend in large part upon the simultaneous elimination of all discrimination based on sex."[33] Just as often, women argued that the common fight of feminism could be won only when white women recognized and took responsibility for racism.[34]

Theorizing the specific situations of Chicanas, Asian-Americans, Native Americans, and Blacks has gone through several waves. The first way of theorizing the position of women of color was that of additive oppressions. One of the first second-wave feminists to do this was Frances Beale, in "Double Jeopardy."[35] The title encapsulates the theory. The situation of Black women was conceptualized as two systems of oppression; racial oppression is distinct from and, for Black women, added to sexual oppression. This does not mean that Black women live their lives in compartments, but rather means that the two systems are analytically and practically separable.

This vision of double jeopardy led to a series of theoretical and political questions that continue to haunt feminism. White socialist feminists who had isolated oppression in capitalism from sexist oppression were in a similar situation. Both political movements out of which feminism grew had suggested that women's struggles for equality and dignity were secondary at best and genocidal at worst. Answering these charges required an analysis of the relations between sexism, racism, capitalism, and heterosexism. Such analysis continually oscillated between "ranking oppressions," labeling one as most basic, as the "independent variable," and others as either consequences of the first or less pressing, and refusing such either/or choices in favor of a developing integrated focus.

Among white women, radical feminist theory moved toward the first option. The defining mark of white "gynocentric" feminism is the priority given to sexism as a system of oppression and the invocation of a unity of "women" across race and class who are oppressed by a unitary group of "men." Of course, every white woman who identifies herself as a feminist is not required to share this view; feminism is too porous and fluid a movement to admit of such a generalization.

The political implication of this appeal was that all women had a common priority in fighting sexism. Marxist feminists retained the Marxist emphasis on class and capitalism as the generator of other oppressions until it became clear that Marxism was unable to account for women's lives; socialist feminism developed out of the quest for an integrated analysis that would acknowledge the differences and the linkages between capitalism and patriarchy.[36]

Even the integrated focus of socialist feminism did not automatically include race. In her comment on Heidi Hartmann's essay "The Unhappy Marriage of Marxism and Feminism," Gloria Joseph focuses on the absence of racial categories and the inadequacy of socialist feminist theory. Joseph argues that "to speak of women, all women categorically, is to perpetuate white supremacy—white female supremacy," because "sexual inequality between Black men and women has very different historical and cultural beginnings than the sexual inequality between white men and women."[37] One of the ways in which supremacy is maintained is by forcing members of subordinate groups to use the categories and assumptions of dominant groups to understand themselves.[38] In the case of Black women, such categories force an impossible choice: are they Black "first," as the Black Power movement insisted, or are they "really" women, as white feminists argued?

The concept of double jeopardy works to refuse that choice. From Beale to the present, women of color have been resisting "ranking the oppressions" in favor of an interactive analysis.[39] A notable feature of the research and discourse of feminists of color is their relative distance from any of the main paradigms of white feminist thought, a distance they maintain precisely because those paradigms have been exclusive, even when there has been an effort, as in socialist feminism, to include considerations of race and class. The main problem is not a refusal to address intersections adequately but rather the inability of global theories to do the work. The solution, one visible throughout the work of women of color in the United States for two decades, is to refuse that model of theory.

Denise Segura makes steps to explicate this resistance in her discussion of "triple oppression" of Chicanas along lines of race, class, and gender.[40] Although the phrase "triple oppression" suggests an additive analysis, Segura tries to work around this linguistic problem. She does use the phrase to indicate the relative deprivation of Chicanas in comparison with either white women or any men, but she is concerned to get at the "interplay" among factors. She uses the example of the relationship between familial expectations and family structure and the labor force position of Chicanas, urging scholars to look for connections rather than accept hegemonic distinctions between work and family, public and private, and the like.

Such work is required to make the contours of oppressions clear. As Aida Hurtado's work on the forms of subordination experienced by white women and women of color demonstrates, we cannot move from the simple category of "oppression" or even "subordination" to assume that the shape and dynamics of that oppression are similar everywhere. Hurtado argues that white women's subordination often took the form of and worked through seduction by men, being "groomed from birth to be the lovers, mothers, and partners (however unequal) of white men," and being granted in return material stability and a certain sense of self-worth. As the "lovers, mothers, and partners (however unequal) of men of Color," women of color have no hope of advancement or advantage. This is not for Hurtado a matter of "more" oppression, but rather of "different forms of enforcing oppression."[41] As a result, the two groups of women have "different political responses and skills," which often lead them to oppose one another or to clash even when they hope to achieve the same aim. This point was made by Mae King in 1975, Beale in 1970, and countless others, but it was largely overlooked by white women until the 1980s. Even in the 1980s (and 1990s), that "recognition" has not been complete; the chaos in the National Women's Studies Association in the early 1990s was partly a result of these different responses, and also of different aims.

A similar point can be made about the positions of white middle- and upper-class women compared to those of poor or working-class women. Whereas the middle and upper classes are most thoroughly hegemonized, which is to say seduced, working-class and poor women walk the line of disappointment in a country where the official dogma is that anyone can rise, and that women can rise through marriage, but the reality is that most women will not. Thus, poor white women face a situation not entirely seductive but not expressing the brutal rejection of racism.

The racial configuration of "women" is demonstrated by Murray when she counters the charges that slavery and racism emasculated Black males with the argument that Black women were excluded from womanhood:

> If idealized values of masculinity and femininity are used as criteria, it would be hard to say whether the experience of slavery subjected the black male to any greater loss of his manhood than the black female of her womanhood. The chasm between the slave woman and her white counterpart (whose own enslavement was masked by her position as a symbol of high virtue and an object of chivalry) was as impassable as the gulf between the male slave and his arrogant white master. If black males suffered from real and psychological castration, black females bore the burden of real or psychological rape.[42]

This exclusion was highlighted and challenged by Sojourner Truth's famous "Ain't I a woman?" speech, but it continued long after slavery. In 1970, Murray makes clear, being strong and self-supporting was virtually a denial of one's womanhood. The treatment of African-American women by whites continued to show the lack of "chivalry" or other acknowledgment of womanhood accorded to (or imposed on) white women. Murray uses this condition to argue that Black women have their own agenda, linked to those of both white women and Black men but not identical to either.[43]

At the close of her article, Murray adds a phrase that is not unimportant in her analysis. She does not say that "the Negro [sic] woman is strategically placed by virtue of her tradition of independence and her long experience in civil rights" to link the two movements; rather, she says that "the middle-class Negro woman" is so located.[44] Aside from this one time, she drops the class qualifier. Why does it appear here at all? Most of Murray's article describes the historical and contemporary conditions of women whom white sociologists would describe as working class. However, Murray tells us that the middle-class Black woman has the education, the "training," and the "values" to "communicate with her white counterparts, interpret the deepest feelings of the black community, and cooperate with white women on the basis of mutual concerns as women."[45] Murray's position as a lawyer may explain her motivation for the remark, but it needs explication and argument to be persuasive.

Among whites in the United States, such a remark would be justified by the tradition in which the middle class is the "middling class," the average, and therefore the representative. In fact, the notion of a middle class is so elastic among whites as to be almost meaningless; in a country that does not officially recognize or endorse class inequality, being outside the middle is fraught with danger. Murray is not making such an assumption of averageness. She is saying that the Black middle class is specifically equipped for an educative role. To understand why, we have to see that class is defined differently in African-American communities than in Euro-American ones. In African-American communities, where poverty has too often been the norm, class distinctions have as much to do with education and social position as with income—especially before 1970, when ghettoization forced middle-class Blacks to remain in the same community with the poor. Unlike whites, who more easily stratified through geographical distancing, African-American communities remained networks encompassing diversity of class. Within these networks, the educated middle class were the standard-bearers for the race, not simply for themselves. The Black women's club movement involved middle-class women in "community improvement" as well as feminist activism, and it did so not as an option, as white women's clubs did, but out of an awareness of the fragility of common survival.[46] Thus, a remark that would sound merely pompous or elitist from a white woman has a background among Blacks that may shift its meaning. Without the specificities of history, we cannot make an adequate judgment of such a statement.

For white women in the 1970s Firestone was the theorist, the author cited in discussions of radical feminism. She had to be dealt with in white women's education in feminism; Murray, Cade, and others were absent. There are two connected reasons for this neglect. First is the straightforward dynamic of racism. White women, as a hegemonic group, did not even notice the absence of women of color for quite a while; when they did, the question asked too often was "Why aren't 'they' here with 'us'?" The implicit privileging of white middle-class women's problems and perspectives led to viewing other women's lives through that lens. In this vision, differences were seen as "exceptions" or "variations" from the "norm" of womanhood. The erasure and invisibility of other cultures that is part of structural racism operated in the women's movement through the assumption that feminism began when white women started to write about it, and through attempts to "reach out" to women of color, to "include" them in white theories and organizations, rather than changing those theories and organizations to account for the rich diversity and complexity that existed.

The second reason for the lack of attention paid to the work of women of color is the conception and position of "theory" in the intellectual universe of Euro-Americans. Until the 1970s it was virtually unquestionable that the criteria for theory were comprehensiveness and universality; the more extensive the theory, the more "territory" it could cover, the better. Firestone's ideas, and manifestos such as that of the Redstockings, are paradigm cases of feminist "grand theory." When this conception of theory is combined with the racist assumption that white women are "generic" women, and women of color the "exceptions," theory will almost inevitably replicate the invisibilities or silences of the hegemonic culture.

In contrast to this vision of theory, we find writers such as Murray insisting on a more specific analysis. Instead of positing a universal connection and hierarchy of oppressions, Murray states that racism and sexism are "deeply intertwined" in the United States. She shares the sense that the elimination of sexism is crucial to the elimination of racism, but her analysis and description are more specific. She does not move to universal hypotheses about the causal priority of sex inequality over racial disparity, as does Firestone, but makes a very concrete argument.

This specificity runs throughout the feminist work of women of color in the United States. Whatever their differences of origin and culture, "women of color" form a unity precisely in their position as nonwhite in a white supremacist society; theirs is a unity of opposition. The racial stereotypes vary from group to group, and often serve to pit one "minority" against another, but they share the feature of opposition, of oppression on the basis of race. Economic subordination is generally (though not always) a concomitant of racial subordination, but we cannot understand these simply by "adding" or substituting class for race in our analysis; the experience and position of a poor Chicana is both different from and similar to that of poor whites (and both vary from region to region).

This is the giant leap in theorizing that must be developed and extended by white women. What looks, from the position of traditional theory, like a step backward from "theory" to "description" (to use Alison Jaggar's distinction) is in fact a move forward, away from the dominance of modeling-type theories to a more concrete, more local, but also more specific and comprehensive way of doing theory. It is part of the shift that Kirstie McClure urges toward "figuring 'theory' less as a noun than as a verb."[47] Barbara Christian's insistence that "people of color have always theorized—but in forms quite different from the Western form of abstract logic" makes this point exactly.[48] The forms she describes—stories, riddles, and proverbs—highlight the view of theorizing as something people do rather than theory as something people have or formulate.

The diverse forms of their theorizing make this point shine through. McClure is Christian's nightmare, in a certain sense—versed in poststructuralism and "high theory," writing dense prose, seemingly forbidding and inaccessible. Christian's directness is not simplistic, but it is direct, straightforward, "more accessible." And yet both these writers agree that theorizing occurs in many forms. The possibility that such diverse writers might read one another as serious contributors to theory is itself a new event, largely due to the work of writers of color in the last two decades. This possibility sets off "new social movements," including feminism and lesbian activism, from older, more scientistic and hierarchical, movements.

Conclusion

What holds for race is also the case for class, for sexuality, and for other axes of oppression. We cannot say a priori what "the" effect of "class oppression" is; we need to know how classes are constructed, how the dominant discourses treat class, how class is inflected across other lines. While we can make general statements about the privilege of heterosexuality, we cannot automatically assume that we know the configuration that takes in a given society. Therefore, we cannot know what is needed in a political program until we understand that configuration.

A specific focus reminds us that even "configurations" within a society are constructions of the analyst as well as of social actors, that configurations will not be complete and comprehensive, and that therefore political programs cannot claim the total quality of revolution for themselves. The dream of revolution is inextricably woven with the dream of totality. A postmodern vision is a modest vision of local, specific actors and struggles. This does not mean the abandonment of the ideal of social change, but it does mean the abandonment of the revolution/reform distinction and of the dream of total, comprehensive, synchronic change.

A critical feminist theory will not shrink from generalizations and prescriptions for fear of antiessentialism, as did many in the 1980s. Feminism has always involved an ideal of justice and (some sort of) equality, and will continue to derive its moral and political power from that ideal. Yet a critical theory must recognize women's unity as articulated, as hegemonic practice and achievement rather than a given. Moral and political claims have their force and their sense only in particular "contexts of action, with all their particularities of history, affiliation, and preconceived value."[49] The task of a feminist theory should not be to describe universal conditions or prescriptions, but rather should be to provide a basis for political judgment and action within a given social context.

The strength of feminist theory lies in the simultaneous recognition that theory is indispensable and that good theory is inextricably bound to the world of which it speaks. The lack of a feminist canon of great works contributes to that strength; rather than argue endlessly about what a given celebrity thinks, as though that would legitimate an idea, feminist theory always returns to the challenge of social change. A critical feminist theory draws on all the resources of political and social theory in order to think about what and how to change, while recognizing that elegant theory is no substitute for justice. The refusal to dispense with politics and with a positive vision, while retaining critical humility about the visions we create, provides the lifeblood for the work that lies ahead.

Interlude I: Getting Specific

In practice, getting specific is a process of weaving threads. It is conceptually possible to separate out one thread and say "This is class" and find another that is labeled "gender" or "race" or "sexuality," but that separation alone will never do justice to the way that the whole fabric is lived. Getting specific therefore is more like storytelling than like analysis, though both are required. I will illustrate this weaving by picking up the thread of class in my life; picking up this thread forces me to carry the whole cloth, and eventually to describe it as well.

Of course, this kind of theorizing implicitly denies all of the tenets of modern social science; instead of removing myself from the field of study, I am placing myself at the center. Getting specific means turning social science and theory on its head; it means working out from the centers of our lives to seeing the connections and contradictions in them. The failure of contemporary political theory, especially liberal theory, to speak to our lives, suggests that such a radical course is at least worth trying. I believe that the actual narrative of my life speaks more convincingly about mutthood, about class and race privilege, and about the oppression of lesbians, than any scholarly treatise or argument.

My parents were both first-generation upper class, though in very different ways. My maternal grandmother was a Latvian Jew who crossed the border from Canada illegally in the 1890s, when she was quite young. My maternal grandfather belonged to one of the oldest Dutch families in the country, a family that has an official society of family members. My grandparents married with the disapproval of both families.

My mother was born in 1918, and her parents divorced in the 1920s. My grandmother had gradually taken legal control of the estate and of my grandfather's magazine. When they divorced, she got it

32

all. *Time* magazine covered the divorce and basically called her a thief. My mother always kept the clipping of the retraction that they later printed. I grew up very proud of my grandmother; she was my model of a woman who did what she wanted and didn't get stuck at home. Only later did I realize that she was also a tyrant, running her daughters' lives with no respect for them as persons.

My father was born in South Carolina in 1916, in a family of poor rural farmers. My grandfather began to work for the Du Pont Company and became a vice president. I know very little of my father's early years. I do know that despite a very privileged boyhood his life was miserable; his mother, one of thirteen children from a Tennessee dirt farm, was critical and hateful until the day she died. She was the first person I ever felt that I hated. I cannot begin to imagine the circumstances under which she grew to adulthood; we have one picture of her family, all tight-lipped, unsmiling people. Knowing what I now know, I suspect she was abused in many ways. My grandfather, an alcoholic, died at forty-nine, before I was born.

I know that my father hated his work. Between my father and his father, my family had sixty-five years with Du Pont. My father told all his children never to work for a big corporation, but he could tolerate no criticism of Du Pont. He acknowledged the criminal mistreatment of workers in business in general, but Du Pont was always the exception. All he knew about cars, about safe driving, about work, he learned at Du Pont. We were a corporate family, moving when and where the company sent us.

My dad worked in middle management for Du Pont all his life, and we never had the kind of money that went with my parents' attitudes, though we had quite a bit. Both my parents had a mix of East Coast wealthy snobbery and Jewish or poor Southern farming attitudes that was quite confusing. They both had been raised with maids and expected that others took care of things; when I took auto shop in high school I was questioned, certainly for crossing gender, but, I think, more for crossing class lines. None of us learned any household maintenance skills, because my parents always paid others to do things and raised us to expect that we would have the money to do likewise. My mother thought I was a genius when I made jam. We always had a woman of color, either African-American or Chicana, as a semiweekly housekeeper.

Living in the Midwest, we were still very "Eastern," meaning upper middle class, in our tastes. We routinely ate things that I later found many people never even tasted: artichokes, asparagus, lobster, and filet mignon, as well as chopped chicken liver and sour cream herring.

We had special plates just for artichokes. We never once in my life had macaroni and cheese or tuna noodle casserole; these were exotica I found while camping or at other people's houses.

Still, class was not monolithic in my family. Both my parents had come from nouveau situations in different ways, and they had achieved very different places. My father's family, though well off, was always in an employee situation within a corporation, whereas my mother's family was capitalist. My father had the identity of someone who worked for others, who couldn't control decisions; my mother always seemed to think that any of us could do whatever we chose and that others would agree to our terms and desires when we talked to them.

In both cases my grandparents had backgrounds that did not prepare them for wealth, so there was almost a covert feeling to some parts of our lives. My father, especially, was allergic to anything that might connect him to working-class people. When I bought a van, we fought over whether I could park it out front: to my father a van was a truck, and only farmers drove trucks.

At one point, however, my mother became willing to associate with "those people." When I was fifteen, I became pregnant. There was no possibility of telling my father, the raging bull with the purse strings, so my mother set out to secure coverage from Medical (the California state Medicaid system) for my abortion. Of course, that didn't mean that I should actually be treated like someone on public relief; my mother also fought for and won the right to have the abortion performed in a fancy private hospital rather than the local public hospital where others went.

In short, my mother and I became welfare cheats. Not only did we drive a big car, as the stereotype of the cheat goes, we also lived in a big house, ate fine food, and went on nice vacations. Yet when we got down to it, my mother and I were tenants in my father's house. Living with the money is not the same thing as controlling it. What can be read as my mother's individual cowardice toward my father can also, and should, be read as her clear perception of the inequality and intimidation in their relationship. We needed public support, not to escape official poverty, but to escape our particular situation of patriarchy.

This episode always comes back to me with mixed feelings. I remember my anger with my mother, who scorned me, but I also remember that she went with me to a place that she could never imagine going, that she protected me, that she fought for me with all the weapons she possessed. I remember my pride that my boyfriend came too, that he did not desert me as my mother said he would, and that these two, who hated each other, sat together with me. And now, years later, I snort with anger when (neo)conservatives attack the poor because we were, in fact, the cheaters, the undeserving unpoor, and people who rail against welfare abuse will never complain against me but will act against those who need decent public support the most.

Class was problematic for another reason. Both my parents were from alcoholic families with lots of emotional abuse. It has been suggested to me that alcoholism is not politically relevant, as are race and class, but I think that this charge misses the point. The emotional, physical, and sexual abuse that occurs in alcoholic families is incredibly disempowering. My father, with his awful life, somewhere learned that raping his daughter was acceptable. My mother learned that pacifying her husband was more important than protecting her children. From the time I was four or five, the message that I could do anything was mixed with the reality that I could not escape the monster in my own home. I blocked my memory of the abuse, but its effects ran throughout my life. For years I lived almost as two people: the class-privileged, powerful, and competent person, and the abused, fearful, self-hating one. I think the divide is related to the public/private separation in contemporary Western culture, in that my public self was confident and competent, while my capacity for intimacy with other humans was destroyed. This incapacity, however, is not just "private" but fans out into all human relations; my own fears convinced me of the importance of examining our personal lives if we are to be effective allies and leaders.

Another common feature of alcoholism is downward class mobility. My parents did not cross class very dramatically, but I did. I began to drink at thirteen and used a lot of drugs. The kids I did this with were uniformly from less well-off families, ranging from middle class to welfare recipients. I was given very little money by my parents (though still more than my friends received), so I did the same things my friends did. I panhandled, I stole booze and cigarettes, I made deals for drugs and alcohol. I spent a lot of time away from my parents, either running away, in institutions, or just somewhere else, and while gone I lived in ways that my parents couldn't stand. They made it clear that the problem was not simply my behavior, but who I behaved with.

Still, none of these experiences ever changed the basic shape of class in me. I was always a visitor in poverty, as I was in the juvenile justice system, mental hospitals, and so on. I know now that the class training I was given has made much of the difference in enabling me to survive the abuses and disadvantages I have faced, because the basic message of that training was that I have a right to be here, that I have a right to be heard, that I have resources. I was sent to good schools, with a good breakfast, and to whatever lessons and activities interested me: piano, voice, flute, dancing, swimming, tennis, baton, Girl Scouts. . . . Incest, abuse, and alcoholism did not change the basic message that I have a right to live well. Because of my problems, I did not get the education that I might have got, but I still ended up in a position of tremendous privilege. I did not, in the end, cross class at all.

Wealth was wonderful, but it couldn't erase Jewishness. My maternal grandmother tried to hide her Jewishness by going to church, but my mother says she always said her Hebrew prayers very quietly. At any rate, if anyone looked Jewish it was Susu; there was no hiding it. My mother later told us about being denied hotel accommodations that they had booked when they arrived and the owners saw they were Jewish. I didn't find out we were part Jewish, or where Latvia was, until we left Ohio in 1966. No one would explain where Latvia was, because the explanation involved describing the Jewish Pale under the czars and the struggles between Germany and Russia to dump "their" Jews. In our nice suburb, Catholics were considered suspect. Jews were not even conceivable.

The lesson my mother learned from all this was that no price is too high to pay for fitting in. Rather than learning compassion for others in similar situations, she tried to make sure that none of her kids would ever experience such things, and she chose to ignore them when they happened to others; in short, she identified completely with the oppressor. One of my most horrible memories of my mother is her description of a shopping trip to Tijuana (we lived then in southern California) and her praise for the tour guide who prevented them from having to see the extent of the poverty all around them. When I told her I was a lesbian, her reaction was simply that I was making trouble for myself. When I told her of rapes and assaults on other lesbians, she replied that that was the price of being different.

As a teenager, I thought of "converting" to Judaism. I was raised as an Episcopalian, but I had not been confirmed, and by my mother's line I remain Jewish by Jewish law. I was fiercely proud of Israel until the 1973 war. I fasted on Yom Kippur throughout high school. My grandmother was dead by then, but my great aunt was exuberant. My sister had married a Jew, and here was another prodigal daughter coming home: my great aunt told my mother, "You can't run away from it." I never went farther into Judaism: the 1973 war alienated me from Israel too deeply, and my Judaism was tightly bound to Israel. When I returned to think about Judaism, it was with friends who were very observant. I went to groups to talk about my confusion and pain at feeling not "in" anywhere.

I think the main attraction of Judaism was that it is a visible, distinct culture, providing meaning, while hegemonic U.S. Christianity does not present itself as such. The need to look elsewhere for a culture is itself one characteristic way of being a middle-class Anglo-American. Another reason for identifying with Judaism was my own history of physical and sexual abuse and consequent identification with any underdog, any oppressed people. If my mother abandoned "all that," I retrieved it. She rejected my grandmother; I embraced her. My horror at my mother's callousness, a callousness that extended to her children, translated into a horror at any pain and a tremendous admiration for those who resisted. Later, I realized that being Jewish was not the only, nor the best for me, way to resist or to find community.

My childhood was dominated by Martin Luther King and the Kennedys, by Vietnam and civil rights, and by the Beatles and the Rolling Stones. I read the paper every morning by age ten, and in 1968 I saw both my heroes die within two months. My parents encouraged me to believe that everyone was equally valuable and that prejudice was bad. My realization that they did not believe these things was a crucial part of growing up.

The loud silence in my parents' house about race did not make sense to me until many years after I had left. I was raised not to say "bad things," and that included racist remarks. Yet my father could suddenly say that the Chicago Cubs couldn't go a whole season because they had too many Black players (who are too lazy to go that long). Arguing with such an offensive idiocy was forbidden. My parents agreed, after we moved to Los Angeles in 1970, that most of the people in the West were stupid. This was not the effect of bad education, nutrition, or other problems, but seemed to be in their nature. Chicanos, Blacks, Okies, all came under fire. When I got into fights at school, it was the fault of the Chicanas with whom I fought, or the poor white low-riders on my side, and it was just the way they were. I had been told that we were all equal and that the civil rights struggle was a just fight, but that didn't mean that we were *really* equal. I was raised to value equal political rights for all, but not to respect others or different cultures. My parents were limousine liberals.

As I look back, I think this was a major turning point for me, the point when I turned away from school and achievement and toward drugs and alcohol, toward despair. My parents were liars, both in the home, where we pretended I was not being assaulted, and in the wider world, where we pretended not to be bigots. The Johnson administration was made up of liars, about the war and about civil rights, but even worse was Nixon's election. Even the Beatles broke up. Everything I counted on as a young girl seemed to fall apart.

I was born fascinated with politics, in all its myriad forms. The play of power and of personality, the complexities of people trying to live together, have always drawn me. So my teen years were spent trying to reach a political understanding of my life. I began as a vague socialist, opposed to capitalism for its inequities of distribution but not very clear about how it worked or what else to do. In high school I read Ayn Rand, and that sent me off on several years of libertarian adventure. Rand told me that I didn't have to apologize for my life, that it was all right to be strong, all right to be alienated. She gave me a measure of pride and self-esteem at a time when I had none. It took several years of voracious reading for me to decide that compassion was too important to forsake. I joined the Young Republicans (who didn't believe I wanted to join), left them for the Libertarian party (for a semester), and then fell into confusion. A course in my final semester of college brought me back to where I began. I have continued to change my mind about many things, but my basic sense of the indecency of capitalism and the need for a democratic socialism has never left.

These resources and problems come together for me when I look at my experience as a lesbian. I was raised in a family that commanded me not to hear, not to speak, not to cry, not to feel. I was a constant failure at this. It never occurred to me to be in the closet as a lesbian; when I decided I was one, I lived that way.

Growing up, the only lesbians I saw were juvenile delinquents and women who looked like they couldn't get men. Neither group seemed particularly happy, nor did they seem very sexual. As a thoroughly indoctrinated girlchild, it simply did not occur to me that there was any joy between women. Since age four or five, I associated sex with penises. I was a "tomboy," but my mother made sure I stopped playing football when my period started. I did not get along well with women. Most that I had known were very straight and teased me for not being a "real woman"—shaved legs, makeup, and so on. It was not until the end of my undergraduate career that I met feminists, who thought and talked and accepted me as I was. That was what I needed.

I became a lesbian in the lesbian capital of the United States—Northampton, Massachusetts. I did so for a variety of reasons. First, I felt a desire for other women, both emotionally and sexually. I had not known many women before, so I had not known what I missed; when I found out, I wanted it. But I also came out, or came out as radically as I did, as a result of the homophobic reactions to the first Northampton Gay and Lesbian Pride March of 1982. I marched in support of my friends, in agony over my attempts to remain heterosexual, but when I came home I found that my neighbors didn't distinguish supporters from queers. For weeks after the event, I was taunted by the neighborhood children whenever I left the house. This treatment convinced me of the importance of the choice; it also left me feeling that there was no longer anything to lose by actually coming out.

As a lesbian, I have had to make strategic decisions in a way that straight women need not. I wanted to write about lesbian feminism—about my community—in my dissertation, but it was the sort of topic that marginalizes scholars, so I had to really think hard before doing it. I did it partly so that I could not tempt myself with the closet when job hunting. I have had to work on self-presentation in order to teach. These are perhaps things that I share with other women, but being a quasi-butch lesbian highlights them in certain ways. What some would call "dressing for success" I experience not as drag but as disempowering, as being awkward and out of my body. Whereas many heterosexual women report a need to assert themselves more strongly, I have worked more at "softening up," being less "threatening."

Because of my class background with its messages of my rights and privileges, I have never had to face a choice between being out and working at the career I want. My lesbianism crosses my class and race privileges, but they are not canceled by it. I am able to "fit" into situations of privilege when I choose, even though I fit a bit oddly.

As a white middle-class woman, I have been granted the privilege of not having to listen to other women. I have been forced to listen to men, though, and to repeat their words, in order to have authority. As a lesbian, I have lost or forsaken other sorts of privilege or subjection. My lesbianism does not necessarily align me with all women, however, or even with all other lesbians. My class inflects everything I am and do, but it is not monolithic; it cannot simply neutralize ethnic or religious prejudice, though it might protect me from some of the worst effects. My race privileges me in a unique way, but it does not remove my lesbianism, nor does it exempt me from incest, rape, or the other violations visited upon most U.S. women. As a theorist, I have participated in the power (and for me, the beauty and excitement) of redefining the existing world and envisioning new possibilities.

None of these lines locates me in an unambiguous way. It is precisely that gap that provides the space of politics, even as it is politics that defines the lines. Politics, as the articulation and negotiation of differences within and for a collectivity, is what takes place in the slippery places, the interstices between elements of power. Getting specific is the prerequisite for a politics that is neither vanguardist nor blandly pluralist, that recognizes differences as important and enduring and difficult and works not to erase or eliminate those differences but to weave the threads that might link us. To that politics we now turn.

Chapter 3

(Be)Coming Out: Lesbian Identity and Politics

Having made general claims for specificity, I would like to move on to consider what can be gained for lesbian identity politics from such a shift in perspective. Because identity is currently so tightly bound to questions of truth, identity politics is tugged along in the wake of modern assumptions about the nature of sexual identity as something that can be known. Postmodernism enables us to challenge the status and nature of truth (and of nature) and so helps us to rethink sexual identity as a process of becoming. Through the concept of (be)coming out, I will suggest a model of sexual identities as works in progress rather than museum pieces or clinical specimens. By getting specific we can understand lesbian identities not as selves that are isolated or removed from our societies of birth but as locations/consciousnesses that position us within them in particular, potentially subversive ways. This subversive force extends far beyond that of naturalized or essentialized sexual identities, for it might extend into the lives of all members of a society who understand themselves in this way. Such a conception serves to equalize lesbians and nonlesbians, especially heterosexuals, removing the crust of obviousness around heterosexuality and its unmarked privilege. It returns us to crucial questions asked by earlier lesbian feminists without mandating the global theoretical responses they proffered.[1] It challenges the essentialism of mainstream gay and lesbian politics without silencing the moments of truth and possibilities for strategic advantage that might inhere in such essentialism.

Postmodernism, Poststructuralism, and Claims of Truth

One of the hallmarks of postmodern theory has been the questioning of what Jean-François Lyotard has labeled the "metanarratives" of Western metaphysics, the stories about progress and freedom that le-

41

gitimate specific knowledges and practices. Lyotard defines legitimation as "the process by which a 'legislator' dealing with scientific discourse is authorized to prescribe the stated conditions . . . determining
whether a statement is to be included in that discourse for consideration by the scientific community."[2] We may generalize this definition
to say that legitimation is the process whereby meaningful statements
are distinguished from those without meaning, and that metanarratives are the systems or code by which we accomplish this distinction.
Thus, not all narratives are metanarratives; metanarratives organize
and regulate narratives.

When knowledge is described in this way, it loses much of its aura.
Whereas Western accounts of knowledge have generally linked it to a
unitary, eternal truth, knowledge is now seen to be internal to systems, structured by and accounted as such within them. As Sandra
Harding has explained, when we view knowledge as a socially located
enterprise, we can see that "epistemologies are justificatory strategies," and then inquire into "the hostile environment that creates the
perception that one needs a theory of knowledge at all."[3] Theories of
knowledge serve to justify claims to specific knowledges; they produce
and legitimate power.

What comes to the fore, then, is not truth but strategy. If we ask
why certain metanarratives function at certain times and places, we
find that the answer has to do not with simple progress of a unitary
knowledge but rather with shifting structures of meaning, power, and
action. For example, the modern European bourgeoisie's self-understanding embodied in liberal discourse centered on a metanarrative of
the progress of truth and freedom through science. This self-understanding is bound to the rise of science and technical expertise to
order and to discipline both the bourgeoisie and workers. From
within this view, order and discipline were the means of freedom,
democracy the fruit of order; from without, the role of power was visible, though differently structured than in earlier regimes.[4] Kathy Ferguson has labeled these perspectives or strategies "genealogical" because they "deconstruct meaning claims in order to look for the
modes of power they carry and to force open a space for the emergence of counter-meanings."[5] Lyotard's "incredulity" is one version of
this genealogical view; he argues that "postmodern" knowledge "re-
fines our sensitivity to differences and reinforces our ability to tolerate
the incommensurable" because it deprives us of the possibility of a
single overarching truth and thereby enables us to challenge scientific
discourses.[6] We cannot, however, simply equate geneaology, poststructuralism, and postmodernism. While both poststructuralism and

postmodernism have genealogical elements, there are differences of emphasis. Most self-consciously poststructuralist work is distinctly modern in tone, retaining some measure of confidence in the Enlightenment ideas of reason and freedom while indicting modern Western societies for betraying these categories while ostensibly serving them.[7] Writers such as Lyotard and Derrida, in contrast, work continually to disrupt modern categories even as they rely on them.[8] Derridean deconstruction is not a process of destruction, as many critics have charged, but a process of revealing the open spaces and gaps beneath seemingly solid foundations for argument. This revelation does not carry with it the command to replace these gaps with a more secure foundation—a typically modern response—but rather bids us to humility before the limits of reason. Although it is, of course, possible to be both poststructuralist and postmodern—many would place Derrida in this position—no affinity necessarily exists between the two.[9]

The gap between postmodernism and poststructuralism occasionally extends to become a contradiction between arguments for politicized, historicized identities and those for a more thorough deconstruction of identity/identities altogether. Much of the debate between Foucault and Derrida, between "New Historicists" and "deconstructionists," centers on this point. These two lines of thought are better seen not as opposites or exclusive alternatives, however, but as the ground of a rich, often internally contradictory field of discussion. As Gayatri Spivak argues, a central lesson of deconstruction is that we cannot avoid being essentialist; rather, we must work on a heightened consciousness of the effects of and ways in which our essentialisms function.[10] Whether to "be" modern(ist) or postmodern(ist) is finally less important than how to bring the postmodern to presence continually within the modern. This process involves, simultaneously, allegiance to categories of truth and reason and continual disruption and questioning—at times even rejection—of these categories.

Neither postmodernism nor poststructuralism has been accepted by feminists without dispute. Many have argued that without transcendental or quasi-transcendental notions of truth and the subject, feminism loses its critical leverage. Many of those who are keenly aware of the role of culture and history in thought retain the idea that cultural variations are legitimated or tested by their approximation to a liberating truth. The suggestion that any truth claim is internal to systems is acceptable, but only with the provision that some systems are better than others—a reintroduction of metanarrative at a "higher" level. Truly facing the possibility of nontranscendental knowledge induces vertigo in most of us. After all, if we cannot refer to this final truth, upon what may we base our own claims for dignity or inclusion or transformation of society? Even those who are keenly aware of the role of culture and history in thought retain the idea that these variations in some way are legitimated by their approximation to a truth that is also liberating.

Speaking of the relation of poststructuralism to feminism, Linda Alcoff argues that poststructuralism "undercuts our ability to oppose the dominant trend (and, one might argue, the dominant danger) in mainstream Western intellectual thought, that is, the insistence on a universal, neutral, perspectiveless epistemology, metaphysics, and ethics."[11] Within such a framework, "race, class, and gender are constructs and, therefore, incapable of decisively validating conceptions of justice and truth because underneath there lies no natural core to build on or liberate or maximize."[12]

Alcoff equates poststructuralism with liberalism by arguing that poststructuralists hold a social constructionist view of the self and that this view makes all differences contingent; "Once again, underneath we are all the same."[13] This characterization breezes through several difficult points. First, there are many different discourses that we may call "social constructionist," because we lack the will or language to distinguish them. Some of these are indeed based in liberal theory. Poststructuralists such as Foucault and Derrida do not, though, hold to arguments that we have an "underneath" to speak of, nor do they suggest that we are equal fields of possibility waiting for formation. They point to our inevitable enmeshment in linguistic and institutional structures, while also arguing that these structures are not in themselves inevitable, and so our identities are not either. As Mary Poovey argues, deconstruction leads beyond "the more common understanding of social construction many feminists now endorse, because it deconstructs not only the relationship between women and certain social roles but also the very term 'woman.' "[14]

Secondly, we may argue that the criteria for justification are not the same in all areas, and that Alcoff is confusing ethics or politics with natural science. Recognition of historical constructions of experience and the implication of power differentials in those constructions is crucial to any critical claims we might make. As Iris Marion Young states, "a theory of justice that claims universality, comprehensiveness, and necessity implicitly conflates moral reflection with scientific knowledge."[15]

More importantly, however, Alcoff's charge begs the question, for it relies crucially upon the "language game" that is under examination: the claim that poststructuralism(s) undermines the possibilities for action rests on the very point of contention between the opponents. Alcoff would propose that we step back and examine the two discourses and their claims and judge between them. Such a possibility rests upon the very claim I wish to contest, namely that there can be an Archimedean point outside of these languages by which we can examine and judge. Her concern that poststructuralists cannot "decisively" ground and justify notions of justice and truth rests on the belief that somehow we might decisively settle these questions.

Alcoff's objection is based on the premise that without a final, stable, eternal truth there is no truth at all; that without a reality beyond words there is no reality; and that without a knowledge that penetrates to this eternal, prediscursive, presocial reality there is no knowledge. These are ideas that have chained women and men of all races and classes into place. They rest upon ancient but recent Greek distinctions between words and deeds, between the seen and the heard, between appearance and reality, that have been used to order the social hierarchy.[16]

Since Plato, Western elites have justified themselves and their claims on the basis of "universal" ideals and arguments, and they have convinced those of us who live and work within that network that we must do the same if we are to protest against injustice. This persuasion has had the effect, not of strengthening the claims of oppressed or stigmatized groups, but of paralyzing them by forcing them to fit within the master's house and use the master's tools. This tendency is so strong that we fail to see when we are being limited by it, seeing it instead as liberation.

Some insist, for example, that the modern subject position is the only basis for legitimate claims, and so must not be abandoned by feminists.[17] This is an understandable position; as Kaja Silverman has recently noted, "Hegemonic colonialism works by inspiring in the colonized subject the desire to assume the identity of his or her colonizers."[18] Male subjectivity in the modern West is not a liberating force, however, but a debilitating one; subjectivity expands as alienation from life and practice expand, becoming the one refuge of freedom in a world of domination.[19] The price of that refuge has always been conformity. Those without power have continually been asked to "show their papers"—their authority to speak—before they have been heard, and the basis for that authority is acquiescence to the status quo. The Western opposition of objective/subjective, in which white bourgeois men have, not coincidentally, been accorded objectivity, translates into fair/biased in politics, and speaking from our own knowledges as members of oppressed groups disqualifies us as "subjective" or "biased."

Feminists have countered with extensive critiques of the ideological nature of the idea of objectivity in these cases, but we have not been able to relinquish the idea altogether. Instead we have produced a wealth of research and argumentation about the "real" nature of objectivity in order to document and support our claims as subjects. Many in the twentieth century have argued that the hypostatized split between subject and object is not only misguided but also serves ideological functions, as some are accorded the status of subject and others are treated as objects.[20] Feminists have objected to the separation of subject and object, saying that such separation is characteristic of the masculine/masculinist mind but is not the way women's consciousness exists. Yet these same theorists have argued for women's subjectivity as a starting point for any feminist analysis, insisting that women should not or cannot surrender claims to subjectivity because such claims are the basis of political claims in this society.[21] In this way, we perpetuate the dichotomy and its results. Alcoff falls prey to this temptation when she argues that deconstructions of categories such as "woman" make it impossible to demand changes in the lives and status of women. Changes are made precisely by challenging the categories that have been used to exclude and include, to explain or leave ineffable. Deconstruction of "woman" does not mean the elimination of the category any more than prior attacks on the ideologies of womanhood have meant the destruction of the category of woman; it provides a certain distancing and flexibility to the category that are required if we are to move out of the space(s) that have been allocated for us. This attitude toward the idea of "woman" is an essential part of lesbian politics.[22]

Poststructuralism in general and deconstruction in particular may operate as a conservative force in the social and academic worlds. Mary Poovey and Leslie Wahl Rabine have recently reminded us of the ways in which deconstruction is used against any active program by feminists. Both Poovey and Rabine present a more nuanced argument than does Alcoff. In her distinction between the "demystification" and "recuperation" modes of deconstruction, Poovey argues forcefully for demystification and decentering while warning against the reinscription of "woman" into "nature," outside of culture. Rabine likewise notes the dangers of deconstruction, but her warnings are more overtly strategic than are Alcoff's; she acknowledges the occasional political need for unities, but does not extend this acknowledgment into an epistemological position. She is acutely aware of the *political* determinants of theory, warning that "Whether (deconstructive) play is progressive depends on who does it to whom, what is its historic or institutional context, and who makes the rules."[23]

These debates are important and vital, but they are not my central concern here. I wish to enact a version of postmodern lesbianism rather than to engage in the more abstract epistemological and ontological debates. This enactment may in turn be of help in thinking about those debates, making them more specific, as it were.

The Meaning of Lesbianism

We can see in the discussion of lesbianism over the past century or so several theoretical strategies and counterstrategies, all of which hinge on the ambiguity of "nature" and its various transmutations, such as "God" and "psyche." These strategies have served either to justify homophobia and heterosexism or to defend against them. All of them have denied their strategic character, thus operating within Enlightenment standards of truth. Lesbian/gay studies scholars have debated the question of nature versus social construction with an awareness of the strategic role of such arguments, but it is clear that full social acknowledgment of the claim to "naturalness" as a strategy would subvert the strategy itself.[24] In the modern understanding, truth and strategy are opposed; thus, open strategizing about whether or not to claim that lesbianism and gayness are "natural" would delegitimate any claims made about it.

Ironically, the appeal to nature used by lesbians has also been used by those who would condemn them. Heterosexists have argued that "God" or "nature" condemns sexual activity outside of certain situations and formats. Some argue for sexual activity exclusively within the bounds of heterosexual marriage; heterosexists do not uniformly envision sexuality as appropriate only for reproduction, yet they are united in their belief that heterosexuality, whatever its particular forms, is natural and therefore privileged over lesbianism. This opinion relies upon a telic conception of nature, that is, a conception in which nature embodies and carries within it certain goals and purposes. Particular beings and activities can be measured by their conformity to or transgression of these goals and purposes.

Opponents of the God arguments assert that if God were opposed to lesbianism then "He" would not make anyone gay or lesbian, and that God loves us all and wants us to express love for others in any way we can. Opponents of the nature argument have also used nature, but differently construed, for their counterargument. Within these arguments, "nature" is simply the totality of what is, prior to or outside of human intervention. We can recognize the natural by its existence. Lesbianism must be natural, because it occurs; moreover, it occurs with great frequency. The battle between groups, then, is over the nature of nature. Nature functions as an authority no less ambivalently than does God.[25]

A modern version of the nature argument has been embedded within psychoanalysis. Freud's picture of human sexual development and his description of homosexuality as arrested development have legitimated calls for proscription of lesbian identity and activity. Psychoanalytic work that attempts to separate sexuality from more general psychic development by arguing that lesbians/gays are "just like" heterosexuals in every way other than sexual preference has been applauded by many gay and lesbian activists. The debate has not been about the status of psychoanalysis as a narrative of psychological development, but simply and narrowly about whether homosexuality is "sick."

In the neo-Freudian schema developed in the United States, lesbianism is the result of arrested development, dooming lesbians to a life without complete adult love. Cures will make us happier. Psychoanalysis continues to describe lesbianism as a variety of heterosexual development, just as Freud explained women as men gone wrong. Both are entrapped within what Luce Irigaray has called the "logic of the same."[26] The argument of so many lesbian and gay activists—that we just *are* lesbian or gay—attempts to counter that logic, but it does so by recourse to the same old metaphysic, in which nature is a privileged, unchanging, unchangeable category.

Arguments within all of these frameworks are predicated on the existence of an overarching "truth" that vindicates them. Evidence is marshaled to demonstrate one side or another. Statistical surveys documenting the percentage of gays and lesbians in the population, clinical tests evaluating the mental health of lesbians and gays, and biblical exegesis all seek to establish a definitive answer concerning the reality and nature of lesbianism.

The important question is not whether any particular theory is "right" about lesbianism and lesbians. Rather, we need to ask, "So what?" Instead of interrogating science or religion or feminism for the "truth," we need to ask why we need to justify ourselves. Why does homophobia exist? Why is heterosexism so central to Western thought, and why is there so little tolerance for diversity? Why should it be important that we all develop heterosexual attachments and desires? What are the stakes here? Why is homophobia virulent in some societies and mild or nonexistent in others? These questions need asking, not because there is a truth out there to be found that will eliminate heterosexism and homophobia, but because they shift the focus from lesbian identity to heterosexist social institutions. This shift has the signal virtue of avoiding the constructions of lesbianism that trap us—constructions based on the idea of a natural or an authentic lesbian identity, by which we can measure and justify our existence. Asking these questions must be combined with a refusal to answer the earlier questions, with a refusal to explain (which is to justify) ourselves, our choices, and our identities.

This refusal was initiated by lesbian feminists two decades ago. The critique of heterosexuality developed by early radical feminists and sharpened by Adrienne Rich's 1980 landmark article "Compulsory Heterosexuality and Lesbian Existence" focused on how women have been defined in relation to men and on the mechanisms that have enforced that definition. Rich points out the ways in which heterosexuality is unquestioned in feminist discourse, rendering lesbianism either "unnatural" or domesticated into "sexual preference," a purely individual "lifestyle." She urges feminists to question the heterosexist linkage between species survival and reproduction on the one hand and emotional/erotic relationships on the other. This challenge is still compelling.

The radical critique notwithstanding, the drive for self-justificatory explanation has also operated freely within lesbian feminism. From the beginnings of contemporary lesbian feminism, women concerned themselves with the question of the "meaning" of lesbianism. The authors of the 1970 essay "The Woman-Identified Woman" answered by crystallizing from their personal experience the essence of "the lesbian": "She is the woman who . . . acts in accordance with her inner compulsion to be a more complete and freer human being than her society . . . cares to allow her. . . . On some level she has not been able to accept the limitations and oppression laid on her by the most basic role of her society—the female role."[27] Lesbianism is about rebellion.

In this view, lesbianism is not simply sexual but is a matter of resistance to patriarchy. Lesbianism is about being fully oneself rather than the stunted person that society thinks of as "woman." The theme of rebellion was blended with the idea that lesbians are those who never turn their backs on their mothers, their first love. What had been seen by psychoanalysts as a failure to separate and individuate became in lesbian feminism the constancy of female love. And this love for the mother enables us to resist the imperatives of male, Oedipal society;

this love for women that we never lose is both the source of our rebellion and the seed of our wholeness.

Feminist and lesbian poets, theorists, and historians have engaged in struggles to reclaim and reshape words to reflect strength and integrity. The debates about the meaning of lesbianism have been waged often in the form of debates about the meaning of the word "lesbian," the history of lesbians, and the reclamation of words that have been used against us.[28] Many of these projects, however, maintain an allegiance to uncovering deep meanings and ultimate truths rather than to focusing on the disruptive strategies highlighted by poststructural perspectives. The difference emerges at the point where the writer takes the new definition or history to be not simply a political strategy conducted within and through language but the deep meaning and truth of lesbianism. The commitment to a final truth—hitherto occluded by sexism, heterosexism, racism, and other structures of oppression—enables (or forces) some of these writers to except their own strategies from their otherwise acute understanding of the strategic use of language. As Fuss argues, "What is missing in many of the treatises on lesbian identity is a recognition of the precarious status of identity and a full awareness of the complicated processes of identity formation, both psychical and social."[29]

An example of this flawed commitment to truth is displayed by Jeffner Allen in her collection of essays on lesbian philosophy. The essays convincingly describe the sexual domination of women by men and question the "phallogocentric" order that makes such domination invisible, and they provide a strong demystification of the heterosexual order. Allen never mentions that men differ across race, class, sexuality, culture, and time; she makes these differences secondary to men's shared status as oppressors. Women are equally unitary, lesbians the most so. She tells us that "although torn apart in its tissue by men's logocentric vision, the world of female friendship has maintained an ethics of care and a metaphysics of touch. Apart from the ties that bind men, *a fundamental ontological rupture is effected by women.*"[30] There is, for Allen, an originally intact world or process of female friendship, which is inherently lesbian. It is grounded on women's ethics and metaphysics. Later attacks weaken and shred this world, but it persists.

But what happens to this vision if lesbians decide that this "ethic of care" has been imposed on us by men, that it is part of the powerlessness of women?[31] Is it possible that such a "metaphysics of touch" is the result of women's lack of access to formal education rather than the "natural" distaste for abstraction that Allen describes?[32] Certainly then lesbians may be the most womanly but not for that the most intact of women.

Allen could (and I think would) respond that such ideas are male identified, a product of an earlier rupture from one's female self. But this response relies on her narrative; it is not external to it, a neutral criterion or explanation, but makes sense precisely within the paradigm I am challenging. Rather than arguing with one another about which story is true, lesbians must look instead at what is at stake in our differing stories; we must examine the consequences of our stories in terms of power and change. If Fuss is right—and I believe she is—in arguing that essentialism is linked to oppression, then lesbian essentialism is understandable; when one is presented with a stigmatized identity, it makes sense to challenge the stigma surrounding that identity. To do so serves, ironically, to reinforce the solidity of that identity even as the stigma is rejected. Maintaining and strengthening such essentialized identities, however, will not end our oppression. We must find the room and the strength to confront the fear that perhaps there is no single core to lesbian identity and thus that our identities rely on politics rather than ontology—indeed, that ontology is itself an effect of politics.

(Be)Coming Out

The privileging of lesbian identity, and the need for truth that underlies this privileging, is displayed in the whole cluster of ideas manifested in the phrase "coming out." This phrase is meant to suggest that the process of declaring one's lesbianism is a revelation, an acknowledgment of a previously hidden truth. By implication, coming out is a process of discovery or admission rather than one of construction or choice.

Lesbians all know how this works. When we meet someone who "looks like a dyke" or who hangs around with lesbians but is involved with men, we wait for her to admit the truth to herself—to come out of denial. Or we might judge the authenticity of other lesbians on our assessments of the "consistency" of their sexuality and their politics. Such discriminations rest on the assumptions that we "are" or "are not" lesbian and that sexuality and politics are part of a seamless whole, sundered only by false consciousness. Collections of coming-out stories document this narrative of discovery.

There are other ways to tell this story. Barbara Ponse describes a "gay trajectory" of identity construction that ranges over five elements, from a feeling of being "different" to finding a community and entering an intimate relationship. Ponse notes that the presence of any of the five elements gives rise to a common assumption among lesbians that the individual concerned "is really" a lesbian and will come to realize that. She describes as "identity work" the "processes and procedures engaged in by groups designed to effect change in the meanings of particular identities."[33] In this account the process of "coming out" is at least as much a matter of "becoming" as revealing.

The idea of (be)coming out also illuminates the concept of "the closet." As a metaphor for invisibility, the closet is spatial. It suggests that our identity is clear, and the question is simply whether or not that identity is visible, whether it takes up space. If we think of identity as a process, the closet changes. Leaving the closet is not a matter of simple visibility, but is a reconfiguration of the self. It is a project rather than an event. Becoming lesbian is indeed a process of resistance to patriarchal heterosexuality. It is not the discovery or revelation of one's resistance but is the resistance itself. Furthermore, this project is never complete. One is never "finally," "truly" a lesbian, but becomes lesbian or not with the choices one makes.

Drawing on the work of Michel Foucault, Mark Blasius has argued that coming out is instead a process of "*becoming* lesbian or gay." This involves a "practical creation of the self" in a community that guides one in the process of becoming lesbian or gay. This process is described by Blasius as a "lifelong learning of how to become and of inventing the meaning of being a lesbian or a gay man in this historical moment."[34] There is in this view a reality, a stable horizon of what it means to be lesbian or gay, but that stability is not given by discovery of deep truth but by participating in particular historical communities and discourses. Coming out is partially a process of revealing something kept hidden, but it is more than that. It is a process of fashioning a self—a lesbian self—that did not exist before coming out began.

I want to illustrate this by discussing my own process of becoming lesbian. When I first came out, I looked into my past for the indicators of my true sexuality and gloried to find them. Thinking that I was discovering rather than becoming, I traced my history of latent lesbianism: being a tomboy, playing sexual games with pubescent girlfriends, being a feminist, not shaving my body hair. This was supported by several friends' response to my announcement: "I knew it all the time." Wow! These people met me when I was married to a man, and they nevertheless *knew!* It must be true.

Now I look at my list and my friends differently. What we all saw as signs of lesbianism were signs of nonconformity to sexist standards of femininity. To see adolescent sex with girls as an indicator, I had to ignore the decade of sex with men. Many lesbians have helped me to do this, arguing that my sex with men was alienated, the result of various forms of compulsory heterosexuality, while playing with girls is evidence of my true desire. But this view is too simple. It rests on the same "principle of consistency" that Ponse notes among heterosexuals: the assumption of a natural linkage among sex, gender role, gender identity, and sexual object choice.[35] According to this principle, deviation from gender role is an indication of deviance, either latent or actual, from heterosexuality. This logic is too often accepted by lesbians as well as heterosexuals and provides the basis for the conflation of feminism with lesbianism.

What is it to become lesbian? At a certain point my focus changed. I agonized, as so many of us do, as I saw the price of being lesbian in a homophobic and heterosexist society. That agony served to make me aware of the power of the system of heterosexuality. And on a day in June, on a street in Los Angeles where I had always felt at home, I became a stranger. I looked around at others, and I felt them looking at me, and realized that I had crossed a line: I was a lesbian. I experienced that moment partially as discovery: so this was the difference I had always felt and never had a name for. But as the days and months and years went on, that feeling faded. Being a lesbian was not the source of the difference I had felt; that difference traced instead to being a rebel: it was wearing denim jackets and old jeans in Beverly Hills (before it was popular), it was short hair in Malibu, it was hanging out with the guys instead of the girls without quite "becoming like" the guys. It was a whole network of identity and power relations that produced my specific consciousness.

Lesbian theorists have been implicated in heterosexuality and patriarchy at the point where we conflate lesbianism and "gender trouble." Being a tomboy is not an indicator of lesbianism except to those who believe that real women do not climb trees. This belief has been embraced by conservatives and by many lesbians, who take tree climbing as evidence of deviation from the heterosexual norm. Linking gender rebellion to lesbianism replicates the binary opposition of "woman" (= heterosexual) versus "lesbian"; it thus effectively discourages women who have sex with men from linking politically with lesbians and in turn limits the potential strength for feminist agendas.[36]

Lesbianism provides a critical space against heteropatriarchy most keenly insofar as lesbians turn from self-explanation to analysis and demystification of the heterosexual order(s) that define "woman" and "man" and make lesbians so scandalous. Examining my own being as a lesbian, even in celebration, reinscribes that heterosexual space within which lesbians are an anomaly.[37] This reinscription does not preclude any self-examination, but it mandates a measure of humility and critical distance on the constructions and narratives of identity that we produce and live within.

Reading an autobiographical essay by Minnie Bruce Pratt, Biddy Martin and Chandra Talpade Mohanty focus on the importance of historical specificity in locating oneself. This approach includes a strong deromanticization of lesbianism. In their reading, lesbianism is not the source of epistemological or political privilege in any simple sense. Rather, it "is that which exposes the extreme limits of what passes itself off as simply human, as universal, as unconstrained by identity, namely, the position of the white middle class." In their view, this critical stance does not eliminate the possibility of community or common action; it is what makes such action possible. "Change has to do with the transgression of boundaries, those boundaries so carefully, so tenaciously, so invisibly drawn around white identity."[38] Or, as Teresa de Lauretis puts it, lesbianism is not "a truer or essential or unifying identity, but precisely the critical vantage point" that operates against unification and simple identification.[39] We must forsake the idea that lesbian sexuality is outside of, or against, or safe from the network of compulsory heterosexuality, bearing in mind Lyotard's warning that being in opposition is one of the modes of participation within a system. I agree that it is possible for lesbian sex and sexuality to present possibilities not comprehended by heterosex(uality), but this possibility is not a given but an achievement, and it is never as total as we might want. Debates over whether butch/femme roles or other forms of lesbian life replicate heterosexual structures have too often foundered on assumptions that some practices or ideas or identities simply are or are not sources for progressive social change. Shifting the debates to how to make these practices or ideas or identities progressive would be more useful.[40] The issue of location is not simply one of whether we are "like" heterosexuals or not but of how, precisely, we live our lives. "Lesbians" occupy more than one position within the structures of patriarchal heterosexuality, even as they push the edges of those structures. As Ann Ferguson describes it, lesbian cultures are "potential cultures of resistance *within* historically specific patriarchal cultures."[41] Were lesbian cultures not within patriarchy, we would not have to engage in so much struggle to define and maintain them. Thinking of ourselves as simply outside is an illusion that denies us any strategic power in patriarchal cultures.

Nature, Truth, and Politics

Like its cousins *am* and *is*, the word *be* implies a fixity and stability to lesbian identity that does not serve lesbians. Insofar as we "are" lesbians, we are caught up in the network of power centered in the medical/psychological structures that grew up in the nineteenth century around the "types" of character that did certain socially proscribed acts—the homosexual, the pervert, the delinquent, and so on. Twist and turn as we might, the imputation of "being" will inevitably implicate us in society's disciplinary structures.[42]

Growing up as most of us have in systems that impute identity to sexual orientation, relinquishing lesbianism as a kind of nature may seem baffling or incoherent. But the defects of "lesbian as being" are evident in questions such as "Can you be heterosexual and feminist?" Heterosexuals "are" no more than lesbians or gays, except that their "nature" has been called into question less than that of others. More productive questions might be: What is it like to live as a lesbian in certain times/places? How are lesbians and lesbianism positioned in a given society? What relations to power are called into play when we assume a "lesbian" subject position? Which of those relations require change, and which might be drawn upon to effect that change? Convinced that sexuality is symptomatic of being, that it is "prior to" convention (except insofar as we are deformed by some occurrence), lesbians have called upon ourselves and one another to decipher the truth of our bodies and to attune our politics to that truth. But my body has had enough truth to last a lifetime. I do not need epistemology to justify my desire, my life, my love. I need politics; I need to build a world that does not require such justifications. The appeal of postmodern theory is precisely due to its rejection of the separation of philosophy from (and privileging over) politics. The space once occupied by the metanarratives that regulate our knowledge becomes an open field for politics, a politics that knows itself to be such and so empowers its practitioners more democratically than do academic and popular discourses of "truth." This (ironically very philosophical) appeal is fulfilled in the "theory in the flesh" being done by many who would not align themselves with postmodernism. Acknowledging that power is at stake helps us to address questions of justice directly rather than allowing claims of authority to silence us (or using those claims to silence one another).

Challenging the naturalism implicit in ideas such as "coming out" may better enable lesbians to formulate identities that foster coalitions and alliances. Gay men, one possible community of allies, have also been struggling with issues of identity and politics. Arguments about whether gays and lesbians constitute an ethnic minority, arguments that I will address in the following chapter, are arguments about what sort of politics to pursue, but they often founder on the shoals of the assumption that the discussion is about what gays or lesbians "really" are rather than about how best to articulate those identities. Similarly, debates about the relation between race and class, about the connections between contemporary racial identities and historical nations, are central to rearticulations of the positions and politics of people of color.[43]

The rebellion against the (meta)narratives of the white, male West deprives us of the legitimation and purity we so often have desired, but it need not deprive us of a basis for action. The rebellion is not against all knowledge, even all narrative knowledge, but against the great stories of legitimation that have served to blind us to the role of power in common life. We may say that lesbianism challenges heterosexual privilege, that it challenges heterosexist gender conceptions, without going so far as to say that it provides us with its own privileged epistemology. Lesbianism provides the vantage point for a negative dialectic, a displacement and critique, what de Lauretis calls "a space of contradictions, in the here and now, that need to be affirmed but not resolved."[44]

Thus, lesbians should not refuse the specificity and reality of lesbian experience, nor should we reify our experience into an identity and history so stable that no one can speak to it besides other lesbians who agree on that particular description of their existence. Getting specific about our histories and the processes whereby we become and continue to be lesbians will enable us to decide when to reach out and when to withdraw, when to emphasize commonalities among and between groups and when differences and inequalities must be highlighted. The following chapters are attempts at such work.

Chapter 4

Lesbians and Mestizas: Appropriation and Equivalence

Early models of oppressions as additive have increasingly given way to an understanding that oppression and resistance are lived as unities, and that another way of understanding the cumulative effects of multiple oppressions must be formulated. The Combahee River Collective described oppressions as "interlocking," stating that "the synthesis of these oppressions creates the conditions of our lives."[1] More recently, Gloria Anzaldúa's concept of the "new mestiza" illuminates a view of multiple oppression as the site of a new consciousness, a consciousness with a heightened appreciation of ambiguity and multiplicity. The effect of interlocking systems of power is to prevent a secure singular identity. This is not a weakness, but is a strength; only such a dislocation can provoke the awareness of possibilities and the tolerance of ambiguity that she sees as requirements for real social change.

Anzaldúa's work on the new mestiza intersects two disparate discussions about lesbian identity. The first is the discussion, largely among white gay men, of sexuality as ethnicity. The second, more "lesbian" usage, refers less to "the facts" about sexuality and more to mestiza consciousness, a possibility of thought that might prove fruitful for all people. In this second conversation, the mestiza appears as an "inappropriate/inappropriated other," as one who challenges existing categories by her refusal/inability to fit within them.[2] After addressing the first discussion, I will return to the question of mestiza position and consciousness as a model for feminist theory. Lesbianism is a locus of social oppression but not one that is simply analogous to race. The simple analogy is culturally imperialist; so is a politics built on the theory that "all oppressions are the same" because they share a pattern of inequality. The image of the mestiza has tremendous power and attraction for many white lesbians, but we cannot for that reason simply adopt it as our own. Nonetheless, Anzaldúa's vision and description provide a sorely needed ontological account of coalitional identity politics.

Race and Ethnicity

In *Racial Formation in the United States from the 1960s to the 1980s,* Michael Omi and Howard Winant describe the paradigms by which races have been constructed and understood in the United States. The dominant paradigm, which they term "ethnicity-based" theory, seeks to describe race as a social grouping rather than a biological one. Ethnicity theory bypasses race in favor of culture, or, more accurately, it rewrites racial difference as equivalent to other cultural/historical group differences. In this theoretical frame, Blacks in the United States are an ethnic group in the same way that Italian-Americans are. Omi and Winant note the Euro-American bias of this equation, both for its rejection of any distinctive difference between "white" ethnic groups and "black" or other racial groups, and also for the treatment of Blacks as a single ethnic group without acknowledgment of either the tribal differences before enslavement or regional differences in the United States.

The central concerns of ethnicity theory desribed by Omi and Winant are the "incorporation and separation of 'ethnic minorities,' the nature of ethnic identity, and the impact of ethnicity on politics."[3] The ethnicity model is the research paradigm of liberal politics. Founded in a rejection of biological racial theory, the ethnicity paradigm spoke to the experience of European immigrants, with their dilemmas of assimilation and "getting ahead" versus maintaining cultural identity. Cultural identity became a "private" matter, irrelevant to one's work and legal position. The affinity of this conceptualization with liberalism is clear. In a liberal world, we are united by laws and, secondarily, by economic interdependence, but culture is irrelevant to the public sphere.

This blindness, or impoverishment, in liberal visions of the polity produces a number of reactions. The most faithful child of this vision of ethnicity is what Daniel Bell has labeled "the new ethnicity." The "new ethnicity" has changed the conception of ethnicity from something private and simply affective to a bifurcation between an explicitly political identity, aimed at the state and interest-group politics, and an "expressive" moment of "community." Bell suggests that the new ethnicity can be seen as either "the emergent expression of primordial feelings" or as "a 'strategic site,' chosen by disadvantaged persons as a new mode of seeking political redress in the society."[4] In fact, the two are not exclusive; as a reaction to the impersonal bureaucratic political and social culture of the United States in the late twentieth century, ethnic identity provides a site for community and interpersonal relations. The feelings expressed may not be "primordial" in the sense of a stable, always-here-though-unacknowledged complex of attachments and values, but they are quickly rearticulated and experienced as such. The new ethnicity may be clearly political, but it is also a response to cultural impoverishment.

A second response to the narrowness of liberalism is the rejection of the ethnicity paradigm in favor of visions that allow for the force of culture as a binding element in human life. Omi and Winant identify class theory and nation theory as the primary paradigms of critical work on race. Class theory seeks to understand race in terms of the "social allocation of advantage and disadvantage," in economic terms, while nation-based theories focus on "cultural autonomy and the right to self-determination" as a people.[5]

Both of these theories gained a certain strength from the historical conditions of people of color in the United States. Segregation, whether official or not, forced the development of institutions and identities for people wholly overlooked or excluded from white definitions of the United States and its institutions of culture and power. White recognition of the "activities and institutions" of people of color relied upon their resemblance to white ones; "truly indigenous activities and institutions qualitatively distinct from majority values," that is, ones that did not simply translate into the cultural language of the dominant society, remained invisible and thus bereft of hegemonic legitimation.[6]

Segregation and poverty lent themselves to two contrasting images of race. Mario Barrera describes how the focus on poverty among Chicanos led many to adopt a Marxist analysis in which all Chicanos were by definition part of the working class.[7] This argument has always run up against the political reality that the call for class unity "has amounted in practice to an argument that nonwhites give up their racially based demands in favor of 'class' unity on white terms."[8] In contrast, the argument for nationhood has relied upon the idea of a homeland, locating racial oppression within a narrative of national oppression and colonialism. The political consequence has generally been separatist, focusing on the development of "indigenous" organizations and institutions and the reclamation of culture. The result has been both culturally strong, vital communities and political marginalization. More dangerously, members of such nationalist communities often became "consumers of their own culture,"[9] and saw this consumption as political activity sufficient unto itself. In this way, nationalism and capitalism intertwine.

Before moving on to consider whether sexuality "is like" ethnicity, it is important to underscore that the ethnicity model does not simply describe something, "ethnicity," that is out in the world, but is rather one articulation of differences. Its historical links to liberalism have made it a powerful articulation for interest-group politics in the form of the "new ethnicity." As an articulation that serves primarily to assimilate and pacify rather than to bring differences into the sphere of critical recognition, however, it is questionable whether ethnicity is an adequate paradigm for any radical social movement.

Sexuality as Ethnicity

Ethnicity has provided a powerful self-understanding for many whites from nondominant groups, such as southern and eastern Europeans.[10] It has spoken to the experience of people whose aim truly has been assimilation, though often they have experienced the loss of historical identification as a result. It has also been one powerful model for liberal feminism, with its agenda of assimilation into the male public world. Racial metaphors, on the other hand, have provided a different ground for political imagination. Race in the United States has been the mark of the unassimilable, the "truly different." As a result, movements defined "racially" have vacillated between the poles of assimilation and nationalism in a manner unavailable to "ethnic minorities."

The project of gay/lesbian liberation was conceived in the United States along the lines of ethnic or racial politics, largely because that seemed politically effective.[11] The impact of the civil rights and Black Power movements on the U.S. political imagination made them ripe for imitation. The white feminist movement as well as the gay and lesbian movement(s) appropriated not only the (often contradictory) arguments for civil rights and for group pride but also the descriptions and metaphors of position; as Kobena Mercer has described the situation in Britain, "black pride acted as metonymic leverage for the expression of 'gay pride' just as notions of 'brotherhood' and 'community' in black political discourse influenced the assertions of 'global sisterhood' or 'sisterhood is strength.' "[12] The large component of cultural nationalism in radical lesbian/gay politics is a result of this "racial" articulation.

Ethnic and racial articulations of sexuality have coexisted in uneasy balances in various cities for almost fifty years now. Both, however, have revolved around the same axis of essentialism that leads to so much confusion and pain. While they are politically efficacious in their hold on popular imagination and in their implicit political prescriptions, they must be carefully negotiated if lesbians and gays are to avoid simple imitation of some of the worst features of those articulations.

Treating sexuality as ethnicity requires a certain amount of essentialism.[13] By this I mean that sexuality must come to seem as much a matter of "primordial affinities and attachments" as ethnicity does to most Americans.[14] Sexuality, specifically sexual object choice, must come to be seen as given and stable over the lifetime of an individual. This stability, in turn, should then be described as resting upon or resulting from a sexual identity, a persistent attribute beyond "behavior." This interpretation of sexuality in fact coincides with prevailing United States characterizations, in which people "really are" heterosexual or homosexual (though homosexuality is a regrettable, hopefully curable, condition). Sexual activity does not inevitably dictate sexual identity—one may occasionally engage in "lesbian sex" while identifying as a heterosexual—but generally such persons are presumed by both lesbians/gays and heterosexuals to be in a state of denial about the "truth" of their identity.

Barbara Ponse describes the heterosexist "principle of consistency" that links sex assignment, gender identity, gender role, sexual object choice, and sexual identity. Through this linkage, "female" comes to be equated with "woman," which in turn is linked to "heterosexual" (in this case, attraction to men). Thus, a lesbian is not "really" a woman. Her gender identity ("woman") conflicts with her sexual identity ("lesbian"), and this conflict is resolved through the stereotype of the "masculine" lesbian as the "real" lesbian.[15]

Ponse suggests that, far from rejecting this principle of consistency, lesbians adopt a corresponding "gay trajectory" of lesbian identity formation that "functions as a biographic norm" among white lesbians.[16] The trajectory moves from "a subjective sense of being different from heterosexual persons" that is attributed to attraction to women, to "an understanding of the homosexual or lesbian significance of these feelings." The third stage is acceptance of a lesbian identity—"coming out." On this basis, the individual searches for a community and for a lesbian sexual and emotional relationship(s). As Ponse notes, any one of these elements is sufficient to establish the belief among lesbians that a woman "is lesbian," whether she acknowledges it or not. Lesbian explanations of sexual identity conform to

what Omi and Winant term the rule of "hypo-descent" in race categorizing.[17] In racial theory, hypo-descent is the rule that "even a little"
makes one "really" one race or another, usually a stigmatized one.
The lesbian corollary to this is the belief that "even a little" lesbian
sexual desire makes one "really" a lesbian, as though desire (and race)
were discrete entities, categorized by nature. Thus, both the heterosexual and the lesbian stories assume a fixed reality about one's "true"
sexual identity and seek explanations for deviations and anomalies.

This assumption has been increasingly problematic for lesbians.
The room for lesbians within white feminism, even to the sanctioning
of lesbian relationships as "feminism in action," has provided a means
for many white women to identify as lesbians on the basis of political
and affective ties rather than sexual activity.[18] Such choices, however,
have given a different twist to essentialism among white feminist lesbians. Here, the essentialism is less about lesbianism as object choice
than it is about male and female natures and heterosexual relations.
Early arguments about "sleeping with the enemy" presumed a monolithic male nature and a correspondingly unambiguous feminist politics. Lesbians, in this interpretation, are the ones who leave the world
of (male or patriarchal) nature for the realm of (female or feminist)
freedom.[19]

Notions of primordial affinities have not been sufficient in themselves to establish an ethnic articulation of sexuality. The second element of the ethnic model is having a culture and a history. Some lesbians and gay men have worked at establishing historical linkages and
claiming ancestors as part of the project of "ethnicizing" sexuality. For
example, Judy Grahn has argued that "Gay [sic] culture is ancient and
has been suppressed into an underground state of being," but that it
nonetheless is "continuous."[20] To make her point, Grahn moves across
continents, time, and sexual desires. She includes as ancestors women
who had sex exclusively with men but who defy modern white stereotypes of "feminine" behavior.[21] For Grahn, the early feminist slogan
that "feminism is the theory, lesbianism is the practice" is transformed
into "acting in ways that feminists now celebrate makes one a lesbian." Thus, the lesbian appropriation of unconventional women described by Ponse is extended by Grahn across time and culture.

Grahn's project belies her experience of growing up in a lesbophobic, medicalized society. For her, the decisive marker of lesbianism in
the past is gender-role inversion. As Scott Bravmann has noted,
Grahn's project ignores the fact that non-European societies do not always assign and link gender and sexuality as European and Euro-
American ones do: thus the berdache, interpreted by Euro-Americans

as "homosexual," is defined (within those Native American cultures where berdache is an institution) not by "sexual orientation" but by a different alignment between biological sex and social gender than the prevailing one.[22] The "recovery" work of writers such as Grahn amounts to colonization of other cultures for the service of a contemporary, largely Euro-American, movement. In doing so, both the other cultures and contemporary lesbians are treated incompletely. The centrality of inversion belies a prefeminist, medicalized understanding of homosexuality. In extending this alignment of gender and desire to other cultures, it misrepresents them as well.[23]

The creation of a history is part of an effort to justify our lives. "Successful" justification will not be a matter of demonstrating longevity, however; Jewish, Christian, and Muslim fundamentalists all agree that sodomy was practiced at Sodom. Nor will the demonstration that "homosexuality is a way of being," rather than a "behavior," be sufficient to end oppression.[24] Medicalization was precisely that demonstration, but it has not served lesbians and gays well. Even the argument that there is and has been a "culture" will not stop the "cultural war" of the Right; Europeans and Euro-Americans (including some white women, gay men, and lesbians) have proved willing, and even zealous, to destroy other cultures.[25] The New Right is perfectly willing to talk of a "gay culture" and to accuse its members of destroying the United States. "Invented traditions" will not do the work of politics for us. I do not mean that all attempts to treat the past and honor heroes are mistaken. I do mean that such attempts must always be modest, undertaken with awareness of their limitations and possible pitfalls.

Postmodern Ethnicity

Postmodernism works to deconstruct not only lesbian claims to ethnicity but the general category of ethnicity itself. In this effort postmodern theorists are not alone but are joined by the whole range of "social constructionists" who have called into question the view of ethnicity as primordial rather than strategic or functional. In the latter view, known variously as "circumstantialist," "optionalist," or "social constructionist," ethnicity is "a strategic possibility peculiarly suited to the requirements of political and social mobilization in the modern large-scale state."[26] Ethnicity becomes a matter of "putative" rather than "absolute" ascription,[27] distinguishable from voluntary affiliation not in kind but in degree.

The conceptual opposition of voluntary association and absolute ascription rests on liberal models of society in which one is either the agent of voluntary association (that is, with no necessary pressure beyond "subjective affinity") or one is fixed in social space by factors beyond one's control. Marx's exposure of the ideological functions of this opposition within capitalism did not enable him to overcome it in his own thought, and Marxism has for a century oscillated between voluntarism and various determinisms. Thoroughly challenging this model requires that we question the idea of "society" as "founding totality of its partial processes"[28] and work instead on describing social relations as articulatory practices that produce and/or modify the identities of individuals. "Ethnicity" then can be seen as one such articulation, a "construction of nodal points which partially fix meaning."[29]

With such a view, the question can no longer be stated as "Is lesbianism analogous to ethnicity?" Instead, the question is "What are the implications of such an analogy? What sort of relations are established through this articulation of lesbianism?"

As developed by writers such as Grahn, the ethnic model has little to offer feminist lesbians. This is so for several reasons. First, the articulation often relies on an essentialist view of lesbianism, a view that I challenged in the preceding chapter. This essentialism may speak to the experience of lifelong lesbians, but it cannot adequately address the desires and understandings of those who came to women later in life. Second, the ethnicity model relies fundamentally on a medicalized view of sexuality, in which sexual object choice and gender identity are "naturally" aligned. Finally, this articulation enacts a "natural" identity with gay men, an identity that many feminist lesbians would challenge. This is perhaps the reason why so few lesbians have involved themselves in the ethnicity debates at all. As lesbians and gays move into open political battles in the United States, however, the ethnic analogy appears more frequently. I will argue later that we do not need this analogy to argue for civil rights. If we do not need the ethnic paradigm for civil rights, and if it poses dangers of cultural nationalism and essentialism, then we can and should dispense with it.

Lesbianism: A New *Mestizaje?*

Another "racial" articulation has attracted many white lesbians: the vision of the mestiza described most notably by Gloria Anzaldúa. In *Borderlands / La Frontera*, Anzaldúa describes and enacts mestiza history and consciousness.[30] The history of the U.S. Southwest, of Aztlán, is a history of conquest upon conquest, of Indian mixing with Spaniard with Anglo with African-American. In this mingling it resembles the rest of the United States—indeed, the rest of the American continents. The distinctive feature of the Southwest is the survival of indigenous people as distinct peoples and as mixtures simultaneously, as living history of rapes and slaughters and loves and memories. This demarcation that is always shifting is evident even in the names used to delineate heritage; "Chicano" has implications quite contrary to those of "Spanish-American" or "Mexican-American," and, as John Garcia notes, "one's ethnic label choice may vary with the social setting."[31] Anzaldúa's self-labeling as a Chicana marks her off as politically radical, proud of her border existence, seeking neither the purity of Indian ancestry nor the privilege of the Spanish, but instead looking for distinctive values in mestiza history.[32]

Anzaldúa's lesbianism prevents her full or easy assimilation into Chicana/Chicano culture, just as her ethnic heritage marks her within white lesbian communities. She compares the two exclusions, treating them as bridges instead:

> As a *mestiza* I have no country, my homeland cast me out; yet all countries are mine because I am every woman's sister or potential lover. (As a lesbian I have no race, my own people disclaim me; but I am all races because there is the queer of me in all races.)[33]

In many ways, Anzaldúa's formulation might be read as a reification of lesbian identity; references to "the queer of me" and statements that lesbians have "no race" qua lesbians might appear to reinstate "modern" universalist notions of identity. That is not Anzaldúa's meaning here. She does not state that she "is" raceless, but that her "own people" reject and deny her. She retains a link to "all races" through her connections with other lesbians. This is clarified in a later essay, when she states that "Though the deepest connections colored dykes have is to their native culture, we also have strong links with other races, including whites. Though right now there is a strong return to nationalist feeling, colored lesbian feminists in our everyday interactions are truly more citizens of the planet."[34] This is not simply a matter of the good will of lesbian feminists but instead reflects that "white culture and its perspectives are inscribed on us / into us."[35]

Perhaps the most important lesson for white lesbians to learn from Anzaldúa's discussion is the rejection of "ontological separatism." The heterosexist rejection of lesbians as belonging somewhere else, usually to an enemy, is matched by a separatist vision in which lesbians are not "really" of the world in which they were raised and in which they encountered their pain or isolation. Ontological separatism is distinct from certain political separatisms that focus on the need for a moment of separation to build and reinforce threatened identities. Whereas the latter treats separatism not as a final solution but as part of a movement toward general social change, the former describes separatism as an acknowledgment of the fundamental and permanent differences between men and women (or lesbians and everyone else) that make common action impossible.[36]

The mestiza has moments of separation, but the more fundamental aspect of being mestiza is the dual inability ever to fully separate or fully belong. If "belonging" requires exclusion of the other(s), the mestiza can belong only by sacrificing part of herself; and in this case, then not all of her has lived to belong. Whatever survives is not mestiza so much as part of a person. Separation likewise is a denial of her own reality, of elements of her life that remain meaningful. As a consequence, the mestiza focuses on blending, on inclusion rather than exclusion. This blending is not simply transcendence of conflict and opposition, but internalization of the struggle. Mestizas belong even where "their own people" deny it.[37]

Thus, mestiza identities are paradigmatic of postmodern social ontology, in which social identities are treated as "the meeting point for a multiplicity of articulatory practices, many of them antagonistic."[38] *Mestizaje* is not an essence but is the very transgression of essence, a "point of departure, a mark of difference, allowing for the expression of other differences."[39] Mestizas "juggle cultures" with "plural personalit[ies]."[40] Describing mestizas in this way does not valorize dissociation or multiple-personality syndrome, as some critics have charged. The multiplicity of the mestiza is not simply internal fracture, a failure to build an integrated personality, but is a sociohistorical reality. Against those who would have mestizas "choose" one aspect of their lives, one culture over another(s), Anzaldúa insists that all of her "personalities" are part of her integrated self. This is evident in Anzaldúa's writing, in which the "we" shifts from page to page, meaning sometimes queers, sometimes Chicanos/Chicanas, sometimes feminists. Her contextualization of this shifting "we" removes the possibility of reading her statements as simple calls for unity, instead calling on us to acknowledge all of her locations at once and equally.

This does not mean that Anzaldúa "is postmodern," or that every aspect of the mestiza is replicated and captured by poststructuralist theory. The belongingness of the mestiza for Anzaldúa is not simply a matter of choice, of voluntary affiliation, but of history and social density. In that evocation of history and rebellion, and in her political commitment, she is allied with Michel Foucault. She is not simply "Foucauldian," however, as if reading Foucault would tell us what Anzaldúa thinks. She retains a sense of the mystery at the heart of being that vanishes from Foucault's later work. In that recognition of mystery she is on the same path as Jean-François Lyotard, Jean-Luc Nancy, and Jacques Derrida, but she provides a more forceful alliance of strong politics and philosophical humility than do they. Her recognition of the incompleteness of every identity and every project does not lead her to inaction, to continual deferral of politics, as has been the case for so many poststructuralists or postmodernist thinkers.[41] Rather, it leads her to a "radical acceptance of vulnerability," in Gayatri Spivak's terms.[42] The mestiza is defined by her shifting territories and incomplete identifications, but the instability and incompleteness of the territories and identifications does not render them less "real" than more unitary ones. They point to the historical, rather than ontological, nature of all territories and identities.

As lesbians, we (both white lesbians and lesbians of color) are often denied by our families or our communities and cut off from major social institutions, but the fact of our birth and life within those communities and cultures is not so easily erased within us. We may be defined as other, but in fact we are always here, always present before those who would deny us. Lesbianism does not locate us as members of one culture who are trapped by birth or circumstance in an alien land. As Iris Young explains, difference "is not absolute otherness, a complete absence of relationship or shared attributes,"[43] but exists within a field of discourse that provides the system of relationships of same/other, similar/different. To the extent that white middle-class lesbians refuse difference and insist on otherness, on absolute exclusion, we/they replicate the prevailing structures of domination.

Rather than being marginal, rather perhaps even than being liminal, lesbians are central to the societies that repudiate them. We are not accepted as lesbians, but our not being accepted does not entail that there is a somewhere else we really belong. It is tempting to think that we must fully belong somewhere, but the temptation must be resisted.[44] The ideal of full and uncomplicated belonging rests on the ideal of the unitary, harmonious self, thus demanding that we seek out and eliminate the obstacles to this harmonious unity.

This lack of "belonging" does not mean that there is not, will not be, or should not be any such thing as "lesbian culture." Lesbian cultures are becoming a social reality; the question is not whether to build lesbian cultures, but what sort of culture(s) we want to build.[45]

The historical development of lesbian communities alerts us to the fact that there is no one such thing as "lesbian culture" for all of us to belong to; rather, there are many lesbian cultures or subcultures. "Lesbian culture" cannot be a monolith or a totality that encompasses all of our lives, and this limitation is actually a strength. We must recognize and retain our positions in the dominant society, both as a group and as individuals, or we risk losing important parts of our selves as well as any possibility for political intervention.

Interpretation and Appropriation

There are two straightforward arguments to be made for the legitimacy of the use of the mestiza concept to describe white lesbian lives. The first is that Anzaldúa understands *mestizaje* in this way, and that therefore such a use is simply faithful to her intent. This argument is easily dismissed by a reading of her later references to mestizas. In her 1988 plenary address to the National Women's Studies Association, Anzaldúa refers repeatedly to "mestiza lesbians" and "mestiza queer persons."[46] She contrasts these people with "white lesbians," the people with whom mestizas must make alliances. For Anzaldúa, it seems, *mestizaje* is a racial or ethnic, not a sexual, category, though mestizas may also be lesbians.

The second, more complex, argument rests on the analogy between lesbianism and *mestizaje* as loci of oppression and oppositional culture. This is the position that, whether or not Anzaldúa intended lesbianism to be understood as *mestizaje*, it is proper to use it this way. There are several elements to such an argument. First, we must argue that appropriation of authors' ideas in a way they may not endorse is "fair" in public academic relations. This is usually assumed in cases where the relevant authors are from dominant groups.[47] But does Anzaldúa's position as a lesbian of color change the rules here?

Several feminist authors have begun writing about the limits of white women's interpretation of the texts of women of color, but there has been less discussion about the appropriate use of those texts for analysis of white women's lives.[48] This gap is primarily due to the hegemonic position of white feminist theory, which leads white women too often to read the work of women of color as anthropology, as learning about others, rather than to use these texts for introspection. Thus, for instance, virtually all feminists now acknowledge that our analyses must allow for the effects of race and class in the lives of those who have been marked as inferior within those structures, but white feminists too often fail to examine the effects of race on white women or of class on middle- or upper-class white women.[49]

Feminists then need to discuss how much or in what ways the theory of women of color can be used by white women in our descriptions of our situations. I don't think that there will be a blanket answer to this problem. Mercer distinguishes, for example, between the appropriation involved in the "White Negro," a figure representative of white alienation from middle-class white culture, embodied most fully in Elvis Presley and Mick Jagger, and the identification of Jean Genet with Black Panthers and Palestinian freedom fighters. The first operates from a basis of unconsciousness and rejection, an unconsciousness that leads to appropriation rather than political solidarity. Genet's position is rather one that "does not attempt to master or assimilate difference but which speaks from a position of equality as part of a shared struggle to decolonize models of subjectivity."[50]

As this example suggests, the first imperative is that identification should always acknowledge the differences between the social location of the original author and that of the user. This acknowledgment includes the willingness to listen and be corrected for one's mistakes, for, as Trinh T. Minh-ha puts it,

> Hegemony works at leveling out differences and at standardizing contexts and expectations in the smallest details of our daily lives. Uncovering this leveling of differences is, therefore, resisting that very notion of difference which defined in the master's terms often resorts to the simplicity of essences.[51]

Resistance to the "leveling of differences" requires a careful attention to the details of history and daily life that produce particular positions and consciousnesses. This must be balanced by a recognition that such details will never fully account for any position/consciousness, that "differences do not only exist between outsider and insider," but also "within the outsider herself, or the insider herself."[52]

One of the consequences of the recognition of difference has been the argument that white women should not presume to interpret the work of women of color, because such interpretation is always an appropriative act performed from a hegemonic position. This argument founders both theoretically and politically. It is not possible to read without interpretation; such an assumption relies on positivistic notions of reading that cannot be sustained. The political consequence of the injunction is to reinforce the gap, to freeze white women into their privilege and its accompanying narrowness, by locking the doors of otherness against them. Such a politics bars any hope of common understanding.[53]

Moving from the idea of "difference," which all too often lends itself to such unbridgeable gaps, toward specificity of locations or "identity points" allows us to acknowledge inequalities of power and position (as well as differences not so easily captured in a linear frame of measurement) while through that very acknowledgment discovering and articulating the linkages between us.[54] Specificity provides the ground for commonality without sameness, and so allows for the possibility of antihegemonic appropriation.

As currently used, *mestizaje* refers to a historical experience of oppression and resistance, of living within and also transgressing categories of race that structure domination within the United States. It does not refer to just any mixing of cultures or identities but to the specific history of Aztlán, with its record of colonization and racial domination. In the United States, this politically important distinction is endangered by white appropriation. The United States is the land of the melting pot, within certain narrow limits. The very term "white" is justifiable largely because Christian European-Americans have succeeded in melting into something of a stew, rather than retaining a central focus on the nations from which they or their ancestors emigrated. What, then, is to prevent white heterosexual males from adopting the label of "mestizo" and claiming equality of position with Chicana lesbians?[55] What is to prevent the total demolition of *mestizaje* into a useless category? The political danger of conceptualizing white lesbians as mestizas lies not in the interpretation of lesbian identity and politics but in making an imitation that obscures relevant distinctions in racial battles, and thereby failing as allies.

Some might take this point into account without abandoning the concept entirely. They might do this by describing clearly the differences between ethnicity and race in the United States, differences that define the limits of the melting pot's ingredients. When this is done, we see that "white" people in the United States are often "mutts," but that their differing ethnic "roots" do not provide a basis for current oppression; they are not publicly relevant, but are now simply matters of affective resonance. This can be seen most clearly in the observation that the law of hypo-descent does not apply among whites; we do not debate about whether someone is "really" Hungarian or French or English, as we routinely do about whether someone is "really" Black" or Native American or Jewish or Hispanic. The essentialism that marks racial discourse off from ethnicity discourse also serves to mark the politically important from the "private." The *mestizaje* lived by Anzaldúa is an experience of conflict precisely because one of her "elements" is privileged over another, and consequently her positioning among those elements has direct consequences for her life. This inequality of position, and the racism that defines the two (or more) positions as discrete, concrete entities (such as "blood"), is what produces the unique dynamism of her mestiza identity and politics. This dynamism is missing from the "mutthood" of white men whenever their melting has been produced without strain.

For example, my brothers have ancestors who are English, Dutch, Ashkenazi Jew, and whatever else may have gone into long lines of life in North America. These distinctions were often relevant for their ancestors, the hub of political struggle between Dutch and English in New York, the source of pain for Jews in twentieth-century U.S. society, and so on. However, these distinctions have not entered into their consciousness as anything more than interesting stories of their ancestors. Raised as Episcopalians, with English last names, they have lived not as mestizos but as "Americans" with no hyphens. I have shared in that mutthood, but somewhat differently. Through my bond to my grandmother, I identified with the Jews more strongly than with the Anglos for a long time. This produced personal tension, but there were no societal effects—no one excluded me from hotels or clubs or made anti-Semitic remarks about me, as they had to my grandmother and my mother. Thus, my "roots" did not automatically place me in a mestiza position.

Lesbianism forced that tension into my life. In heterosexist society, as in racist society, one must be one or the other—there is no room for sexual mutthood. Laws of hypo-descent apply here, as they do in racial discourse. Those who identify as lesbian and experience themselves through that self-conception live in a constant either/or situation: either one is "in the closet," passing for straight and experiencing the loss of self that that entails, or one is "out" and facing the harassment, economic deprivation, threat of violence, and loss of family support that so often follow.

This tension is still not enough for *mestizaje*, however. Most fundamentally, lesbianism is a difference that most of us can choose to manifest or not. Although needing to hide is oppressive, being able to hide still marks lesbians off from racially defined groups. Anzaldúa acknowledges the pain of heterosexism and homophobia, but she ranks this pain below that she experiences when white women seem to rank racism below sexism as an issue, when she feels, "after all our dialogues and struggles, that my cultural identity is *still* being pushed off to the side, being minimized by some of my so-called allies who unconsciously rank racism a lesser oppression than sexism."[56] "Lesbian cultures" in which white women predominate have too often provided a place in which the experience of *mestizaje* is avoided, not celebrated. Lesbians of color are "world travelers" in such lesbian cultures, as they are among heterosexuals of their various races.[57] As Anzaldúa describes it, being a mestiza has to do with the integration of difference as a daily lived reality, and not simply with "belonging" to multiple and seemingly opposed groups.

Historically, white feminists in the United States have articulated their oppression along lines borrowed from movements of racial liberation. In so doing, they have sometimes failed to explore the particulars of white women's oppression as such, instead linking prematurely to frameworks developed in other struggles. A central moment of getting specific is the description and theorization of our own positions. We need not and cannot abandon analogy and metaphor (those crucial tools of political struggle), but we must not allow these to take the place of consideration of the ways in which race, class, gender, and sexuality (among others) *all* inflect *all* of our lives. Appropriating *mestizaje* does not serve to build alliances; it serves to convince mestizas that white women don't get it, that white women are blind to their own privilege and oblivious to the force of history. Our alliances cannot be built by grafting ourselves onto others' identities. The process of democratic articulation is not one of equation, or even of simile, but is one of linkage between disparate elements. Such linkage must recognize those disparities, or it simply renews colonization.

Mestiza Consciousness

Rather than appropriating the position of the mestiza, white middle-class lesbians can learn from Anzaldúa's discussion of mestiza consciousness. The power of mestiza consciousness lies in the refusal of dualisms and boundaries that have worked to limit and separate us, from one another, and from the fullness of our selves. Mestizas, Anzaldúa tells us, cope by "developing a tolerance for contradictions, a tolerance for ambiguity."[58] This tolerance allows for the acceptance of conflict as necessary and fruitful rather than threatening. However, such tolerant refusal of those boundaries that have worked against us need not be extended into a blanket rejection of all boundaries. As Anzaldúa notes, bridging is not merging.[59] For instance, insisting that white women are not mestizas does not work to "divide" women in any new way; in recognizing the historical and social weight of the mestiza identity in the Southwest we prepare ourselves for responsible alliances by acknowledging our differences.

In her acceptance of conflict, Anzaldúa is in sharp contrast with theorists such as Nancy Hartsock, who repudiates an "agonistic" world view as essentially male.[60] Hartsock's gender dualism, in which women are fundamentally cooperative and community oriented and men are disposed to individualism and domination, continues the tradition of either/or thinking against which Anzaldúa struggles. Anzaldúa does not deny the fundamental asymmetry of power between men and women, nor does she call for a romantic politics of reconciliation, but she does insist on understanding the lives of men of color within the context of oppression that makes them potential allies as well as opponents.

The idea of *mestizaje* has been an avenue for white women to develop a new understanding of alliance. This theory has developed through the 1980s and into the 1990s into visions that blend the abstractions of poststructuralist theory with the "theory in the flesh" that Anzaldúa and Moraga brought forward in their collection *This Bridge Called My Back*.[61] The theme and the politics of bridging is what is so crucial for white lesbians now. This lesson may be learned without resorting to appropriations of *mestizaje*; indeed, such appropriations are a refusal to bridge.

In discussing the theory implicit in *This Bridge*, Alarcón argues that "the theory of the subject of consciousness as a unitary and synthesizing agent of knowledge is always already a posture of domination."[62] She indicts Anglo-American feminists for their continued refusal or inability truly to grasp the meaning of this point, and she argues that the continual return to the unitary subject limits the possibilities for solidarity with feminists of color. This drive for unity extends to the idea of "reclaiming" an identity; such reclamation "means always already to have become a subject of consciousness" capable of simply authorizing or denying a given identity.[63] Alarcón argues that "to be oppressed means to be disenabled not only from grasping an 'identity,' but also from reclaiming it," because the force of oppression works not simply to disadvantage some on the basis of a given identity, but creates and disintegrates identities themselves. On this basis, she urges her readers to treat consciousness "as the site of multiple voicings" that "transverse [sic] consciousness and which the subject must struggle with constantly." Refusing this consciousness in favor of a unitary, stable self is described as a "refusal to play 'bridge'" and as "the acceptance of defeat at the hands of political groups whose self-definition follows the view of self as unitary, capable of being defined by a single 'theme.' "[64]

Although she refrains from adopting the poststructuralist language of "subject positions" or "deconstructive identities," Anzaldúa's "new mestiza" does not transcend race but transgresses it, refusing to collude in the homophobic demands of some Chicanas/Chicanos or in the racist invisibility that is too much part of white lesbian communities. Anzaldúa and Alarcón agree that such a position involves forsaking the safety of the familiar or the stable for flux and struggle. Yet both recognize that only this renunciation makes change possible. They agree with Bernice Johnson Reagon that coalition politics is not about nurturance but is about stretching past the limits of comfort and safety to the work that needs to be done.[65]

This ambiguous, simultaneous recognition of alliance and opposition, friendship and alienation, support and betrayal is what makes mestiza consciousness so important. One of the lessons of the past twenty-five years of lesbian organizing is that communities and identities built on the expectation that "we" will only be allies, friends, and supporters of each other will inevitably fail. With such expectations, conflicts can only be understood as betrayal, and opposition can only mean exclusion.

Mestiza consciousness moves away from false oppositions between reform and revolution, separatism and coalition, and the like. These distinctions, though seemingly clear when written down in analytic fashion, are in fact of little use politically. The reform/revolution split has operated within a Marxist paradigm of history that is too thoroughly modernist, too monolithic, and too antidemocratic to be truly helpful. The separatism/coalition divide has similarly been the product of totalizing theory at its worst, the analytic intellect run wild. Both of these dualisms force us to unsatisfactory choices that we need not make, and rarely in fact make, in political life. Mestiza consciousness honors the complexity of political life.

The history of nationalist movements is one of internal strife and the failure of self-criticism, and thus of eventual irrelevance or co-optation.[66] The strength of mestiza consciousness is a result of its multiplicity and ability to sustain contradiction and ambiguity, and this includes the ability to withstand conflict and misunderstanding. The revolutionary force of the mestiza is the ability to refuse the reifications of cultural nationalism without abandoning the nation entirely, and to provide links to class-based movements without becoming subsumed within them. Because she never simply "is" any one element of her blended being, the mestiza cannot be captured in the oppositions that are presented as inevitable; class *or* nation, sex *or* race, or any other reified opposition. The mestiza does not dispute the historical or contemporary reality of these designations, but she does operate constantly to undermine their unitary solidities.

To the extent that any lesbian politics, separatist or not, relies upon the fiction of a unitary self and its autonomy, that politics will fail to do justice to the multiplicity of mutually irreducible struggles and "identity points" at which we live our lives. As Jacquelyn Zita describes it, "claiming a lesbian identity often diffuses into difference, once its locations are made physical, real, and lived."[67] This is the linkage between the ethnic experience of *mestizaje* and the experience of white lesbians who were raised and live in a heterosexual world; not ethnicity, an ascribed identity, but the specific differences that preclude any settled unity. In the chapters to come, I will discuss what sort of politics this unsettled unity may produce and foster.

Chapter 5

Getting Specific about Community

Mestiza consciousness rests simultaneously on two ideas that might seem contradictory. On the one hand, mestiza consciousness refuses the unity of identity, urging us to explore the constructions that would purport to tell us who "we" are and therefore where our allegiance lies. On the other hand, this consciousness provides the ground for common action by denaturalizing fixed identities. To minds used to identitarian politics (not to be confused with "identity politics"), this combination might seem impossible. Identitarian politics presumes that common action must be based on an identity among partners; for example, the belief that only lesbians can be trusted to work for lesbian concerns is not identity politics, but is identitarian. Identity politics, as a general name for social movements based on categories not adequately captured or valued in Marxist theory, does not require such exclusion or demarcation. Getting specific about identities leads to the recognition of similarities as well as differences between forms of oppression. It also, as genealogy, opens solidarity across the differences by virtue of the historical contingency of existing social formations and divisions. Getting specific thus leads identity politics away from identitarian formulations and toward alliances.

Getting specific requires that we explore some of the concepts that structure our expectations for lesbian politics and collective life. If we accept a postmodern social ontology, we must reexamine the constitutive categories of Western political thought and of contemporary Euro-American lesbian politics.

One of these constitutive categories has been that of community. Community has been an ideal of Western political thought at least since the beginnings of Christianity. In its related form of nationhood, it has been an intimate, ever-present part of the fabric of political theory. Whether in Plato's abstractly ordered republic, in the lives and writings of the Hebrews, in Augustine's City of God, in Marx's vision of communist society, or in feminist models of political structure and process, the desire for mutual belonging and recognition has been central to politics and theory.

The past century has shown us the potential horrors of a politics conducted in the name of peoples or nations or ideologically constructed communities, but the latter half of that century has also witnessed a resurgence of the claims of communities and peoples. In forms as diverse as Sandinista Nicaragua, Lithuanian self-determination, lesbian and gay politics, the nationalisms of peoples of color in the United States, and contemporary conservatism, we see the continuing appeal of community as a vision of human relations that resists the advance of the modern state. This return leads us to ask whether it is possible to honor the desire for community or whether this desire is a relic of an immature past, occasionally bursting forth but never to be fully let loose. We can and must, however, move beyond those alternatives, based on that vision and desire, to see whether there is another way to think community that is neither tragic nor totalitarian.

Identitarian Community

What differentiates community from other social interactions and structures? This may be the hardest part of theorizing about community/communities, for there is tremendous ambiguity about the term. In a survey of the sociological literature on community, George Hillery found ninety-four different definitions of the term. He grouped them into several categories and subcategories. For instance, in the category of "geographic area," he distinguishes those definitions that focus on "self-sufficiency" from those that look at "common life," "consciousness of kind," "possession of common ends, norms, means," "collection of institutions," "locality group," and "individuality." Definitions that do not rely on geographic location refer to many of the same criteria, but include other possibilities, such as "totality of attitudes," as well.[1] In the end, Hillery finds that the only thing shared by all the definitions is that "they all deal with people."[2] He finds definitions that deny the relevance of social interaction as a criterion, and so declines to insist even on this feature. Although there may in fact be more to the notion of community than Hillery discovers, his general point is well taken.

In contrast to empirical sociology, philosophical work on community does manifest some common features. Thomas Bender defines community as "a network of social relations marked by mutuality and emotional bonds," by "shared understandings and a sense of obligation," by "affective and emotional ties rather than by a perception of individual self-interest." Communities are not oriented toward specific aims, but are "diffuse in their concerns."[3] R. M. MacIver and Charles Page assert that "wherever members of any group, small or large, live together in such a way that they share, not this or that particular interest, but the basic conditions of a common life, we call that group a community. The mark of a community is that one's life *may* be lived wholly within it."[4] Anthony Black argues that a community is "the unit upon which every human being depends for his or her sense of who they are and where they stand in the scheme of things."[5] For such theorists, community is precisely that which we do not notice or question except in times of disturbance or conflict. It is not a matter of shared goals or principles (except secondarily) so much as one of shared lives.

In many of these definitions, a community is defined by the common characteristics of the membership. Within community, these become something more than characteristics; they stretch out to become identities. Thus, when Michael Sandel says that communities help members to become less "opaque" to themselves, he is referring to the ways in which common understandings and practices create not only the knowledge that comes from familiarity but the knowledge that comes from common identity.

There are several versions of this sort of argument. In the ascriptive presentation, our common identity is based upon a primordial bond, a "natural" basis for community. For example, Judy Grahn's search for lesbian history ascribes a common identity based on sexual practices and cultural roles across times and cultures.[6] Here the identity precedes the community that would recognize it. The identity in question is not one of group identification, but of essence: she does not argue that there have always been people who called themselves lesbians or thought of sexuality as we do, but in a dazzling conflation of sexuality and gender identity she does argue that there have always been "odd girls" who have a historical continuity with contemporary lesbians.

Even many ascriptivists recognize that the "natural" basis of community can develop into full community only through social relations that foster a collective consciousness, a recognition of others as like ourselves. The relations of consanguinity, temporality, or spatiality provide the possibility of community but do not guarantee it. The recognition of others as bound to us and like us is crucial. At that point, self-reflection can aid us in knowing about others, and observation of others may tell us important things about ourselves. Further, this identification requires that we understand ourselves not simply as

"like another" but as sharing a common identity, a common membership within a concrete community. Although Grahn does not assume
that lesbian communities have existed over time as a result of this
identity, she sees them as always potentially available through mutual
recognition.

We can also imagine and form nonascriptive communities that are
nonetheless based in mutual identification or consciousness of kind. In
this view, communities are voluntary associations of individuals. They
are distinguished from family, geographical, or political units into
which we are born: we choose to enter and remain and can choose to
leave without logical contradiction or legal consequences. Thus Julia
Stanley says that a community is "composed of individuals who have
many ideas and experiences of our lives that we share."[7] She states
that "one joins a community because she finds companionship, support, and commitment to common ideals within that community."
This community is "internally defined by its members on the basis of
shared experiences and common interpretations of events in the real
world."[8] Here a community is fully voluntary: Stanley distinguishes a
community from a subculture, which is based on external definitions
of the identities of the members. A community and the identity of its
members, on the other hand, are consciously chosen and fashioned by
those members. Here we see both a voluntarist conception of community, shared by many modern thinkers, and a use of that conception to
distinguish stigmatized, externally imposed identities from valorized,
self-fashioned ones. It is, in Gramscian terms, an attempt to wrest
hegemony over the definitions of the members' lives from the dominant culture. The community is defined not simply by interaction or
bonds or understandings but is also (at least implicitly) defined as autonomous from a "society" or "culture" that marginalizes a given
group. In the community, it seems, one is always in the center.

In this case it appears that a community can never be ascriptive. If
we choose our community, the identity we achieve or recognize there
is not previously given. Yet things are not so simple. What is involved
here is a process of rearticulation that reascribes us, as it were, not
necessarily by challenging notions of primordial or "true" identity,
but by relocating our identities. We may thus refer to "created communities," not in stark contrast to "natural" (ascriptive) ones, but
along a continuum of relations between space and time on the one
hand and consciousness on the other.

This voluntarist notion of community goes back at least to the
early Christians, who distinguished their religious relationships
among themselves from their political, kinship, economic, or gender

relations. As Sheldon Wolin has explained, the Christian vision of community contained "ideals of solidarity and membership that were to leave a lasting imprint, and not always for good, on the Western tradition of political philosophy."[9] The early Christian church arose in a period of empire, in which most people (and especially women) had no say in the major issues of political life. Increasing inequality and popular disempowerment left a ripe field for a religion that urged its adherents to focus on another world. This search for God's will, this focus on the next life, in fact bound Christians together on earth. The Christian community was one that denied the spiritual importance of temporal inequalities among its members, though it did not require their elimination. Through a sharp separation of physical from spiritual, Christianity could reject hierarchies and still coexist with them.

This "community of believers" provided a counterweight to the alienation of imperial subjection and loss of public meaning. The community shared a common goal, common norms for behavior, and common values: Augustine's distinction between the City of God and the City of Man rested precisely on this point. Not the condition of one's body but the aim of one's desire located each person in one or the other.

While the church and its priests were acknowledged not to be perfect, the contrast between the "community" as a nonpolitical entity of common values and understandings and "society" or "polity" as a realm of limited bonds and veiled force has continued to dominate Western thought to this day. Today the community is the other of the state: whereas the state, center of power and force, operates through regulation and bureaucracy, "community" is seen as the spiritually rich site of meaningful interaction and voluntary action.

There are several questions for us to ask of this other. We can easily undermine the presentation of community outlined above by pointing to the play of power within understandings, values, and norms. We can deconstruct the oppositions between meaning and power and between understanding and power. This deconstruction is especially urgent for groups and individuals who are consciously aiming at greater diversity and openness in their theory and practice, and it has been done extensively and thoroughly by many women. Iris Young argues that traditional understandings of community as the alternative to the impersonal state "can reproduce a homogeneity that usually conflicts with the organization's stated commitment to diversity."[10] She locates the problem in the model of community as "copresence of subjects" that mandates self-transparency and transparency to others. This vision of community rests on the same logic as that of identity as self-presencing, as a place of noncontradiction. This latter vision in turn assumes that the self is a unity, that it need not be accounted for. The consequence of such an assumption is a failure to inquire into the technologies of self that have gone to construct that self and its desires and aims and self-understandings.

Community as Compearance

Shared characteristics are not sufficient for community; "shared characteristics," in fact, exist as such only within a given community of understanding. Without such understanding, there is no reference by which to characterize anything. Thus, communities are not formed of or by individuals with preexisting "characteristics," unless they are sharing a characterization borrowed from another community. Such was and is the case for gays and lesbians; the fact that we generally find the question of characteristics unproblematic reflects our common upbringing in heterosexist communities and societies.

Thus we see that community is constitutive in an important sense. Communitarians, however, have too often taken this constitutivity to mean that the community exists before its members. This move simply begs the earlier question, and so is unacceptable. If questioning stops here, we find a reified "community" that constitutes individuals, without itself requiring constitution. Community does not preexist its members, but consists in "the singular acts by which it is drawn out and communicated."[11] It does not follow, however, that "we" perform "acts" that we thereby designate as "community"; this interpretation would be a return to liberal positivism. Rather, community/communities exist only in our common activities. We are still constituted by community, but community does not thereby acquire a prior, separate existence, for community is simultaneously constituted by us.

In *The Inoperative Community* (*La communauté désœuvrée*) and later work, Jean-Luc Nancy argues that community is a matter of "being-in-common," in which "being-with" is not a modifier or predicate of being but is the ground of being itself. Thus the way in which beings are is always already in common; there is no such thing as being without community, being without being-in-common. As Nancy puts it, "community is simply the real position of existence."[12] Humans do not arise in isolation, as the communitarians remind us, but neither does "the community" exist beyond the being-in-common of particular people. Community is not only constitutive of us; community is performative, consisting only in the process of being-in-common. There is no "community" beyond this, though there are institutions, geographical locations, populations. These, the centers of communitarian thought, are more often the sites of the denial of community in favor of identity, of the common, the same.

This usage of "community" seems to defy our common understandings of the word. Generally, community appeals not just to that which is simply "in common," but to "the common," the *same*. Community has been firmly entrenched within the logic of the same that mandates self-identity and unity among members. In such definitions, community becomes an essence, a thing to be studied and acted upon and used. In Nancy's terms, such essentializing amounts to "the closure of the political."[13] It is a closure because it shuts us off from the insecurity and instability of actually being-in-common and wraps us in common being, in sameness. Politics, the art of being-in-common, is eliminated when we fix identities and locations in this way. This reasoning helps us to see that our "common understandings" of community trap us into antipolitical postures even as we try to valorize "differences."

Although Nancy's description has something in common with the sociological descriptions of community/communities as sites of human interaction, there is a crucial difference. Most of the sociological definitions fall into one or more of several errors. The first error, already discussed, is the assumption of the autonomy and stability of the self. If communities are seen as sites for interaction among preexisting persons, then the assumption is that the self is not substantially formed by its environment—the liberal fallacy. If they are treated as sites of constitution of selves, then the self is historically denser but not necessarily problematic: we can now say that "the community" shapes the individual, without questioning the identity of that community. In order for this to be satisfying, however, we must make the second error: assuming the stability and sufficiency of community. By "stability" I mean relative harmony and sufficient univocity that the person produced by the community will "have an identity" with herself.[14] The "commmunity" that constitutes us is then presented as unified and fixed enough to have an identity ("the community") with a clear history, values, and aims. This assumption leads communitarians to see community as a source of strength, as "home," as the opposite of alienation. The self is reinforced by its community.

Nancy's presentation differs from these in its questioning of the root of community, being-in-common. Rather than being a source of support, Nancy's being-in-common is the locus of anxiety and vertigo that the Western philosophical tradition has fled from. Drawing on Heidegger's instruction about Being, Nancy argues that being-in-common means not stability and identity, but "*no longer having, in any form, in any empirical or ideal place, such a substantial identity, and sharing this* (narcissistic) '*lack of identity.*' "[15] Community is the place where we are forced to recognize the play of forces and desires that are human experience. Identitarian accounts and expectations of community are precisely the repression of this anxious reality.

A mundane example will serve here. Robert Nisbet states that the "archetype, both historically and symbolically" of community "is the family, and in almost every type of genuine community the nomenclature of family is prominent."[16] Some have argued that family is a dangerous metaphor for community, and I concur. But what is important here is the crucial question: How many of us experienced a family or home that was in fact what the rhetoric of community invokes as a model? Not only is "home" a bad metaphor for "community," it is a false model of home! Most homes are probably a perfect example of Nancy's description of community—as the primary site of being-in-common, they exemplify all the terrors and conflicts he describes. While Nancy's discussion is more focused on the ontological than the ontic or everyday, this example points to the uses of deconstructive thinking about community. It is not sufficient to "wean ourselves," to give up the security of home; agency requires that we confront the myth of the secure home, the myth of the origin itself.

So far, it may not be entirely clear what separates Nancy from thinkers who bemoan our inability to achieve community. Nancy is not arguing that community is an unachievable ideal, as many have. Nor is he arguing that it is a lost mode of existence, a hostage of modernity or capitalism. Rather, he is arguing that it is a fact of everyday existence, but that it is suppressed in the search for "community"; because it does not look like the Greco-Christian model that fixes community as "the common," as identity of selves and interests, community is overlooked and denied. For Nancy, community is the ground of all possibility, but an unstable, shifting ground. Attempts to fix it are flights from community toward identity, flights from being-in-common to being common. The danger in this flight is precisely the "complacency that threatens any discourse of community," which is "to think that one is (re)presenting, by one's own communication, a co-humanity whose truth, however, is not a given and (re)presentable essence."[17]

The danger is easy enough to see when we remember the history of lesbianism. "Lesbian" is not an ontological category divorced from social reality; it is an appearance of being that occurs only in certain places/times. There is no such thing as a lesbian without the category "lesbian," and there is no such category outside of a human community. Lesbians "compear" (in Nancy's term, literally "appear together") only in and through community. This does not mean that lesbian identity is solidified in community. Compearance does not mean mutual support for stable identity, but continually threatens it. Compearance, Nancy states, "is of a more originary order than that of the bond" of one subject to another; "it consists in the appearance of the *between* as such."[18]

Being-in-common means being with others, but being with others is the opposite of "being common." Being common is the continual denial of community in favor of oneness. Community in fact works to destabilize identity, as our being with others brings us face to face with multiplicity and differences. Thus, community is not a place of refuge, of sameness, but is its opposite.

The essentializing of community replicates the essentializing of identity and the subject. For example, the struggles among lesbians over race and class have produced a situation in which these characteristics are not only important, but vital; failure to address them and their effects is unacceptable. Too often, however, middle-class white women have participated in these struggles in ways that prevent us from fully addressing "others." We learn the words to use, the adjectives that I suspect for many are modifiers of the basic noun "lesbian." We are nonetheless continuing to essentialize when we simply use these words—"Chicana," "working class"—as though they refer to stable, homogeneous characteristics or identities. This sort of essentializing tells us that we already know about those with whom we are in common, because we know some labels and so (think we know) some characteristics. It enables us to retain the idea of community as a thing by compartmentalizing it, accounting for its various segments and spaces.

This approach reveals the retention of the reified subject that limits our thinking of community. The modern subject, the unified, self-reflective, and autonomous originator of its actions and emotions, is a concept that makes being-in-common impossible to conceive. Even as we are drawn to community, the allure of the subject limits our ability to think beyond models of association or ascription. As Nancy puts it:

> Communication and the alterity that is its condition can, in principle, have only an instrumental and not an ontological role and status in a thinking that views the subject as the negative but specular identity of

the object, that is, as an exteriority without alterity. The subject cannot be outside of itself: this is even what ultimately defines it—that its outside and all its "alienations" or "extraneousness" should in the end be suppressed by and *sublated* in it.[19]

A full thinking of community requires that we move past the subject as origin or fixed point to a self that is a node of communications.

What is left if we give up that subject and its objects? We are left. We "lesbians." We who live in the density of immanence, but never wholly so. As compearance, we live our lives immediately, in the given, but never simply *as* the given. As a space for presencing, community is more of a continual possibility, and an urging toward possibility, than a reality. Invocations of community/communities are calls for spaces of presencing, but when those calls become criteria for membership they betray community.

Compearance as presencing together, community as compearance, is a "negative" concept.[20] "Lesbian" here has no positive content, no "meaning" by which we measure ourselves. Lesbian is a name given by heterosexuals to designate those who differ from them, and a criterion for designation.[21] "We lesbians" may reverse that, saying that we can change the meaning of the word, but this is simply substitution. In either event, the naming of lesbians appears here to be an injustice. The naming of lesbians is an attempt to fix identity, to provide a determinate content by which we shall know ourselves and one another.

The rejection of fixed identity on the part of lesbians contributes to the destabilization of the idea of the "feminist community" as well. The "women's community," lesbian code for the lesbian community, has always been an inadequate way to express the plural alliances and affinities of lesbians, or of feminists of any sexuality. The reassuring unity prescribed by simpler theories of lesbian identity has increasingly given way to recognition of the diversity of lesbian lives. "The community" has become a "place that is unknown and risky, that is not only emotionally but conceptually other; a place of discourse from which speaking and thinking are at best tentative, uncertain, unguaranteed."[22] This is always the fate of the ideal of community and is due not to a failing of a conception nor a political defect but to the tension within community itself, that is, within being-in-common. As an ideal of harmony and wholeness, community can never satisfy its own demands. As the lived ground of human existence, community is never whole or harmonious, but it is precious nonetheless. We can best realize community in our lives not by willing it directly, but by continuing to call it into existence, by compearing as our never-the-same selves.

Getting Specific about Community

These are important points about community, but their political implications are somewhat vague. The strong communitarian position seems to lead too often toward direct entailments between personal identity and political position; the deconstructive view leaves too much room. The space is too often filled in with a vague pluralism, the fate of "difference." The antidote to totalitarian thinking seems to be continual deconstruction of identities and ways of life. This is a crucial and unfinished project for a planet filled with resurgent nationalisms, but it is insufficient to address concrete political struggles. Without some fixing of identity, however provisional, common action will not occur. At this point we need to make the leap from thorough antiessentialism to Spivak's "strategic essentialism." Here specificity becomes crucial. Getting specific can make the link between the recognition of the ontological insecurity of community and the daily solidity and reality of particular communities.

It might appear that ethnographers could provide this greater specificity. Ethnographers, after all, study particular groups and persons, seeming to think "from the ground up" rather than uncritically categorizing people into previously designed slots. This appearance is mistaken, however. While ethnographers are certainly in no worse a position (and quite possibly are in a better one) than others to work toward greater specificity, their training nonetheless inscribes the world that they see.

Denyse Lockard's study of "the lesbian community" is an example of both the strengths and weaknesses that are possible in such an approach. Lockard works to define "lesbian community" as distinct from lesbian population and lesbian subculture. In her ethnography, Lockard notes that "the lesbian community" that she studied maintained ties with other feminists more than with gay men.[23] This simple observation cuts through much theoretical rhetoric about whether gays and lesbians "are" allies or not, exposing the normative element in such formulations. Whether they are allies or not is not a matter to be solved by theorizing but is a question of political action.

On the other hand, Lockard's criteria for a community define the community she studied as white, and define only the white lesbians as participating in community. Because Lockard's definition of lesbian community includes "gay-defined places and organizations," what she calls "an institutional base," she looks only at participants in such locations. Without that base, she argues, there is a social network but no "community." On the basis of that definition, she finds that people of color in her study do not participate in "the community," and therefore do not *have* community. While Lockard's concern for institutions as places to find other lesbians is valid, her argument finally rests on beliefs that only such institutions can provide continuity, and that such institutions do in fact provide it—both of which are subject to challenge. Lockard remains within the realm of identitarian community.

Nonetheless, there is much for political theorists to gain from following ethnographers and anthropologists on their travels. Most importantly, we can gain an awareness of the process nature of community.[24] Communities may be named by nouns in the English language, but that does not make them things. While the above example demonstrates that anthropologists do not automatically understand that community is a process, the studies they conduct can be read to see that point.

Rather than abandon "community," I would like to think of it as a process. In the process of community, personalities are created. Persons do not simply "join" communities; they *become* microcosms of their communities, and their communities change with their entrance. As Mary Follett puts it, "our loyalty is neither to imaginary wholes nor to chosen wholes, but is an integral part of that activity which is at the same time creating me."[25] In her focus on process, Follett shares with Nancy a certain awareness of the becoming of community. She does not, however, use that awareness to abandon identity altogether. She is a communitarian, but certainly no lover of static communities and traditions. Her focus on process impels us toward a vision of communities, as of individuals, as constantly becoming.

Using Follett's notion as a guide, let us return to the problem of lesbian community. I want to argue that "lesbian communities" engage in four major processes. These processess do not all occur in every community at every time, but if none of them are operative I would not say that there is a lesbian community. First, a lesbian community insulates lesbians from hostility to their sexuality. That community is the place or space (in a nongeographical sense) where it is "all right (or even better) to be a lesbian," where being a lesbian is simply not an issue. Thus, lesbian community/communities may enable a lesbian to stop reacting to heterosexual presumptions, anxieties, attacks, and imperatives and to envision and build a life she chooses.

Secondly, a lesbian community can be a beacon for lesbians or for those who would become lesbians. It does this by breaking or easing lesbian invisibility. This process is not the same as insulation or protection. A lesbian community may insulate its members by protecting them, as some Daughters of Bilitis chapters did in the 1950s,[26] without breaking invisibility to a noticeable extent. It is true that the very existence of lesbian organizations or institutions such as bars breaks invisibility to an extent, but a given community can refuse to focus on this, can minimize it. In contrast, when the founding Daughters of Bilitis group included in its objectives "public discussions 'to be conducted by leading members of the legal, psychiatric, religious and other professions,' " they moved toward breaking invisibility.[27]

Communities also model behavior and help members and new entrants interpret their lives—show them "how to be a lesbian" and what it means to be one. This is a crucial function of any community, ascriptive as well as elective. Even "ascriptive" communities do not accept that everyone of a certain heritage is doing that heritage right— one may be called a "bad Jew," a "traitor to the race," and so on. These statements rest on an implicit nationalism, an assumption that identity is known through group membership and that that membership carries unambiguous mandates for living one's life. Barbara Ponse, Joan Nestle, Audre Lorde, and others have given us descriptions of this process of socialization and interpretation.[28]

Finally, communities may provide the base for or result of political mobilization. By "political mobilization" I mean the movement out of the community into the hegemonic cultural, legal, and political systems to challenge the status of lesbians in the larger society/societies. The gay liberation movement was built on the communities that earlier activists had fostered, but lesbian feminist communities arose out of shared opposition to gay male and heterosexual feminist politics. Early 1970s lesbian feminist groups were explicitly feminist and political.[29] These locations and their descendants operate/operated as "free spaces," training centers for citizenship and activism that extend beyond the group itself to form alliances with other groups for common ends.[30]

Now clearly a given community can engage in some of these processes without the others. Just as importantly, the nature of a community will depend crucially upon which of these are seen as central to it. The aura around the word "community" leads us to certain expectations that rest on and reinforce the call of identity, of sameness, and these expectations do require analysis. Nancy's deconstruction, however, is insufficiently specific to serve as more than a philosophical reminder against identitarian hubris. We need an analysis that bears his points in mind while recognizing the political necessity of common construction and (limited) identity.

Although we cannot hope to eliminate by magic the aura around community, we may be able to limit it by getting specific about two aspects of our communities: their histories and our expectations of them. A genealogy of modern communities and identities can provide us with the denaturalization and the historical location that are simultaneously needed to rethink community. I will make this point by contrasting a genealogical, "specific" approach to community with the two alternatives I have just outlined.

Against communitarianism, genealogy brings a recognition of the price of communal identities, traditions, and institutions. Often this recognition may amount to nothing more than shifting perspective to see who is excluded within "one's own" community. For example, Jewish women are and are not "Jews." Cynthia Ozick describes this beautifully and painfully:

> In the world at large, I call myself, and am called, a Jew. But when I sit among women in my traditional shul and the rabbi speaks the word "Jew," I can be sure that he is not referring to me. . . . When my rabbi says, "A Jew is called to the Torah," he never means me or any other living Jewish woman. . . . My own synagogue is the only place in the world where I am not named Jew.[31]

Ozick calls attention to the very concrete, everyday way in which she is not included in "her" community, in the community in which Jewish men would surely locate her. This sort of exclusion occurs for many of us: women in male-dominated institutions, lesbians within the category "women," people of color among "nonracially defined" groups. Calling attention to the actual implicit requirements for membership is part of getting specific about whom and what we are discussing.

Susan Okin has performed this task for the communitarian theorists who present a harmonious and ordered world. By pointing to the domination and exclusion in the traditions they celebrate, and by calling male communitarians to task for their failures to acknowledge these, she reveals their communities to be just that—*their* communities.[32] This critique is needed, and it is familiar to all feminists and lesbians. In one way or another, we have been made acutely aware of our exclusions or silences. This critique is not enough, though. A further examination is needed of the exclusions and productions *within* the "central" population, of the production of the hegemonic selves celebrated by the communitarians. This study has been the forte of deconstruction, the source of its disturbing power. All those who have been attached to the idea of stable, unitary identities as the basis of order or change have been distressed at the disruptive effects of such views. To conservatives such as Allan Bloom, deconstruction destroys the basis for moral order; to Marxists and many feminists, it deprives us of a basis for resistance and claims to change.[33]

Although I am not persuaded by these charges, I am disturbed by the lack of specificity provided or endorsed by deconstruction *simpliciter*. A view that serves only to remind us of the provisionality of our identities is a step in the right direction away from identitarian politics, but in itself it is only a step. Though the fixing of identity is a form of oppression, it is crucial that we examine the particular identities provided or imposed on us. Rich white heterosexual men do indeed "suffer" from identity and its discontents, but their suffering is rather drastically different from that of welfare mothers or people of color or gays and lesbians or any other stigmatized or deprived group. The virtue of specificity as a methodological imperative is the ability to demarcate various overlapping sites of struggle in a social space. Where the communitarians would cover struggle up or sanitize it, and the deconstructionists sometimes express unease with a politics that rests on identity (which is to say, virtually any group politics), the genealogist can and must recognize both the ultimate provisionality of identities and their daily solidity in relations of power.

Genealogy and Exclusion

Such genealogies have been developed in the past few decades by radicals of all sorts who have challenged the centrality of the center. The use of the category of liminality is aimed at precisely this (true) fiction. The liminal is what marks the border between categories; it is a frontier of sorts. The liminal is not the marginal, for "marginal" is a notion based on centers. The liminal is a more spacious location, a position between multiple territories without a simple center/margin dichotomy. Thus, lesbians are marginal only from the perspective of heterosexuals; most lesbians, however, are acutely aware that they negotiate multiple locations with differing codes and expectations.

As the liminal provides a means for thinking through identity, it opens a new thinking of community as real but not essential, not transcendentally founded but produced through discourses carrying power. I will give an example of this work that focuses on the politics of the discursive construction of the center by the periphery, while it provides an implicit account of individual identity in such a construction.

In an article on sexual-morality laws in Trinidad and Tobago,

Jacqui Alexander describes three mechanisms of the process by which "normal" sexuality is constructed.[34] In the first, an "outside" is formed. Rather than starting from the "inside" position, as many would, Alexander's genealogy points out that inside positions are built on the exclusion of others not as a result but as a precondition. Secondly, centrality or normality is defined less by what people do than by what they don't do—they don't do all the things the outsiders do. Thus, dominant sexual standards or identities are shown to be reactive. Finally, the "outside" is presented as having its own location, such as "the red light district" or "the Black side of town." This last mechanism serves to fix the source of danger to the hegemonic self, simultaneously bolstering the separation and locating the source of anxiety.

An account such as this can help us to begin a genealogy of white lesbian communities. White middle-class lesbians' position as insiders on the outside while outsiders on the inside requires attention to the ways in which we, as insiders, build "our" communities. The process of becoming central is always a process built on a logic of opposition.

Who is sent to the periphery when lesbians become central, that is, when a "lesbian community" is created? Most obviously, men are outside. Women who insist on identifying as heterosexual, or who others insist are heterosexual, are not in the "center" of such a community. Indeed, the phrase "lesbian community" implies not just marginality but exclusion, a more complex and dangerous process than may appear at first. In justifying the exclusion of nonlesbians, we necessarily rely upon implicit or explicit ideas of what "those people" are like. What they are like must be contrasted to what "lesbians are like" if we are to be able to distinguish lesbian contexts, subcultures, and communities from nonlesbian ones. Although we may be able to make a contrast that appears nonhierarchical, such as that lesbians sleep with women and heterosexual women sleep with men, the contrast can become meaningful for us, can be relevant, only if certain virtues or vices are associated with these practices. Thus a genealogy of lesbian communities must first examine whom lesbians contrast themselves to in order to become lesbians.

Generally, we know the answers. Contemporary lesbian identities are the product of medicine, of heterosexist popular culture and media, of religion, of semiautonomous lesbian subcultures, and of lesbian involvement with and resistance to both gay male and heterosexual feminist ideas and practices. They are also the result of lesbian creativity, of women living together and creating lives not modeled in the hegemonic society. What is missing from most accounts, however, is the process of exclusion needed to create "lesbian" practices and institutions. The essentializing of sexuality and desire has made that a nonquestion, for lesbians just are lesbians.

The construction of "a" lesbian community has also excluded lesbians who do not fit the implicit model of a lesbian. Such models not only are imparted through words and pictures, through direct statements such as "lesbians are/do such and such," but also are transmitted through the concrete daily practices of such a community. A community centered on a bookstore will not be a community that values illiterate lesbians. A community that is monolithically aligned with feminism will feel alien to lesbians who either are not feminists or have no interest in feminism.

Lesbians of color have written clearly and forcefully about their difficulties with white lesbians. As an example, I want to focus here on a conversation between three lesbians of color that is included in a recent collection, *Piece of My Heart*. The three women give only pseudonymic first names and discuss their fears about coming out, citing homophobia in the Toronto Black community and the need for family and community unity as immigrants. They quickly move on to discuss their invisibility as lesbians among white lesbians. This invisibility, two of them note, is based on two assumptions made by white lesbians. The first is the mutual exclusivity between the category "lesbian" and the category "woman of color." This is a result of categorical rather than social or contextual thinking. As "Anu" describes it:

> I remember I was applying for a job a few summers ago within a feminist organization and I was competing for the job with a white lesbian. I was hired over her. Later on, I heard that I was hired because they "already had enough lesbians," and so they didn't need any more, but what they did need was a woman of color because they had no contacts in those communities. . . . When they hired me their underlying assumption was that a woman of color could not be a lesbian.[35]

She goes on to relate the ways in which her lesbianism was overlooked or denied: though she lived with a woman, she was asked during the interview whether she would have problems working with lesbians, and the people in the organization never revised their early belief. She states that she has decided not to identify herself as a lesbian to white women anymore, because she is met with "curious disbelief" or sexual racism.[36]

"Pramila" identifies the second, related source of invisibility. Noting that "there are a lot of unspoken and unwritten laws in the lesbian society of how to dress and how to look," she points out that "women in saris and salwar kameez would never be seen as lesbians."[37] She thus points to the damage done by implicitly Western, falsely totalizing notions of lesbian identity and politics. This damage is both personal and political and affects both lesbians of color and white lesbians. Any potential solidarity is undermined by easy generalizations about who "we" are and what "our" politics, our fashion, or our lives are like.

Constructions function through opposition and difference, and will not cease to do so just because "we" want to be inclusive. Lesbians of all positionalities may strive for nonreactive constructions, those that begin in affirmation of self rather than denigration or expulsion of the other. Such constructions are not a goal to be fully achieved, however, but a limit to be approached. My purpose here is to suggest that rather than finding a way to eliminate this dynamic entirely, we must urge ourselves toward greater self-consciousness about the political and cultural contexts and effects of our constructions. We (all of us, not any one group) need to be willing to face this process if we are to engage in it responsibly. Denial that "we" exclude others (whichever "we" is in question at the time) serves not to convince those excluded that they are welcome, but to prevent solidarity across differences and exclusions that might even be productive. It is to present ourselves as unreliable and irresponsible. Exclusions, to the extent they are needed, must be acknowledged and argued about.

Again, the distinction between mutts and mestizas can make this point. Although we differentiate between blue-eyed, brown-eyed, black-eyed, and green-eyed persons, this is, in the United States, not a reactive or politically charged distinction. In Germany in the Nazi era, the distinction was slightly more dangerous. Mutts (northern-Euro-Americans of mixed ethnic backgrounds) are not all politically equal, but the distinctions are more cultural curiosities in a culture-consuming society than they are the basis for political inequality. Where these identities are more politically relevant, it is precisely because those people have endured or experienced something important together— the Irish in Ireland and in the United States, southern-Euro-Americans, Jewish Americans. These group constructions often partake more explicitly of reaction precisely because there is a past or present reaction to respond to. The answer then is not the fully deconstructive dismissal of group distinctions in the laudable desire for nonreactive politics, but is the acknowledgment of the specific factors that have shaped possibly dangerous personal and communal identities.

Specificity and the Limits of Identity

Specifying is crucial for white middle-class lesbians because, as we think our way through community and political allegiances, we face two temptations. On the one hand, it is tempting to forget that we are in fact central within our communities. This oversight leads us to retain self-images as marginal, as powerless, as necessarily radical and democratic. On the other hand, we may celebrate our centrality within "lesbian communities," replaying the motifs of harmony, of univocity, of free self-disclosure and transparency. Both of these are inducements to avoid the pain of liminality.

A more specific theory aids in resisting these temptations by bringing us face to face with the multiplicity of factors and forces that have made our lives. When I refuse to essentialize or naturalize lesbianism, when I say that there is no such thing as a lesbian without the category of "lesbian," I do not do so to deny that women in the past loved other women, had joyous sex with women, or lived their lives centered on women. I do not mean to say that there were never butch women or women who saw themselves as liminal. I mean to highlight that contemporary lesbian identity is inextricably bound up with the rise of sexology and other discourses about sexuality that did not just liberate but created and targeted populations for policing. These discourses are not relics but still play a large part in most of our lives. We must acknowledge that lesbian community will never be simply a place of coming together as whole selves but will be the site of pain, confusion, and anxiety as well as love, acceptance, and security.

We have begun, but only begun, the process of acknowledgment, and there are many pitfalls ahead. The first is to imagine that we can solve this problem by pluralizing community—to refer to "communities" instead and have done with it. Thus we might have a "white lesbian community," a "Chicana lesbian community," a "disabled lesbian community," and so on. This multiplicity is useful in some cases, where there actually are communities of the sort being referred to. But two problems arise.

First, we have the problem of internal difference. No matter how many modifiers we attach to "lesbian community," we will not eliminate difference(s). The modifier approach enables us to shut down some conflict by making implicit exclusions explicit, but it does not deal with the basic problem. How do we decide which modifiers rate a "community" of their own, and which are simply characteristics of individuals? This question cannot be resolved theoretically; it is a matter of politics, confrontation, and contestation. Further, this approach continues to rely on the logic of the same by implying that when we parse them down enough, we will find groups that are the same enough—common enough—that they will agree on how to live and what to do.

This belief rests on the fallacy of identity—the belief that our actions and ideas are *simply* the product of social location, so that if we "specify" the location tightly enough we will be the same. bell hooks addresses the defects of this position when she argues against feminism as an identity and in favor of feminism as a position that one advocates—a "movement to end sexist oppression."[38] As an identity, feminism becomes a "lifestyle" that allows one to feel radical without doing anything—"withdrawing from the system" becomes as valuable as changing it. A focus on identity also forces people to polarize between "feminists" and "nonfeminists," whereas a political commitment is more flexible. This is the second problem with simple multiplication of communities: as a single strategy, it does not provide members of different communities with any reasons for common action. The usual situation, an external challenge to a shared characteristic, is not a reliable basis for common action because it is too easy to get disgusted with or tired of the "others" that one is "forced" to work with. Simply put, adjectives will not a political force make.

Though lesbianism and feminism are very different formations, I believe that hooks's point is useful here. Lesbianism is an identity for many women in this society. Lesbian sexual practices are engaged in by many more women who do not identify as lesbians, and the dominant discourses concerning lesbianism inform their sense of what they are doing or resisting. Sexuality in general is an overwhelming identity in modern Western societies. Radical change will require a challenge to particular identities and to identities in general.

A specific theory of community, then, will acknowledge that communities are indeed locations for the production of meaning and value, that this is a worthwhile, even vital function in human life. This production is not simply the manifestation of what we have in common (this elusive "we"), but must be the site of questioning who "we" are and what "we" are doing together. Rather than basing community on what we have in common, we can come to community only by negotiating about what we will have in common, what we will share and how we will share it. This requires historical investigation into the factors that have produced lesbians as a population as well as philosophical reflection and political confrontation concerning who we wish to be. Our language cannot be that of simple ascription, where we know who we are in advance, nor can it be that of total voluntarism. We are thrown together, we lesbians, we women, we humans; but we are not thrown randomly into a world without history.

Against strong deconstructionist views, specifying insists on the reality of provisionally fixed identities and locations and mandates that we examine not just the differences/*différances* between us but also the linkages. If we are to embark on political change, we need something between old-fashioned interest-group liberalism and strong community (which for lesbians in the United States means withdrawal from the larger political community).

Let us now return to the processes of community that I described earlier. How does a specific theory of community help us understand these more flexibly?

First, a specific theory does not "insulate" us from hostility, if by "insulation" we mean never having to be conscious of it. Lesbian communities are not simply detachable from the social formations that surround them and in which we lesbians grow up and live much of our lives. Therefore, we cannot ask that "our" communities do so. They can, however, provide a space for critical distance from the compulsory heterosexuality of those larger formations. This distance, this "breathing room," is a crucial function of a lesbian community, but it is not to be bought at the price of grand theories of lesbianism and its difference from heterosexuality.

As a visible space for the "presencing" of lesbianism, a community of lesbians is responsible for refusing the bait of identity. Visibility should not be the visibility of "the lesbian," the archetypal lesbian, but must be the visibility of *lesbians* in our irreducible plurality. Thus, our visibility needs to be strongly detached from the temptation to present icons of lesbianism. Such a community will know its own history and will know where that history fades into obscurity. It will not be afraid of the truth of its history, especially of the truth of the instability of lesbian identity. This forthrightness includes acknowledging that many women who have loved women also love(d) men or will love them in the future; it means acknowledging "bisexuality," the inevitable supplement of sexual categorizing, at the center of lesbian existence.

Thus, the process of interpreting lesbian life and modeling lesbianism will change. Rather than engaging simply in identity consolidation of the sort Ponse describes, a lesbian community informed by its own specificity will welcome the specificity of each new member's mode of life. The role of interpretation must be separated from that of gatekeeping, or to put it differently, our lesbianisms must become more porous and plural. This change requires a shift from logical discourse (Someone is a lesbian if and only if x . . .) to narratives of lesbian lives. How then does one know if a given person is a lesbian? This paranoid question must give way to others: What does this person's lesbianism mean for her? What does her life have to teach us? This is a move from a logic of exclusion through demarcation to a logic of inclusion, enlarging both the community and the meaning of lesbianism. Lest anyone fear that this meaning will become too vague to be useful, we must remember that this process is occurring within a society with its own strong notions of what a lesbian is, that it will police our borders for us. If that society loses its clear sense of lesbianism, then "we lesbians" needn't worry too much about its vagueness, for its political force will be less urgent.

Finally, more specific theories will foster political mobilization. Genealogies of particular communities can show us exactly what forces are working to produce a community and to make the other three functions so necessary. They will lead us to the avenues of change in particular places. While grand theories posit single causes and huge, monolithic forces, genealogies help us to see the cracks and breaks, the places to drill and chip and huff and puff. They show us particular "local" causes of situations and thus aim us toward their elimination or transformation.

Getting specific about community/communities means that we acknowledge both the appeal of the communitarian call to wholeness and the deconstructive challenge to such calls. More importantly, it moves at a tangent from this debate to address the historical and contemporary foundations of these processes/entities we call "community" to address, not what needs to be done to really have community or how to live without it or with the recognition of its instability, but how we have and do construct the communities we live in, what discourses we are living within, their costs and hidden implications. Getting specific provides the link between identity politics and broadbased movements for change by bringing identities out of their isolation and into a world of multiple locations and discourses. In consequence, we move beyond (but do not dispense with) community to alliances; we move from identity to justice.

Chapter 6

The Space of Justice:
Lesbians and Democratic Interests

In the face of the diversity and dispersion of lesbians the question of a common social or political agenda is greatly problematic. There are, in the United States, many publications focusing on lesbian concerns. There are local and national organizations aimed at securing legal change, protection from violence, education about lesbians and lesbianism, promoting pride, and the like. Very often, however, these organizations have few members, with little outreach to lesbians. They purport to speak for lesbians, but it is not clear how many lesbians are listening or agreeing with them. The recent rise of lesbian and gay studies has produced an explosion of theoretically sophisticated and exciting work, but discussion of political goals is often limited. The major "gay" issue of the 1980s, the one primarily responsible for renewed coalitions between white lesbians and gay men, was AIDS. The reason for this development is obvious: AIDS provides us with a clear material interest, addressable by the state, that is shot through with cultural baggage about sexuality. It thus lends itself to overlapping agendas of cultural critique and interest-group activism.[1]

The task of formulating visions of prolesbian society and of its means of achievement has been blocked by the seemingly incompatible aims and perspectives of the two major white discourses on lesbianism: lesbian feminism in its 1970s version and poststructuralist challenges to lesbian identity. Although lesbian feminism provided a powerful analysis and vision of the future, it was too often perceived and used as a "party line" from which individuals strayed only at the cost of a loss of membership in lesbian community. Deconstructive treatments of lesbian identity, on the other hand, have been leery of positive formulations. Thinkers such as Judith Butler and Diana Fuss have called for coalition politics, but even the most subtle and original thinkers have failed to flesh out what this coalition politics would mean.

Fuss has noted that politics is the "aporia in much of our current political theorizing," and she has linked the popularity of the " 'politics of x' " formula, such as "the politics of theory" or "textual politics," to this ambiguity; "politics" denotes struggle and activism, but so vaguely that it can satisfy a myriad of needs by its invocation.[2] I would go even further. The term "politics of x" has thrown political theory into a crisis as we try to untangle the implications of new social movements that do not operate simply on a logic of self-interest or a fight for material goods. Nevertheless, the idea of a wider "politics" has also served those who resist large-scale institutional politics but who want to discuss power. This broadening has been an important avenue for new insights, but the "politics of x" idea has sometimes led to the refusal to discuss institutional or movement politics, leaving us with the narrowest, popularly U.S. American, vision of "politics" as the terrain of power, but never of common vision or justice or citizenship. Simply pointing out and condemning oppression or inequality become political activism. That one can do this as an isolated academic as well as in concert with others means that this version of politics serves to neglect the force of atomization and isolation in modern U.S. society.

Judith Butler's call in *Gender Trouble* for coalition politics is hedged by cautions that such politics must not "assume in advance what the content of 'women' will be," nor can we predict the "form of coalition, of an emerging and unpredictable assemblage of positions."[3] I agree that political agents are constructed through their political action, but this condition need not entail abandonment of all categories of identity; recognition of their provisional nature, a key element in both postmodern and poststructuralist theories, allows them to be retained but mandates caution and humility in their use. The realities of institutions and U.S. politics require basing common action on the provisional stability of categories of identity even as we challenge them.

Several issues need to be addressed in order to begin to theorize postmodern lesbian politics. First, we need to discuss our goals critically. We remain within dichotomies of assimilation versus transformation, reform versus revolution, and the like that can limit our conceptions. It is time for lesbians to confront whether we can and should envision a future and what that future should be. Following that, we need to examine how to achieve these goals. Specifically, we need to think in more detail about what postmodern coalitions might look like. That will be my task in the final chapter.

In this chapter and the rest of the book, I will increasingly refer to "gays and lesbians" rather than simply "lesbians." This is due to the differential distinction between the two groups at the level of identity and community versus that of more institutional politics. Although many lesbians may live lives that have little presence for gay men as friends (although many do have such friendships), the 1990s are seeing a renewed sense of a common political purpose. It is this renewed alliance that I will signal through the inclusion of gays as subjects in the following chapters.

Outlaws and Solid Citizens

The most striking thing about lesbians is not our difference(s) from heterosexuals or something distinctive about lesbian cultures and communities; it is our diversity. There are politically conservative lesbians, antifeminist lesbians, separatist lesbians (both feminist and nonfeminist), Marxist lesbians, radical feminist lesbians, liberal lesbians, apolitical lesbians, and others. This variety was a problem for traditional identity politics because such politics posited an intimate connection between one's sexual orientation or preference[4] and one's political sympathies or "true interest." This was best conceived along the lines of standpoint theory. A given lesbian might not presently adopt a "lesbian" standpoint, seeing things from a "prolesbian" perspective, but the elements of that standpoint are implicit in her life, waiting for consciousness to catch up.

Many lesbians may believe that the daily texture of lesbians' lives in the United States provides the ground for a common vision, but the experience of the past twenty-five years indicates that a broad or comprehensive vision is not in fact shared at this point. Although white lesbians are notably and consistently more liberal in their voting patterns than are either heterosexual women or men of any sort, they are far from monolithic.[5] Even among feminist lesbians, there are many disputed questions. One example is the question of marriage between lesbians. The question is, should lesbians fight for the right to be legally married, with the tax preferences, property understandings, and other legal powers that currently accompany marriage in the United States, or should we critique an institution that is inherently patriarchal? Would legal marriage present an improvement for lesbians, or would it signal their assimilation into a heterosexual paradigm? Similar questions arise concerning issues of lesbian motherhood. An even more painful case is that of lesbians in the military. Should we fight for the chance to serve in the military or be grateful and even proud that we are unwelcome in a destructive and oppressive institution?

Ruthann Robson refers to the two sides in these arguments as "separatist" and "assimilationist." The debate in general, as she puts it, is this:

> Are we sexual outlaws, and perhaps political outlaws as well, who recognize that the law is founded upon the rule of men, upon enforced heterosexuality, and upon violence? Or are we legitimate citizens who have been wrongly excluded from legal recognitions and protections because our private lives are slightly different from some mythical norm?[6]

This is a hard choice. Even more, as Sandoval has shown, it is a mistaken one. First, the exclusive choice between being law-abiding and being criminal, between being within (and under, subject to) the law and being an "outlaw," is not logically given but is socially structured by the current regime of power/knowledge. In this regime, breaking the law "makes" one into something—a "criminal," an "outlaw"—that then, for many, becomes a badge of pride. For others, the encompassing nature of the identity becomes a deterrence to certain sorts of activity. Although I wouldn't mind stealing, someone might say, I wouldn't want to "be a thief." We already see this pattern of thinking in the many men and women who have regular sexual relations with those of the same sex but refuse the identities of "gay" or "lesbian" because these are stigmatized, "outlaw" identities. Full assimilationists are those who accept the label but refuse stigmatization; they say, "Yes, I am a lesbian, but I'm not a criminal; I'm a law-abiding normal citizen."

This dynamic relies on the assumption that "everyone else" is in fact law-abiding and "normal." This is the hegemonic assumption, the assumption that exempts (white, middle-class) heterosexuals from problematization. This assumption assigns difference to the underprivileged side of what is actually a relation of difference. Instead of noting that both sides of an opposition are "different" from one another, the hegemony works to render the relation invisible and to describe difference as something inherent in one side.[7] For example, research and discussion into how Blacks differ from whites presumes a white viewpoint as given; from that perspective, it is the difference of Blacks that emerges as a question. Whites may be shocked and offended to hear or read Blacks discussing the differentness of whites, hearing in it the assumption of superiority that is so common as to be invisible among whites when they discuss Blacks.

In this (hetero)sexist social ontology, there are two distinct groups: "Americans" and "gays and lesbians." This ontology is shared among Americans of all political stripes: remember Ross Perot's statement in the 1992 presidential campaign that he would not have "homosexuals and adulterers" in his cabinet because they would be "controversial" with "the American people." This pronouncement erases the huge incidence of heterosexual adultery as well as the presence of homosexuals among "the American people." The strength of feminist and separatist positions has been the ability to question this hegemonic presentation, to challenge the "normality" of the normal citizen/subject. These analyses have exposed the assumed maleness and heterosexuality of the citizen. Problems reemerge when we accept the idea that lesbians should not or cannot become citizens. This persuasion serves to erase all the (usually, but not always, closeted) lesbians who live "normal" or "exemplary" lives.

The second mistake implicit in Robson's choice is the belief that "legitimate citizens" must not be subject to (or aware of?) social dominance. The guiding assumption of assimilationists is that heterosexuals are not daily coerced and shaped into fit subjects. Because of this assumption, they can see inclusion as enough; if only "outsiders" are coerced and subjected, then becoming "insiders" will suffice for freedom. But they are mistaken in this belief. "Other" populations can be effectively targeted only when the "core" population is safely domesticated. Thus the question should be, where and how do we want power to move through our lives? Do we want to experience power as heterosexual white people experience it, or do we want to experience it some other way?

In fact, Robson argues, assimilationists and separatists are not necessarily opposed: their divergence is instead the result of legal thought that occludes recognition of differences as other than dichotomous and enduring. "The law's pronouncement that a person is either law-abiding or a criminal may be a dichotomy that serves the law's interests and does not serve lesbian interests."[8] This question presumes in its very structure that lesbians are distinct from "the society" in which they live. Such questions work for those who experience themselves as true insiders mistakenly disenfranchised, but they do nothing to problematize the inside. And without that problematization of the "inside," the hegemonic core of social structures, we will continually return to unsatisfying choices.

One of the most important insights of poststructuralist work has been the strong deconstruction of "society." Although Marx recognized that societies were processes as well as structures and that the conceptual separation of the individual from society was deceptive, liberal political theory has never made this leap. In Marxism, the problem of society has been that of viewing these systems of processes as a monolithic structure, ruled by "the economic system." This formulation still assumes a unity of system in the economy instead of a plurality of processes and events and positions. Increasingly these systems, and thus "society," are giving way to "the social" as the theoretical space of negotiation of identity and difference. Thus the liberal vision of the individual and his/her society finally breaks down. We are "society," we shifting, incomplete beings. We do indeed live within social formations that possess a certain fixity and provide channels and links and productions of power and meaning, but these formations are not, strictly speaking, separable from us. We are, we speak, those formations.

The question is not, do we "fit into" "society" or not, but where and how do we find our places in social formations, and where do we want to be? This is not a question that admits of a singular answer, such as "Lesbians fit x" or "Lesbians are y" or even "Lesbians should do/be z." It is a postmodern question, which is to say, it is a question that cannot be answered through the metanarratives of the last several hundred years. We cannot simply piggyback onto metanarratives about the progress of freedom and enlightenment that were partial and flawed in their formation without being carried along by their defective assumptions. Lesbian political theory requires differential consciousness to move through these dilemmas, exploring our interests and how to further them.

Lesbian Interests

What is to be done is not obvious. Robson urges us to center "lesbian interests," but it is far from clear what that means. For her it seems to mean the ability of lesbians to choose their circumstances of life. In her desire to "put lesbians at the center," to construct a "lesbian legal theory," Robson argues that such a theory must center lesbians over any others. She gives as an example child-custody rules. She reminds us that not all lesbians will want custody of their children. If the lesbian does not want custody, then "lesbian legal theory" should support that decision regardless of the desires of the child or other parents. If a lesbian desires custody, such a theory must "privilege her position to choose custody."[9] For Robson, then, lesbian legal theory privileges any given lesbian over any nonlesbian. This may sound inviting to those of us (most of us!) who have been told in our lives to subordinate our desires and needs to those of others, but her alternative is not an improvement. First, this rule presumes that we know who lesbians are, a presumption belied both by current theory and by political controversies. Are women who occasionally sleep with men lesbians? How often is too often? If a lesbian were to become heterosexual, would Robson recommend that her ex-lover be given child custody? The instability of lesbian identity makes Robson's proposal much more difficult than it first appears.

Second, Robson's recommendation rests on an impoverished conception of the social landscape. Lesbians become the privileged, whose desires are the command of the law. If I can certify my lesbianism, and I want to abandon my child, then Robson's theory would support that decision. Although Robson is not intending a world of all-powerful lesbian choosers, her theory does not sufficiently address the networks of relationships from which lesbians emerge and within which we live.

Robson's proposal in fact has no content beyond particular interests at particular times. It is not a standard that is appropriate to any real humans in relation, much less a full public life. It speaks only to lesbians as consumers of rights, characterized as social or political goods, in a world in which choice is the greatest good. Such a conception of a desired end is unable to articulate with other struggles in any terms other than "choice," which will not do. At some point, individuals' choices will conflict. If we do not have some sense of how to adjudicate these conflicts beyond the a priori privilege given to one party over another, we will be unable to sustain a common world. Such a "lesbian legal theory" as Robson proposes guarantees that lesbians will be isolated from others, both in the rigidity of our identities and in the privilege accorded us as consumers of the law.

Behind Robson's recommendation lies a conception of interest that is inimical to building democratic alliances. This conception assumes, first, that identities are easily demarcated, and, second, that interests are attached to identities. A more specific analysis calls into question the simple delineation of identities. If our basis for theory is social practice and structure, rather than rational/logical categorization, it becomes immediately clear than no one fits within any identity; we are all "citizens of the lack," as it were, all members of an incompletely filled or stable social space. We all live within multiple valid descriptions of ourselves, choosing from situation to situation which description—which identity—shall come to the fore.

The full political implications of this awareness emerge only when we look at the second assumption. Its message is that each "identity" carries with it an identifiable "interest." Thus farmers have an "interest" in keeping agricultural prices high, in maintaining farm subsidies, and so on, whereas consumers have an interest in low prices and abundant food.

Both interest-group liberalism and Marxism embrace these two assumptions. They differ in their conception of the goal of politics. For interest-group liberalism the goal of politics is the adjudication through compromise of competing interests. For Marxism, "politics" is largely secondary, if not distracting; while democratic socialists allow for parliamentary, democratic forms of change, Leninists and many others disavow it. For both orthodox Marxists and liberals, politics is the work of advancing essentially prepolitical or nonpolitical "interests."

Theodore Lowi describes the "model" of "interest-group liberalism" as follows:

> (1) Organized interests are homogeneous and easy to define. Any duly elected representative of any interest is taken as an accurate representation of each and every member. (2) Organized interests emerge in every sector of our lives and adequately represent most of those sectors, so that one organized group can be found effectively answering and checking some other organized group as it seeks to prosecute its claims against society. And (3) the role of government is one of insuring access to the most effectively organized, and of ratifying the agreements and adjustments worked out among the competing leaders.[10]

Thus interest-group liberalism gives us a description of politics in which the business at hand is that of effecting compromises between farmers and consumers. To the extent that justice surfaces at all, it is a matter of optimal (that is, satisfactory to all parties) distribution of goods. Within this model, the purpose of coalitions is to lend support to another's interest in return for their support of yours.

Albert O. Hirschman has noted that the new construction of "interest" in the early modern period was intended to moderate "passion" and thereby tame politics; even before the term came to have a strongly material flavor to it, it "denoted an element of reflection and calculation with respect to the manner in which these aspirations were to be pursued."[11] The major advantages of thinking in terms of interests were the predictability and constancy they imposed on politics: "in the pursuit of their interests men were expected to be steadfast, single-minded, and methodical,"[12] in contrast to the behavior of those moved by passions. It is assumed that interests themselves are stable;

were I to be singleminded and methodical in the pursuit of fluctuating interests, I would perhaps be tenacious, but I would not be easily predictable.

This model works best for interests that are economically defined. The rise of "interest thinking" coincides with and reinforces the modern capitalist state, with its primary business of negotiating between competing classes. James Madison underscores this point when he argues that "the most common and durable source of factions has been the verious [*sic*] and unequal distribution of property. Those who hold and those who are without property have ever formed distinct interests in society. . . . The regulation of these various and interfering interests forms the principal task of modern legislation."[13] The modern category of the "consumer" has problematized even these identities and interests. A farmer is also a consumer. If interests are attached to identities, as interest-group pluralism suggests, then most of us will find ourselves in positions of internal conflict. When we move beyond economic "identities" to sociocultural ones, things get even more confusing.

Interest talk may make sense if all the members of a group share every "relevant" social characteristic or submerge difference/differences among themselves, but this condition is increasingly unlikely. In modern societies, where overlapping social movements and identities are increasingly present, interest becomes as unstable as identity. It is at least in part this instability of overlapping identities that has given rise to the attacks on identity politics from across the political spectrum. Seeing interest as concretely and stably linked to particular social identities, such commentators have seen in the proliferation of identities a fragmentation of the social world and the impossibility of common action.

Interest and the Space of Citizenship

If this is all there is to interest, then the poststructuralist critique of identity and the identity politics of new social movements seem to demolish the possibility of interests as the basis of politics; yet a shift of focus enables us to see these proliferations as the opening to a new citizenship and public life, to a new interest. Without the presumption of stability and predictability of political subjects, the position of "interest" is opened for reexamination.

Anna Jonasdottir has begun this task. She reminds us that in its root "interest" does not simply refer to the content of people's desires, needs, or demands, but to the space of politics itself. Its initial construction, from the Latin *inter* ("among," "between") and *esse* ("to be"), suggests that interest is also the claim to *publicity* of certain needs or wants; that is, the concept of interest marks those things that are of legitimate public concern, in contrast to those desires and needs that are "private," my business alone. Thus claiming something as an interest is both a substantive claim to a good and a formal claim to participation and public recognition.[14] Martha Ackelsberg develops this line of thought as she argues that "political interests are not analogous to an interest in football," because political interests are public and of general concern.[15] Conceiving of politics in terms of (privatized) interests removes the possibility of genuinely public—that is, noninstrumental—discourse and action.

Jonasdottir argues that the formal claim of interest is more "relevant" than the substantive (content) claim. The formal claim of an interest—say, as a lesbian—does not yet commit a lesbian to a particular desire or need. It establishes lesbianism as a relevant political identity from which to proceed. The claim of interest provides the space to articulate a "lesbian good" without predetermining what that good will be. It also opens the category of "lesbian" to negotiation—claiming lesbianism as a relevant identity cannot simply avoid "commonsense" notions of what such an identity is, but it need not rest with those notions either. The identity itself becomes open to politics.

This is not a situation unique to lesbianism, or to sexual categories in general. Consider the case of the farmer again. Claiming an interest as a farmer will lead many to conclusions about what that person— the "farmer"—will want and support. It is not given from the establishment of that interest/identity exactly who will be defined as a farmer, however, nor is it given that the farmer *must* support subsidies or oppose decent wages for migrant workers or, in general, think only in the narrowest terms of individual economic advantage. The farmer is also (at least potentially) a *citizen*—not as "another" identity, but as the basis of the claim of interest. The farmer may conclude that the nation cannot afford subsidies, or that decent wages and living conditions are a requirement of justice, without abandoning her "interest" as a farmer.[16]

In the same way, claiming an interest as a lesbian in this view is a civic act. It embeds the lesbian in her political community/communities, implicating her in responsibilities as well as rights and demands. This point is often missed, both in mainstream political science treatments of interest and in discussions of lesbian politics. Claims made on a community are inseparable from recognition of that community.

When we lesbians seek to further our interests in U.S. society and law, we are at the same time involving ourselves in the larger affairs of that society. And this involvement is crucial if we are to actually have the option to live "lesbian-centered" lives. As Michael Walzer points out, within a political community "the denial of membership is always the first of a long train of abuses,"[17] and thus anyone interested in eliminating persecution and oppression must work immediately for recognition of the membership of lesbian citizens. If lesbians are to claim any interest at all, the first interest must be recognition as members of the political community.

If we transform our identity politics from one that assumes an automatic correlation between identity and politics to one based on the spaces of citizenship itself we might, ironically, find more to share both with other lesbians and with nonlesbians. Such a politics will recognize relevant differences in the specific situations of our lives while leaving the political meaning of those differences open to negotiation. This need not be contradictory, though it may sound paradoxical.

We can get at this problem by considering what counts as a lesbian issue. Some might argue that lesbian issues should be only those that concern all lesbians or affect lesbians qua lesbians, but these categories break down quickly. Lesbian motherhood is not an issue for all lesbians; many cannot have children, and others are not interested. Although lesbophobic violence against lesbians may seem a clear "lesbian issue," it is irrelevant in less violent cultures or locations in the United States. More basically, any such requirements for lesbian issues presume a stability to lesbian identities that is belied by recent theory as well as many women's experiences. What is it to act "as a lesbian," or to have a concern "in one's capacity as a lesbian"? These essentialisms and reifications have broken down, and with them falls the question of a lesbian issue construed as unique.

Consider the goal of decent housing for all. Surely this is a concern for many lesbians, and is therefore a "lesbian" issue. It is also a concern for many others, however, and for them it is not configured as "lesbian." The difficulty that poor lesbians face in finding decent housing, especially if they try to live openly as lesbians, is lesbian specific but also reaches beyond lesbians to the problem of decent housing at affordable cost for all. Here we can distinguish the difficulties faced by women marked as lesbians, stigmatized in a heterosexist identitarian society, without attributing to them any essential features or qualities. We can thus establish a limited political agenda without essentializing or overgeneralizing.

We could approach this problem in several ways, but I will focus on two here. In this first, lesbian-centered approach, lesbians will work with other lesbians to provide decent housing for lesbians. This will include construction, oversight of landlords and municipalities for maintenance and rate fairness, and work to ensure that lesbians are not discriminated against on the basis of their sexuality. Nonlesbians will be ignored, except insofar as they either control housing or provide something desirable. This is the separatist solution, and there is much to be said for it as an occasional tactic. Working with and for other lesbians is exhilarating and empowering. It cannot be our only position, however.

In the second approach, lesbians will work with everyone concerned to provide decent housing to all citizens. This effort will look like the first approach in many ways, but there are some differences. First, the nonlesbians will need continual prodding to understand and work on issues of discrimination. Second, the lesbians will have to commit to working with and for people who are not lesbians. In so doing, they will not be able to focus simply on lesbians, but will have to work for and talk about the problems faced by the other members and potential members of the group. This responsibility does not make decent housing no longer a lesbian issue; it simply removes the divide between lesbians and everyone else. Making decent housing a lesbian issue does not remove it from the public agenda, or from that of any other identifiable group. The lesbian concerns may be specific to lesbians, but it does not follow that those concerns cannot be shared and fought for by all.

In this second scenario, the specific problems and desires of lesbians are relevant to the whole group, insofar as it wants to include lesbians as equal members of a democratic organization or polity. This relevance does not mean that the specifics of being lesbian are irrelevant to membership in the group; each is welcome and has an equal voice without regard to sexuality. The equality of membership in the group requires that the group treat all equally, and that means paying attention to the situations and needs of all. It does not mean allowing only those in a given situation to participate in decision making, however; that violates equality.[18]

Such a politics allows both for the presentation of something like a "lesbian interest" and for the recognition that many (if not most) lesbians will not share that interest. In the model described by Lowi, an interest was a "real" interest only if it was shared by every member of the homogeneously defined group. Thus if not all lesbians agree on a policy, it cannot be a "lesbian interest." If we abandon presumptions of homogeneity and identity, however—if we get specific—we can say that nondiscrimination in housing is a lesbian interest without thereby excluding others from having that interest or requiring that all lesbians share it.

This move has an effect that some may find ironic, even unpalatable. Removing interest from identity forces us to end theoretical imperialism. It makes it impossible for anyone to tell another what the other's interest "really is." It seems, therefore, to pull the ground out from beneath any shared goals. We are forced to recognize nonfeminist lesbians as lesbians nonetheless; outlaws and solid citizens must both relinquish any claims to the truth of lesbianism. We seem to have very little left to share politically.

This is only half the story, however. If we now have a less monolithic agenda, the focus on the public nature of lesbian interest invites us into a realm of shared concern extending beyond lesbian communities or groups. Feminist lesbians may be forced to admit that not all lesbians share any version of a feminist agenda, but on the other hand we have a greater opening to work with feminist nonlesbians as well as others with whom we may share a great deal. If the above treatment of interest lowers the substantive goals of lesbians, it raises the procedural/formal ones to the demand that lesbians be acknowledged as equal citizens, with equal participation and recognition not "in spite" of our lesbianism, but simply regardless of it. Our membership is not qualified or limited by our lesbianism, and thus our concerns, even our concerns as lesbians, are legitimately public ones. Our compearance as lesbians is prior to any particular claims we make and does not require proof of our sameness with heterosexuals. Membership as compearance acknowledges our existence, our presence; this acknowledgment is what interest-group politics collapses. It is not a liberal abstraction but is the claim of specificity.

Rethinking interest moves us from identity, with the assumptions of homogeneity and privatized consumerist concerns and agendas, to politics as an activity that is valuable in itself. The result is not the subsumption or transcendence of "identity politics" but a recognition of the fullness of politics that cannot be encapsulated by identity. It is the return of identity politics to its formulation by the Combahee River Collective. They did not say that their only political concerns would arise from their self-interest, which was to be unquestioned and unchallenged; they said that they would no longer accept other people's agendas and models for their politics, that they would look to the specific circumstances of their own lives for their politics. The later problems of identity politics have had less to do with this vision than with its corruption into interest-group liberalism. This corruption was not the exclusive product of middle-class whites, but we had most to do with it. The homogeneity that appears from the hegemonic position contributed to a vision of masses of women, of lesbians, and so on, with a unified interest. The recognition of the diversity of these groups gave rise to descriptions of "difference," but for many white (and probably many nonwhite) people this looked like the end of politics, the death of a shared world, because "differences" appeared as discrete entities, singular atoms on a blank social space, rather than as nodes in social constellations. The refiguration of differences as specificities enables us to return to the strength of identity politics without leading to abandonment of those who do not obviously share our identities.

Lesbian Citizens

Getting specific shows us that lesbians both are and are not different from nonlesbians. We cannot simply say "lesbians are different from nonlesbians" without gross generalization; neither can we deny that there are systematic differences.

We can see this in current battles for lesbian and gay rights in the United States. Rights bills have generally taken the simple form of statements that ban discrimination on the basis of "sexual orientation," defined in both bills as homosexuality, heterosexuality, and bisexuality. The rhetoric used to support these bills is largely liberal univeralist: sexual orientation is not a publicly significant difference, though it is currently a basis for discrimination. Gays and lesbians are just like heterosexuals. This argument is conveyed in television specials that show lesbian or gay parents and couples, and portray their opponents as intolerant bigots. Such presentations imply that inclusion of lesbians and gays as equal members of society will not significantly change or threaten it; it will simply extend full membership to people who have been unjustly excluded or victimized.

This picture is not simply wrong, but it is not simply right either. Passage of rights bills that ban discrimination in housing, employment, or public accommodation are just the opening wedge. If discrimination in employment on the basis of sexual orientation is impermissible, then eventually lesbians will demand spousal benefits and privileges comparable to those enjoyed by heterosexuals. The existing argument against this demand, that withholding of these goods is not discrimination but is simply based on marital status, will give way before the fact that lesbians and gays are not allowed to marry and are therefore systematically deprived of the possibility of participating in benefits open to heterosexuals.

So far, the process looks like more assimilation—inclusion by arguments that we are like heterosexuals, and so should be treated like them. Similarly, recent controversy over lifting the U.S. ban on "homosexuals" in the military has proceeded on the terms of whether gays and lesbians are "really different" enough to justify exclusion, with the "progay" group claiming minimal differences and the "antigay" group appealing to the discomfort of heterosexual soldiers. Neither side is fully prepared to consider that the military, like marriage and family, may indeed change profoundly as a result of inclusion. The ban has served to police "heterosexual" soldiers as well as "homosexual" ones, fostering an atmosphere of anxiety and homophobia that were not extensive before exclusion. Contemporary American gender-role linkages among masculinity, violence, and male heterosexuality as predation and conquest of women are extremely powerful in the armed forces. Visible gay men disrupt these linkages, detaching masculinity and violence from heterosexuality. They do this regardless of their personal sexism or lack of it. A military with openly gay men would not be the military we know now.[19]

Think, too, of what inclusion in family law and policy would mean. Family policy is made in the clear light of the nuclear patriarchal ideal, and those who do not fit (most Americans) are judged in that light. Actual nondiscrimination against lesbian families requires thorough rethinking of that ideal, because there is absolutely no policy—no bridefare, no AFDC police—that will introduce a male head of household into that family.

Getting specific introduces the possibility of thinking of lesbians not as outlaws or as solid citizens but as lesbian citizens. These lesbian citizens are "queer" in existing models of citizenship, but this queerness is not itself a virtue. The revolutionary potential of lesbian citizens lies not in separatism nor in continual elaboration of the law to privilege "lesbian interests" but in forcing the political and legal systems to stretch and re-form to do justice to our lives. Legislators and judges would indeed have to consider lesbian interests, but not as a list of criteria based upon known characteristics. They would have to learn to frame legislation and adjudication from the standpoint of a lesbian in a given case, to ask what she needs as well as what nonlesbians need. This is not a privileging of lesbians above others; it is, in Martha Minow's words, a process of "making all the difference," moving to see fields of relations rather than discrete persons labeled as "different." If "difference" is no longer the property of one group but is the mark of a relation of (dis)similarity, then it is not enough to fit "others" into a previously existing frame, nor can we simply modify the frame to include them. There is no avoiding it; what is needed is not a specific result, but a process—that of public deliberation among a group all of whose members are treated as equal participants. Although certain particulars, such as civil rights, are a prerequisite for this process, they are not the sum of the goal. The other part is our need for choice if we are to truly reshape institutions and practices. Lesbian citizens will thus be part of the larger project of radical democracy that aims at making all the difference, at eliminating the privilege of hegemonic identity.

Opening the space of citizenship addresses the needs of U.S. lesbians for recognition and self-determination, inclusion, and safety. It also provides a means of linking lesbian struggles to other demands for these same things without assuming a priority among those struggles or suggesting a hierarchy of oppressions. It enables lesbians and others to be specific about their own circumstances, to make connections between their circumstances and those of others, and to formulate a common agenda for concrete changes that does not play into zero-sum games of power. The demand for the broadest range of civil rights is not a "special interest" demand, sought at the expense of the civic good or that of another "group," but is a demand for equal membership in a democratic polity.

In the end, our goal should be to articulate a lesbian agenda as part of a radical democratic creed shared across sexualities and other differences. In such a future, the interest of lesbians in their lives will be shared by others, and will not need to include reminders that we should not be raped, killed, intimidated, "cured," or ignored. We will thus be ready for specific citizenships, entry into the multiplicity of public realms that await postmodern citizens.

Chapter 7

Oppression, Liberation, and Power

As a result both of AIDS and the heightened attacks by fundamentalist Christians and conservative bigots, the past ten years have witnessed broader coalition building among and between gays, lesbians, and others. These new coalitions have focused on legislative battles for civil rights for lesbians and gays and on anticensorship struggles as well as on AIDS—and have raised new problems. Lesbians have been divided by analyses that either placed rights at the center of a lesbian agenda or those that eschewed such a focus, labeling it narrow and reformist. As the New Right increases pressure to deny us the marginal tolerance we have been gaining, momentum has built for an assimilationist agenda. With this shift, the debate between being "in the system" and not being in it appears to be mistaken and unfruitful. Rather than debate whether to "be in the system" or not, we need to shift our ground to talk about *how* to be in the contemporary United States and what must happen for us to fully be members of the multiple societies within the nation.

Can we create ground to speak as democratic citizens? I think that we can, but this creation involves revision of some liberal concepts. I will argue here that we should abandon the metaphor of liberation and work instead for power. An analysis of the sort of oppression operative in heterosexist societies will lead us to see the limitations of "liberation" as a goal. As a metaphor, liberation has been inextricably bound to modernity and its forms of power and has been unable to address contemporary configurations that are not recognizable within that framework. Fully thinking about power locates us within a framework of common citizenship rather than "consumption" of rights in the liberal model or "authentic selfhood" as a liberationist goal. It provides us with benchmarks for evaluation of progress, progress conceived not as exemption from an oppressive society or state but as its transformation. A focus on power will also help us to

114

evaluate alliances on the basis not of identity but of common goals and the actual position of lesbians within those alliances.

Oppression

Iris Young has recently argued that justice is a matter of societal support for and furtherance of the conditions for two core values. These values are, first, "developing and exercising one's capacities and expressing one's experience" and, second, "participating in determining one's action and the conditions of one's action."[1] She contrasts this view with the predominant liberal treatment of justice as a matter of distribution of goods. With Michael Walzer, she is focusing on "the naming of the goods, the giving of meaning, and the collective making" of goods, what Nancy Fraser describes as "the politics of need interpretation."[2] From this perspective, justice is not simply getting "goods" in a ratio that is defensible, but involves the power to develop oneself and share that development with others and the power to share in decision making for the community. Justice is about the ability to set the agenda as well as voting on the items presented.

Oppression, in this analysis, is a denial of justice. Young identifies five "faces" or forms of oppression and argues that not all forms coincide. The five faces she explores are: exploitation, "the steady process of the transfer of the results of the labor of one social group to benefit another";[3] marginalization, in which "a whole category of people is expelled from useful participation in social life and thus potentially subjected to severe material deprivation and even extermination";[4] powerlessness, "a position in the division of labor and the comcomitant social position that allows persons little opportunity to develop and exercise skills," as well as the lack of power in relation to others;[5] cultural imperialism, in which "the dominant meanings of a society render the particular perspective of one's own group invisible at the same time as they stereotype one's group and mark it out as the Other";[6] and systematic violence. These five "faces" serve to make the concept of oppression more specific and analytically useful, and in so doing they help us to see some problems with earlier theorizing.

The central failure of modern political theories has been their attempt to incorporate all forms of oppression within one rubric rather than recognize the plurality of forms of oppression. Liberalism's focus on state power and individual powerlessness enforced denial of other forms of oppression. Marxist theory is a powerful tool for analyzing exploitation; its downfall occurs when other oppressions are redefined as exploitation, so that the anti-imperialist struggle or feminism or gay/lesbian liberation may be subsumed within the class struggle.[7] Much of women's oppression does indeed take the form of systematic transfers of products and wealth, as in female agricultural work that is appropriated by male family members. We cannot adequately theorize the sum of women's oppression under the heading of exploitation, however. While many groups suffer from several forms of oppression, and for them those forms are interrelated in various particular ways, it does not follow that "true oppression" requires all of the forms or that the connections between one group's marginalization and another's powerlessness are automatic. Oppression is not a monolith.

Aida Hurtado presents a fine example of the necessary distinctions between forms of oppression. She argues that although within the United States all women are subordinated to white men, the form of subordination is very different for white women and for women of color. Specifically, she argues that though white women are "seduced" into subordination through promises of benefits and privileges, women of color experience subordination through rejection: "the avenues of advancement through marriage that are open to white women who conform to prescribed standards of middle-class femininity are not even a theoretical possibility for most women of Color" (her capitalization). She does not mean to suggest that women of color are "more oppressed than white women, but, rather, that white men use different forms of enforcing oppression of white women and of women of Color. As a consequence, these groups of women have different political responses and skills, and at times these differences cause the two groups to clash."[8]

It is important to note the blind spot in Hurtado's otherwise strong analysis. She nowhere refers to lesbians or to the institutions of heterosexuality, and as a result she invites lesbians (especially white lesbians) to make the arguments of the early 1970s: because lesbians don't relate sexually to men and generally don't marry them—because, that is, they are more independent—their experience crosses the racial divide of subordination and rejection. And certainly something of the sort is true: heterosexual men try to seduce lesbians, both sexually and emotionally, and if they fail, lesbians are rejected. But this condition is not enough to make oppression on the basis of lesbianism equivalent to racial oppression. We need to insist both that white lesbians are not seduced in quite the same ways as heterosexual white women and also that white lesbians remain open to seduction (through access to education, career advancement and pay, and so forth) in ways that lesbians of color are denied.

We thus see that discussions of "the" oppression of lesbians are doomed to work within the false unification mandated by language. We can try to distinguish forms of oppression suffered by lesbians qua lesbians, but these forms will always be shot through with other structures of power and identity. Clearly, traditional theoretical language is severely challenged by a thoroughgoing identity politics. The answer to this obstacle is not to stop theorizing, and not to stop making generalized statements, but to remain open to the challenges and qualifications that must inevitably result.

With this caution, can we go on to make such generalized statements about the oppression of lesbians? I think we can. A concrete example will serve. In the 1980s, with the influx of women into the military, many men sought to stem the tide. Sexual harassment was and is pandemic, but if women complained they were placed under investigation for lesbianism. "Women" were officially welcome in the military, but "lesbians" were not, and so many women were ejected through charges (accurate and inaccurate) of lesbianism. Thus at a time when investigations against men had virtually ceased, women were being discharged at a growing rate.[9] This example reminds us of the relative powerlessness of lesbians qua lesbians both against the state and against individuals: without state support, crimes against lesbians are ignored or used as the opening for state harassment. Hate crimes against lesbians are only beginning to be recorded, and only a few are reported, for the remedy, many feel, is worse than the disease.

Cultural imperialism is both a cause and an effect of other oppressions in lesbians' lives. Living under the threat of violence, many lesbians live invisible lives. They thus leave a vacuum of representation, a vacuum obligingly filled by homophobic and heterosexist forces. This dominant representation then makes it very unattractive for anyone to become visible or public as a lesbian—who wants to be seen as a pervert? Discounting news reports on lesbian or gay issues unless they are reported by a heterosexual—someone who "can be objective"—is a further instance of cultural imperialism.[10]

We might indeed imagine that violence and powerlessness are both effects of cultural imperalism without arguing that "lesbian oppression" is really, fundamentally, a matter of cultural imperialism. Violence is a distinct problem, related to but separable from cultural imperialism. Powerlessness is more problematic, for many lesbians are not powerless in U.S. society even though the group "lesbians" are disempowered and recognizable membership in that group often has disempowering results. Throughout the United States, lesbians have to make choices between being fully visible as lesbians—a central part of being empowered, in Young's terms—and being empowered in the other ways she describes. We may say that lesbians are relatively disempowered in U.S. society, in that they are barred from full development of self and the opportunity for social/political power, but we cannot say that lesbians are powerless; for many of us, it is a matter of trade-offs, of degrees of visibility in exchange for degrees of opportunity. Oppression is more complex than slogans would make it.

Liberation

When we examine these forms of oppression, it becomes clear that "liberation" is an inadequate way to express their elimination. Only perhaps of violence could it be said that its opposite or elimination would be liberation, and even in that case there are better ways to express the opposite, such as the absence of violence. Exploitation, marginalization, violence, powerlessness, and cultural imperialism are all differentially present among lesbians, and none of these is remedied by "liberation." They are remedied by (em)power(ment).

The metaphor of liberation assumes a social landscape in which power is something that forbids certain actions and commands others. Unjust limitation is oppression, and the opposite is liberation. Whether the identified form of oppression is exploitation, violence, or any other, the metaphor of liberation conceives of oppression as imposition on an otherwise free subject and liberation as its antidote.[11] Under this sign, theory is treated as the means by which groups identify the sources and methods of limitation in order to eliminate them, to throw them off. The metaphor of liberation suggests that when we have done this, we will be free and the world will be just; that is, justice is also a matter of liberation. The eternal question for libera(l)/tion theories then is, What sorts of limitation are justified, and who gets to decide?

This is an important question, but it is not the only important political question to be asked. It is a question of government, of ordering and authorizing. It evades questions such as: How do we live together? How do we decide how to decide? What are our common purposes, and what purposes might we share? Libera(l)/tion theories are fundamentally individualistic, even when the "subject" of liberation is a people. They suggest that the oppressor and the oppressed can be treated as coherent unities within themselves, that ideally those unities are coherent rather than fractious and partial. They imply that when "liberation" is achieved, the individual or "the people" will be free, and that this position is unproblematic. They evade questions that are the core of politics; for if we did not live together, we would not need to decide who governs.

The libera(l)/tion model treats power as either wholly negative, something to be eliminated, or as something to be used against "others," but only with carefully prescribed limits, such as in wars of liberation. If power is negative and prohibitive by nature, we cannot ask what we wish it to achieve; we can only ask what we wish it to prevent. Thus proceeds old-fashioned rights talk, in which rights are a claim against state power.[12] Thus proceeds Marxism, in which workers' power is meant to limit, then finally eliminate, the oppression perpetrated by the bourgeoisie.[13] The end result of this limitation is self-management, the internalization of rules into habits. The vagueness of so much Marxist theory has much to do with the purely negative quality of liberation; though the idea of liberation expresses the desire for release and for self-determination, it offers no real help with questions of how we should live.

Without a context, the self of self-determination is lost, perpetually hungry, in exile. As Dennis Fischman explains:

> The theme of exile portrays the breakdown of meaning between self, situation, and other that recurrently plagues a people which is partially constituted by a compelling purpose. When changes in the world they inhabit make the tasks pertaining to such a group impossible to fulfill, its members suffer. They are injured in their identity, in their claim to social resources that they need, and in their ability to participate freely in everyday social life, as whole selves. Most poignantly, however, the notion of exile implies that members of such a group will find themselves dispossessed of the language they need in order to formulate and communicate their predicament. They are psychically isolated as well as socially disempowered.[14]

In Young's terms, exile is constituted in large part as powerlessness and cultural imperialism. Lesbians do not constitute a "people which is partially constituted by a compelling purpose," but the theme of exile applies to lesbian existence in (post)modern societies. To the extent that lesbians can be spoken of as "a people" at all, to the extent that there are such things as lesbian identities, these identities are injured by heterosexist oppression. Lesbians have faced continuous deprivation of social resources that we need; denied membership as lesbians in our societies, we find ourselves forced to speak in the language of heterosexual, male-dominated regimes. Lesbians, though they are not a people in Fischman's sense, are indeed in exile.

As Fischman's analysis suggests, the remedy for exile is never as simple as "liberation." The liberation framework has historically been valuable for men subject to colonial oppression, slavery, and violence. These situations present the possibility that merely ending the existing situation of truly forbidding power would be enough for justice and freedom. Many other situations that are justly labeled oppressive do not fit this mold, however. The use of "liberation" in these situations may in fact both occlude existing power relations and incite disputes and anger between groups that need not be opposed. The oppression of marginalization or invisibility is not relieved by the absence of force simply conceived. Lesbian invisibility is an instance of social power that operates by refusing the possibility of action within recognized forms. When lesbians can receive no social or legal recognition of their domestic or life partnerships they do not suffer from laws that officially target them but from laws that implicitly refuse to acknowledge their possible existence. Such laws and practices aim to reduce being-in-common to being-common, denying the compearance of lesbians (and of everyone else). The antidote is not more legal neglect but is increasingly visible entry into and transformation of a system not designed by or for lesbians.[15] This visible entry is inseparable from the project of power.

Power

The vitality of the liberation theme has less to do with the actual workings of power than it does with fear of power. Euro-Americans are raised in a culture in which power is an entity to be used by some over others, and in which this power is always suspected of being used for selfish ends. They seem to agree with Lord Acton that power corrupts, and absolute power corrupts absolutely. This suspicion is intensified among women, trained not to want power. As Jean Baker Miller's research has shown, too often white women in the United States associate women's power with selfishness and destructiveness.[16]

Given this equation, it is hard for white lesbians to seriously envision public power in positive terms. "Liberation" suggests a world without power, and thus avoids the question. This difficulty has crippled our thinking about politics. Lesbians often move to eschew power entirely, or to talk vaguely of "empowerment" as a personal issue, rather than discussing the acquisition and creation of power as a political project, as a public, collective process, a power with others, that acts both as power over and as power to, as ability. The radical democratic project in which lesbians must engage is a project of power. Whereas the liberal model leaves us with nothing more than continual suspicion of power and the sense of the need to escape from under it, a radical democratic politics invites us to share power and to transform it. The question is not how to eliminate power but how to re-create it and how to figure it democratically.

"Democratic" re-creation should not be understood to mean forms of power that never exclude anyone or anything. Such an ideal is fundamentally incoherent. All identities, even democratic ones, are formed through contrast and exclusion. These are operations of power. The individualism latent in modern liberation theories obscures the constitutive role of power in identity formation and thus obfuscates this problem. By imagining a universe of self-contained individuals whose political problem is simply one of governance, rather than one in which politics provides the forum by which we create and negotiate identities, individualists can imagine a "world without power." The premise is false, however, and so the dreamed-of utopia is simply a recipe for disaster. Rather than providing the space for egalitarian community and individual liberty, "the radical disappearance of power would amount to the disintegration of the social fabric."[17] The work of social change cannot be a project of power's elimination. Rather, we must face up to the responsibility of creating new power, with new exclusions and contradictions.

As a central term in political discourse, "power" is a term loaded with resonances; loaded, one might say, with power. This resonance does not contribute to univocity or clarity, however. Power is one of the terms that William Connolly describes as "essentially contested": there is no single "true" or "right" meaning to power.[18] Rather, "power" as a term embodies cultural assumptions about human agency and relations. In Euro-American society, power is usually a thing rather than a relation (as in statements such as "she has a lot of power"); further, it is a thing held by individuals or groups that allows them to achieve their desires. Power is appropriately a thing used to achieve other goals; one of the ways we can slander another is to say that she wants power for its own sake. This charge, of course, rests on the idea that power is power over discrete others, that it operates in a world of stable identities and desires and interests, and that those identities and desires and interests are definitively lodged in individuals.

If we move out of that ontological individualism, however, we may be able to understand power more democratically. Hannah Arendt's discussion of power is suggestive of this nonindividualist social ontology, and thus may provide a beginning.

Arendt argues that "power is never the property of an individual; it belongs to a group and remains in existence only so long as the group keeps together." She continues:

> When we say of somebody that he [sic] is "in power" we actually refer to his being empowered by a certain number of people to act in their name. The moment the group, from which the power originated to begin with . . . disappears, "his power" also vanishes.[19]

For Arendt, power is a collective property, and it is an ephemeral, processlike property at that. While the English language pushes us to treat power as a thing, Arendt reminds us that this thing is in fact always a relation, of varying levels and sorts of stability.

Nancy Hartsock has argued that Arendt's understanding of power is closely linked to her concern for community. She suggests that "power" is for Arendt "the means by which community is constituted" and "the 'glue' that holds the community together."[20] Arendt argues that "power and violence are opposites," because violence destroys the freedom and the solidarity required for power.[21] Power as a collective relation requires freedom, most basically the freedom to associate and discuss common affairs. This power is a good in itself; it is the creation and maintenance of community, of a common life.

Arendt's understanding of power rests on a distinction between politics and government that is all too often lost in American life. The equation of these two leads to the eclipse of a common, public world in favor of an instrumental polity of governed subjects. In such a world, the relevant questions do indeed seem to come down to those of the "business of domination."[22] This is a misunderstanding of the public world, though a self-fulfilling one; to the extent that we fail to distinguish between the collective enterprise of power and the particular forms of violence used to enforce obedience in the absence of power, we condemn ourselves to the mistrust of power and of politics.

As a collective enterprise, the development of power serves to "empower" community members and representatives. This "empowerment" is simultaneously the creation of new political subjects. The process of empowerment produces active citizens where before there were none; it produces lesbians where previously there were "spinsters" or "old maids" or "inverts." The articulation of battered wives was inseparable from the feminist project of empowerment of those women, and this empowerment did not consist simply in making them "safe" or "increasing self-esteem" (though these were important). It included exercising power over batterers, now articulated as such, excluding them, and resisting them. While it may be argued that the goal of work against violence against women is the integration of all people into a humane society, in the immediate term there is no escape from the need to exclude.

Nonetheless, an increase in one group's power does not necessarily imply a loss by others. Rather, it shifts the differential of power. Groups may increase their power even as they lose battles. Gay and lesbian politics show us numerous instances of this phenomenon. We are still (as of this writing) officially excluded from the U.S. military. Forces of reaction are rising to strip us of civil rights in numerous states. These events do not mean a loss of lesbian and gay power, however; they have contributed to its formation. The mobilization of lesbians and gays for and against various causes; the increasing sector of "straight but not narrow" allies; the public discussion, depressing and infuriating as much of it has been—all have contributed to a climate that makes it easier for individuals to find others like them and resist the attacks of bigots. The increasing antagonism between these groups does not spell a clear loss of power for either; rather, it involves the creation and funneling of power to this particular antagonism.

It is easy to think that the mobilization of lesbians and gays, and our occasional political progress, are again instrumental, that they are prerequisites for the real good, "liberation." This is a mistake. Certainly simple visibility and acceptance are not enough. Yet liberation retains its contentlessness. Power, fully understood, is still the better goal. The full development of power includes the formation of collective ways of being. Changes in the law to reflect our realities, changes in the structure of the law itself, are a matter of power. They are not "results" of having power; they are part of the power itself. The ability to define our lives and our values is not a matter of release from another's bondage (though that is a prerequisite) but is a matter of (em)power(ment). These goods rise and fall with the power of the community. And though the community may face violence, and that violence can destroy power if it is brutal enough, relief from violence will not make a community. Communities are constructed as webs of meaning, structures giving content to "common life" as well as individual lives. This construction is inescapably an act of power, one which must be actively engaged in if U.S. society is to become democratic and lesbian friendly.

Pursuing the question of social transformation, Ernesto Laclau and Chantal Mouffe have called for the "construction of a new 'common sense' " about the nature of the social, of identities, and of democratic politics. This project requires that we use power even as we transform it. Laclau and Mouffe argue that this construction must go beyond the calls for "subversion" or "rejection" that are so often the sum of political theorizing. Rather, we must create a new landscape, a new democratic space:

> If the demands of a subordinated group are presented purely as negative demands subversive of a certain order, without being linked to any viable project for the reconstruction of specific areas of society, their capacity to act hegemonically will be excluded from the outset. This is the difference between what might be called a "strategy of opposition" and a "strategy of construction of a new order." In the case of the first, the element of negation of a certain social or political order predominates, but this element of negativity is not accompanied by any real attempt to establish different nodal points from which a process of different and positive reconstruction of the social fabric could be instituted—and as a result the strategy is condemned to marginality.[23]

Taking this lesson to heart, lesbians will work not to eliminate power per se, either among lesbians or between lesbians and nonlesbians, but will work to relocate truth from forms and forums in which it has worked against us to those in which it will aid us. We will, in Laclau and Mouffe's terms, work to "establish different nodal points"—different linkages and articulations between people and positions—so as to "reconstruct the social fabric." This goal requires, for example, the rejection of scientific and medical discourse about lesbians and lesbianism. These discourses work inevitably to place lesbians as subjects/objects of medical description, locating our sexuality as in need of explanation by those who are not lesbian. The implicit privileging of heterosexuality in questions such as "What causes homosexuality?" perpetuate our isolation and individualization under a prurient medical gaze. These research questions often doubly degrade us through the examination of gay men for answers about both men and women. Whether or not such discourse is surrounded/appropriated by those who desire to eliminate lesbians, it is not a democratic discourse.[24] Scientific/medical discourses in themselves remove power from the political community and invest it in "experts." The answer to this movement is not "liberation," the absence of restraint, but is power: the power to define ourselves, to describe our lives, and to be heard.[25]

Rights and Power

The democratic tradition has provided a strong critique of liberal individualism, and especially of "rights talk." Liberal discourse has been centered around rights, conceived as the limits of state power. It has been challenged from virtually all quarters as barren, superficial, masking social power, and the like. The rejection of a liberal framework need not mean the elimination of "rights" in the face of popular power, however. Rights are assertions about the subject of entitlement (she who is entitled), the substance of that right, its basis, and its purpose.[26] They therefore make implicit or explicit statements about the nature of the social world. Though liberal theory generally construes rights in the form of private property, it does so because of a particular articulation of and between liberalism and individualism that is neither historically inevitable nor logically entailed.

Rights are a form of power that have been mistakenly construed as the antithesis of power. As "negative power," rights function to ensure that some minimal membership is guaranteed.[27] This is a vital precondition for a democratic society, but the understanding of rights as negative power is mistaken. Rights are a form of power. They authorize people to perform certain actions, largely by forbidding others to restrain them. This prohibition is not a reduction in power per se, however, but is a shift in the differential of power toward those with the right in question. The right is inseparable from that differential of power.

Rights look more attractive when we consider them as one moment in oppositional politics rather than the whole and only goal. Patricia Williams forcefully argues for the centrality of rights for disempowered people. She challenges the disdain for rights talk on the part of scholars in critical legal studies by looking at the importance of rights in her life as a Black woman in the United States. Critical legal-studies scholars have attacked rights talk as alienating, introducing separation and contractual modes of thought into what can and should be more trusting, informal relationships, but Williams points out Blacks' historical need for rights in countries whose majority populations consider them inferior. In such situations, rights take the form of active intervention against oppression. The critique by critical legal-studies theorists, like communitarian critiques of liberalism, has one resonance for those mourning the loss of community under capitalism and quite another for those who see their communities under siege from racism and heterosexism. Thus Williams asserts that the important goal is not "deconstructing rights" or "constructing statements of need," but is "to find a political mechanism that can confront the *denial* of need."[28] Although she acknowledges the problems with the discourse of rights, she is firm that simply abandoning rights and formal structures is a mistake so long as the informal structures of societies perpetuate oppression and hatred. In such a context, the assertion of rights is a prerequisite to any form of common action. Without rights, without the formalities of legal bans on discrimination based on sex or sexuality, lesbians will be fair game for oppressions ranging from marginalization to violence.

Thus, as uninspiring as it may sound in a world of cultural warfare and subversion, lesbians need to fight for civil rights legislation. These rights are part of our collective empowerment. We need to fight for them even when the terms of legal discourse do not square with our understandings of ourselves (which is to say, most of the time). We need to do this quite simply because without the safety afforded by these minimal guarantees we will never get to change anything else. At the same time, we must not rest with hegemonic articulations of our situations and those rights, but must continually struggle over them.

Many might think this declaration is too pessimistic. After all, we aren't in the same place that we were twenty years ago—tremendous change has occurred, even though very few localities have civil rights laws covering lesbians and gays. Twenty years ago neither this book nor many others could have been written before tenure. Though all this is true, it is only part of the picture. On my university campus, among the many lesbian faculty whom I know of, only four or five are "out" in any public way. There are tenured professors who will not come to events that might label them, and live in fear of exposure. Those of us who are out rely on the decency of our colleagues rather than the law, even though the university has a sexual orientation clause in its nondiscrimination statement. Teachers in the public school system and many others face the same concerns. Without local, state, and federal laws to enforce that clause, very few feel safe. This is not the position of citizens—it is that of well-treated subjects. If we view rights as the condition for democratic government, we can support a political focus on rights as part of a radical agenda rather than assimilation. Rights can become a means to collective empowerment as well as individual insulation.

These rights cannot simply be the ones currently taken to be at the center of American citizenship, however. If lesbians are to be empowered in the political life of the United States, we need rights that are currently not recognized or under negotiation. Rather than resting with being "for" or "against" a "rights-based" approach, we need to ask what we want rights to do and what sorts of rights would achieve our desires.

As one attempt at this questioning, Mark Blasius has formulated a "relational right" as the basis for lesbian and gay claims vis-à-vis the state. This right would address what he identifies as the "three major 'moments' of contemporary lesbian and gay liberation" that are concerned with power and the state: "sexual freedom" *simpliciter*, the freedom to relate to those we choose and who choose us; the "necessity for social recognition and equality before the law of relationships," ending lesbian and gay invisibility; and "the more recent concern with access to education about sexuality (both in formal schooling as well as through voluntarily obtained informational media)" and the right to be "protected from any biological risks involved in the exercise of one's sexual relational freedom."[29] Although we can argue about the specifics of this vision, this list represents a step toward reformulating rights. Rather than trying to "fit" lesbians and gays into quasi-existing rights such as that to privacy, Blasius provides a new basis for claims that address existing forms of power rather than ancient ones. He argues that this right is different, first because it is not simply exercised against "the state" as the source of prohibition and punishment but addresses "technologies of government that set the framework for what kinds of relationships it is possible to have in our society," such as tax and inheritance structures. This right is different also because it is "grounded not in a juridical concept of a subject whose rights are recognized by the state or not but rather in a relational subject whose subjectivity is created and recreated through sexual affectional relations with others and who decides for her/himself how society's technologies of government should recognize these relationships."[30] The subject who is the target of juridical, liberal discourse is conceived as an atom or monad, an independent entity whose being or nature can be labeled (as, for example, "wife," "citizen," "parent") and dealt with on the basis of the label. One's rights depend on where one fits in the taxonomies of identity. In contrast, the relational right is held by a subject that is continually reinventing categories and reevaluating their relevance to her life.

As an example, consider the dilemma of marriage. The debate about marriage has polarized two points that falsely define the issue. One side, the "promarriage" faction, focuses on the right to relate to those we choose. The other, "antimarriage" group contests the patriarchal and statist implications of marriage today, arguing that any marriage is slavery at worst, legal domestication of lesbian relationships at best.[31] A relational right would address both of these by requiring recognition of those we consider most important in our lives, valuing relationships themselves, rather than "allowing" lesbians to fit within a form that is centered not on the participants but on the state and property rules. Blasius is aware that relations will transform identities, and thus will center not one class of person but (relationally conceived) persons in general.

In so doing, Blasius retains both the rights focus and the universalism of liberalism, but he does so without abstracting from the conditions of people's lives. His is not a universalism that subsumes/conquers/silences people under the heading of "individuals" but is a universalism that works toward historical specificity.[32] It provides the space for those who have been subjugated and silenced to elaborate their own visions of sexuality and relationships without simply taking a stance "outside of" or "opposed to" public power or the state. It is not a right of withdrawal, but a right to formulate a certain entry into social relationships.

This reconfigured right is a democratic goal. It does not speak to lesbians only, though it directly addresses many of the problems we face. It does not mandate that everyone like our ways of life, but it does require that the state not erase our existence or condone violence against us. It is a right that can call forth the allegiance of heterosexuals as well as lesbians and gays, in that it promotes legal recognition of extended family networks and alternative families of all sorts. It does not rest on ahistorical notions of the person or the family but allows for these to be configured by the individuals involved.

As a result, such a right enables lesbians to emerge within the polity in which they might live *as lesbians*. This move remedies the blind spot in liberalism, a blind spot around the specificities of actual lives and thus around the social and political privilege of certain classes. As Marx explained in "On the Jewish Question," an "equal right" that can be exercised by some only at the price of their cultural identity is not an equal right at all.[33] Elections held on Saturdays exclude observant Jews from the political process without ever mentioning them by name. Similarly, provision of benefits only to couples whose union is sanctioned by the state under current law systematically deprives lesbians and gays from these benefits, under the name of equality for all.[34] As noted, a relational right could address this problem. This right is not, however, an end in itself. While new rights are crucial to the task of improving lesbian lives, the larger project must be empowerment as democratic citizens. This empowerment will be aided, though not guaranteed, by such rights; yet the rights will come only as a result of the acquisition of power.

Democratic Empowerment

Clearly, new rights are needed if lesbians are to be full citizens. By "full citizens" I mean people who can speak for themselves and be heard. Under current conditions lesbians cannot do so. At this writing, fewer than ten states ban discrimination on the basis of sexual orientation. Initiatives to deny the possibility of equal protection have succeeded across the country, and more are pending. The U.S. Congress has mandated by law the exclusion of gays and lesbians from the military. Under such conditions, no one can seriously argue that lesbians have equal rights. Without guarantees that lesbianism will not be grounds for dismissal, eviction, denial of credit, uninvestigated violence, or other calamities, lesbians cannot become public. Without such publicity, without the ability to live as who they are, people live in exile. Thus, our first job must be to fight for existing rights (rather than newer configurations of rights). We need minimally to be safe in our various social locations.

That safety cannot be an end in itself, however. Here lies the problem with liberalism. Liberals too often envisage government simply as the guarantor of safety, whether that safety includes only police or extends to financial support, health codes, or other public welfare items. This vision leaves the public realm as simply technical/legal, with no value of its own. Thus is liberalism complicit with bureaucratic and private discipline and subjugation.[35]

If rights are needed for effective power to exist, the converse is also true. Without power lesbians cannot hope for rights. This is the intuition behind exhortations to "come out" and to vote as a bloc. This intuition has merit: if gays and lesbians in San Francisco had not become politically self-conscious and begun to act together, that city would not have the representation of lesbians and gays, and the relatively safe environment, that it does. When lesbians and gays in the military began to challenge mass discharges and kangaroo courts through the media, refusing to slink away separately, the military was forced to give some ground.[36]

Political empowerment takes us beyond a minimal concern for

safety to collective determination of the conditions of our lives. This collective determination is not simply an instrumental good, valuable for its results, but is the process of coming into freedom. It is also a continuing need: we will not win our rights, or transform the social world, and then be able to abandon power. No people are ever finally free or beyond challenge. Democratic empowerment is both necessary for personal safety and a provision of something far beyond safety. It is the process of participation in self-definition; it is politics itself.

Interlude II:
Lost in the Land of Enchantment

The early months of 1993 were exhausting for many lesbians and gays, and certainly for me. Between Clinton's blunted attack on military exclusion and the fight for civil rights in New Mexico, a fight lost, it was an exhilarating, terrifying, hopeful, and anguish-filled winter. An article about the defeat of Senate Bill 91, the New Mexico "gay rights" bill, quoted a local legislator expressing his relief that the fight was over and hoping to get back to normal and "enjoy life in the Land of Enchantment." I share his exhaustion and a certain relief that the legislative session is over, but I cannot share his desire to return to "normal." In his normal life, everyone is happy. In my normal life, friends are physically attacked by bigots, in and out of a number of uniforms. For years the district attorney's office has known of police assaults on gay men, but until recently no one could be found who would risk being out of the closet and so these cases were never brought to trial. In my "normal" life, my ten-year relationship cannot be safely manifested by publicly holding hands. In my "normal" life, I worry about whether my students will hate me for being lesbian, and whether their hate could cost me my job. No, I do not want to get back to normal. I am comforted, however, by the knowledge that the fight is not nearly over, that it has indeed barely begun.

I want to look here at these recent and continuing struggles, to examine the arguments used against rights for lesbians and gays, and to think about citizenship. For these barriers to equality are fundamentally barriers, not just to a decent private life, but to equal citizenship for gays and lesbians in the United States. A clearer recognition of this fact may help heterosexuals to understand why our fight is their fight, why it should be the fight of every American.

Many have heard the argument that "gay rights" bills are about "special privileges" for lesbians and gays. This was and is simply false. These bills state that no one shall be denied employment, housing, public accommodations, or credit on the basis of sexual orientation, perceived or actual. "Sexual orientation" in these bills refers to homosexuality, heterosexuality, or bisexuality. Clearly this does not say that employers must have quotas for queers. It does not make us "special." It recognizes that the current state of affairs allows employers, landlords, hotel operators, and financial institutions to discriminate on this basis. Although it could be the case that this discrimination was aimed against heterosexuals, it has not been the case. The reality of the world is that the discrimination has been against gays and lesbians, and against bisexuals when they are in same-sex relationships. Heterosexuals have not needed special rights, any more than whites in the South needed legislation guaranteeing these rights. The legislation would not disadvantage heterosexuals, any more than earlier civil rights legislation disadvantaged whites, unless by that we mean the loss of privilege and power. Heterosexuals would be protected as well, by law as well as custom.

Now, what arguments could people use to reject this principle of fairness? We have seen many. The first and most direct are the overt statements of rejection. These say simply, "Our traditions tell us this behavior is abominable. These people engage in this behavior; therefore, they are abominable. They threaten the moral fiber of our communities, and the best we can do is to eliminate them; next best is to force them to live their lives in secrecy and shame." It's easy to see in this argument the exclusion of lesbians and gays from their communities. The myth of "the community" and its "standards" persists only if we willfully ignore the fact that communities throughout the United States include lesbians and gays. The Right would like us to believe that homosexuals live only in big cities, but the work of writers such as Neil Miller shows us that we live everywhere. In his recent book *In Search of Gay America*, Miller introduces us to the openly gay mayor of Bunceton, Missouri, to the church council president in Fargo, North Dakota, and to activists all over the country.[1] Not everyone approves of their lives, but they are respected and integrated members of these communities. There are indeed huge concentrations of lesbians and gays in cities such as San Francisco; this condition is a testament to the rejection so many of us face and the relative freedom and anonymity that urban environments allow.

The overt bigots have the virtue of being honest in their beliefs, and with them we can wage an honest war over membership in the political community of the United States. Other arguments are more insidious. What they share is a power play that Marilyn Frye has called the "politics of reality."[2] In the politics of reality, battles are fought not only over particular policies but over whose vision, whose perspective, is valued. We can see that all of the arguments against equal rights for lesbians and gays, like those against our overt presence in the military, come back to the systematic refusal to include the perspective of gay and lesbian people as equal participants in our common life.

My personal favorite from the SB 91 hearings was the "business realities" argument. This goes as follows: "If we pass this law, either businesses won't come to New Mexico, or existing ones will leave. They cannot afford the costs of suits against us, so they'll relocate." This one requires a certain awareness to see through, and that awareness has been sorely lacking in press accounts of the issue. Translated, this argument says, "We don't care about the rights of queers. We don't have any intention of hiring them or of keeping them if they come out, so we would have to leave. We are obviously more real than they are, so they have to yield." This translation emerges when we ask: Why would a company choose not to come? Not because of the fear of being sued, unless they had no intention of complying with the law. If they comply, there will be no costs.

The full impact of the politics of reality becomes clear when we ask what sort of nation would put the discomfort of a few bigots over the equal rights of a portion of its citizenry. The answer can only be, a nation that does not consider those citizens to be full citizens. The business argument asks heterosexuals to privilege themselves so thoroughly that they write us out of existence.

This is also the argument at work in the debate over "gays" in the military (note that in this debate lesbians are virtually never mentioned). Here the privileged group is heterosexual male soldiers and potential soldiers. Advocates for the ban argue that "soldiers" will be uncomfortable with "homosexuals." Now let's look at this one. First, we have the assumption that all currently serving soldiers are heterosexual—an assumption we know to be false. This assumption is not a factual one, but is ideological: it works to erase gays and lesbians, to exclude the possibility in people's minds that we might be both soldiers and homosexuals. We know that the ban has never excluded lesbians and gays—it has simply made their lives miserable.

The second stage in the argument suggests that heterosexual males will be so uncomfortable with gay men that they will refuse to serve, that we will need a draft to provide for our defense needs. This is like the business argument, in that it suggests that the citizenship of lesbians and gays should take a back seat to "practicality." Would anyone today say publicly that white soldiers' discomfort should exclude people of color from the armed forces? That would be quickly seen as racist, and condemned. But when Harry Truman ordered the racial integration of the armed forces, we saw exactly that argument used. In 1941, when enlistment of Blacks for general service was contemplated, the Special Committee to the Secretary of the Navy stated that "the enlistment of Negroes (other than for mess attendants) leads to disruptive and undermining conditions." Today, even the words are the same: during the hearings, an analyst for the Congressional Research Service testified that exclusion and forced closeting "prevents empirical research from discovering whether or not open homosexuality would, in fact, prove to be disruptive."[3] This is a sympathetic researcher, but he persists in the belief that the relevant question is whether our presence would be "disruptive," as though a positive answer is prima facie evidence against inclusion. But any lesbian or gay man can give the answer: Of course it would be disruptive! Of course adjustment and change would be required! But that is not the issue. Only those who are content with the existing order, who are not bothered by questions of justice and equality, can argue that exclusion of whole classes of persons from national defense is acceptable, justified by a fear of "disruption."

The moral of the struggle over racial integration is, they got over it. They learned how to work it out when they were forced to. It is ironic that Leonard Matlovich, the first to legally challenge the military's exclusion of homosexuals, was a conservative Republican who was trained by the air force to lead antiracism workshops. It was precisely his positive experience with this work that led him to challenge the military ban. But that process of change cannot occur unless there is a commitment from the top that justice is more important than discomfort. We have read that soldiers have been refusing to serve with Keith Meinhold, and these reports are used as evidence that ending the ban is unfeasible. But if we abandon the heterosexual lens, we can see that these soldiers are disobeying orders, and should therefore be subject to disciplinary measures! They should be told to shut up and do their jobs! And they would be, if their commanders knew they had to. But these stories are presented to us as beyond the control of the commanders, as inevitable. This is the politics of reality.

Here's another argument that was popular in Santa Fe in the spring of 1993: "The research that said gays and lesbians constitute 10 percent of the population was false. In fact, they are no more than 3 percent of the population." This assertion was never followed by a direct statement, but the implication was clear: there aren't many of them, so who cares? They don't have many votes, so don't worry. Now first off, we should note how upsetting this argument should be to Jews, Native Americans, and many others. For homosexuals are not the only ones to be written off by this argument, and other groups have seen the horrific consequences of arguments like it. Jehovah's Witnesses, Seventh-Day Adventists, and many other small groups have been told in our history that they had to fit in, and they have successfully challenged those claims. The idea that rights should be proportionate to numbers is repugnant, but it recurs whenever minorities get in the way of powerful majorities. We need to say that rights are rights and justice is justice, and not one individual should be deprived of either.

I want to follow up this analogy to religious groups, and especially to Jews. Many lesbians and gays are making the analogy between heterosexism and racism, and I think there's some value there, but the arguments against lesbian and gay rights also bear a strong odor of anti-Semitism. Most noticeable among these is the argument that "gays" make more money than heterosexuals, that we have power beyond our numbers. First, to the facts: the statistics about gay income are badly biased. They do not account for lesbians as a group, who as women earn much less than men, and they do not accurately represent people of color. There are wealthy gay men and lesbian women, and there are hardworking poor and middle-class lesbians and gays. There is as much diversity among us as among any large group. There is as much diversity among us as among Jews. Jews have been represented by anti-Semites as uniformly wealthy, good at business, smarter than Christians. This representation serves to divert resentment away from powerful Christians and toward a powerless minority group. Jews have also been portrayed as predators, stealing Christian babies for sacrifice. This accusation bears an uncanny resemblance to the mythology about lesbian and gay "recruitment." Both anti-Semitism and homophobia reveal deep anxieties within individuals and cultures, and neither is sufficient justification for the denial of rights.

Let's imagine for a minute that the statistics were valid. Let's imagine that gays and lesbians were better off economically than heterosexuals. Would that justify depriving us of equal rights? How many heterosexuals would trade money for freedom and citizenship? Should we argue that because men as a group make more money, or whites as a group make more money, that the rest of us can deprive them of equal rights? While money does translate into a certain power in this society, it is not the same thing as equality.

Let's remember, too, that the true agenda of the homophobes is not simply to leave us where we are. Their agenda, once our rights are thoroughly stripped, is to see us fired from our jobs, and denied credit and housing. It is not to "live and let live," allowing tolerant employers to tolerate us. It is to forcibly convert us, under the name of a cure. Their agenda is to eliminate us, as many Jews were eliminated through forced conversion to Christianity and as many Native Americans were eliminated through forced removal from their families and home-lands.

Many of those fighting for rights have compared our struggle and our status to that of Blacks, Chicanos, and other historically op-pressed groups. At its extreme, this has taken the form of an argument that there is and always has been a "gay culture," often invisible to dominant cultures but with stable mores and patterns of relating. Others have not seen such a continuity of culture, but they have ar-gued that lesbians and gays currently face oppression as a group on the basis of a fixed feature, and that therefore our struggle is like that of other stigmatized groups. Opponents have sought to argue that sexual orientation is not fixed, that in fact homosexuality is a choice, a bad one, or an illness that should be treated. Both sides seem to agree that the fixity or stability of the attribute is determinative of some-thing about rights, and in this they are mistaken. The question of rights has nothing to do with the question of the etiology of sexual orientation.

Whatever the experience of men may be, I know that a great num-ber—in some samples approaching 50 percent—of lesbians have had extensive histories with men, including marriage. Though many les-bians report the lifelong feeling of desire for women, many others had no such experience until well into adulthood. Whatever scientists try to tell us about the origins of homosexuality, we know that it would be a distortion of our lives to tell one story about our sexual histories and choices. There is not one true homosexuality.

Our opponents use this fact to argue that our sexuality is a choice, and therefore we do not deserve protection from violence and oppres-sion on the basis of this difference. They argue that we are not an op-pressed group, that our difference is not inescapable and publicly visi-ble, and that therefore it's our own fault if a bigot decides to hunt us down and kill us. We have argued that we can't change our sexual ori-entation at will, that this is a fixed feature of our identities, and that therefore we should not be stigmatized for what we cannot change. But this response is a mistake. We need not make this claim to argue for equal rights, and our rights should not depend on it.

During the debates over our rights we have heard that all other protected categories are of this unchangeable and visible nature, but that is not the case. Though national origin, race, gender, and physical disabilities are largely fixed, religion is also protected. Religion is unlike these other categories, and a comparison with homosexuality is useful.[4]

First, although many of us are born into a religion and remain in it throughout our lives, many others change religious affiliation during their lives. The law does not protect only those who remain in their religion of birth; it protects against discrimination on the basis of religious affiliation, current or past. There is no requirement that one show that a given religion is the person's "true" religion, except in the case of conscientious objectors. Thus, the analogy to religion tells us that the issue of whether we are "really" gay, lesbian, or bisexual is irrelevant to our right to protection against discrimination on that basis.

Second, even if the religion holds as sacred practices that are illegal, such as peyote use or polygamy, the law forbids discriminating against people simply because they are Mormons or members of the Native American Church. In this regard, their protection resembles that that should be afforded to gays. Opponents of both gay rights and the end to the military ban have argued that it is incoherent to have sodomy laws on the books and simultaneously protect people who practice sodomy. Sodomy laws are an anachronism and morally wrong, but there is no inconsistency in arguing that those who desire to do something forbidden deserve protection. Mormons desired polygamy; some still do. Polygamy was forbidden, yet Mormons are still afforded religious toleration. Peyote use is banned, but membership in the Native American Church does not make one a criminal. Sodomy laws are addressed to particular behaviors, as are rape laws and antifraternization codes. But holding hands is not sodomy. Loving another person is not sodomy. Wanting another person so bad your knees get weak is not sodomy. The argument from sodomy laws is right on a par with banning Jews from citizenship because they don't believe Jesus was the Messiah. Stories about extraordinary power or viciousness are simply the ideology avoiding the true heinous crime: thinking and desiring differently than the majority.

This persuasion, not any innate features of lesbians and gays, makes the ethnic analogy work. We are like ethnic groups not in having a distinctive culture that exists over time and place. We are like them in being the targets of oppression, in being defined *by others* as a group, solely on the basis of one feature—and a pretty widely differing one at that. We have been defined by heterosexists and homophobes as outside, not just as different, and this exclusion is now the basis for a shared politics. We do not need to claim that we're born that way. We do not need to claim that we can't help it. We need to claim simply that a free society cannot obsessively contain the sexuality of its citizens, and that ours need not. We are uncommon citizens, both in our sharp critiques of the institutions of this country and in our fierce desire to get into so many places that heterosexuals perhaps value less than we do. We have a potential power of pride and gratitude that could energize this country for the many other tasks facing it, if we are allowed to become citizens. I am proud to be a lesbian, because I know how hard it is to live this way, and I'm excited to be alive at a time when I may live to be a citizen of a thoroughly disrupted and newly just nation.

Chapter 8

Alliances and Coalitions: Nonidentity Politics

The vertiginous appeal of poststructuralist theories is due precisely to the rejection of the move in which philosophy is separated from and privileged over politics. As Gayatri Spivak puts it, "deconstruction teaches one to question all transcendental idealisms." In so doing, it does not provide a new idealism, a new metanarrative, but "is always different from itself, always defers itself. It is neither a constitutive nor, of course, a regulative norm."[1] The space once occupied by the metanarratives that regulate our knowledge becomes an open field for politics, a politics that knows itself to be such and so empowers its practitioners more democratically than do academic discourses of "truth."

Any real transformation of the social and political landscape will require lesbians to form coalitions and alliances with nonlesbians. This common action cannot be simply the strategic alignment of diverse groups over a single issue, nor can it mean finding the real unity behind our apparently diverse struggles. It means living in tension with the fact that humans share important needs, desires, hopes, and fears, but we do not share every important thing, or agree on the nature of those we do share. It means that we have long-term interests in helping one another to be heard *in the language that we each speak* rather than by simply convincing those in power that we are really part of their whole. This is the stance of radical democracy. Such a stance enables us to join with others to fight our oppression and theirs without having to find the thread of the grand theory that connects us.

Lesbians have been denied the right to be heard, not simply by forced silence, but also by having our phrases deprived of authority. So the first need for our politics is the guarantee that we will be heard. As Sandra Harding has said, "the right to define the categories through which one is to see the world and to be seen by it is a fundamental political right."[2] This right cannot be achieved, however, by isolating ourselves and our discourse from others; to do so will serve only to perpetuate public silence. We must enter the arena of public discourse without vanishing, though also without falling into essentializing or naturalizing narratives of lesbian existence.

In this chapter I will look at what sorts of alliances are viable and necessary for lesbians in the 1990s and beyond. Successful alliance requires rethinking our assumptions about *everyone's* identity and sexuality, and also about politics. Interest-group pluralism rests on assumptions about natural identities and memberships that are barriers to politics. Further, the pluralist conception of justice in distributive terms, and of our claims as ones of private interest, implicitly opposed to a common good, makes justice alternately unachievable and limited.[3] It thus blocks discussion and debate, and occludes the social foundations of ideas that are needed for critical thought. Interest-group pluralism is also the culprit behind the idea that these many memberships (Black, female, class, and the like) conflict within us; we are trained to think of these as memberships in interest groups, and so the political question becomes, to which group do I give primary allegiance? If we get past interest-group pluralism, however, the questions open up. Who are we? What do we have in common? What might justice be among a diverse people?

"Postmodern" politics means that as we enter public discourse we do so, not as "Lesbians" with a fixed, eternal identity, but as lesbians, people occupying provisional subject positions in heterosexual society. As such, we must acknowledge that speaking and being heard does not mean simply drawing on our "experience" in an unmediated way but means articulating our lives, interpreting and reinterpreting them in ways that link us to others. Coalitions of the future will require us to maintain the subject position of lesbians and our belief in our voices with the growing awareness that our own subjectivity is part of the terrain of possible change. To paraphrase Foucault, "we must insist on *becoming* [lesbian], rather than persist in defining ourselves as such."[4] Thus, the problem for coalition politics is not "What do we share?" but rather "What *might* we share as we develop our identities through the process of coalition?" Coalition cannot be simply the strategic alignment of diverse groups over a single issue, nor can coalition mean finding the real unity behind our apparently diverse struggles. Our politics must be informed by affinity rather than identity, not simply because we are not all alike, but because we each embody multiple, often conflicting, identities and locations.[5]

Interest in the House of Difference

Most discussions of coalition presume an interest-group model of politics. The model assumes that each group is self-contained, and thus does an injustice to many of their members; for example, separating "Blacks" from "women" renders Black women invisible.[6] The possibility of this oversight rests on the relative privilege of those making the assumptions. When the constructors are WASP middle-class heterosexual men, it is easy to neglect the overlaps between class, race, sexuality, gender, and other "interests." It was easy to talk of "Italian-Americans" as a cohesive group, especially when women of each group were overlooked or defined by the men of that group.[7] Similarly, it is possible for white lesbians to privilege "lesbian" as a coherent category, so long as our daily lives do not force us to notice our overlapping membership as whites.

Many gay men have insisted that lesbians are gay, just as "Blacks" are both male and female. And indeed, many women refer to themselves as "gay women." We should not confuse the English grammar with social structures of equality, however. The nonneutral generic male extends to the nongeneric gay; if "gay" refers to a "social identity and consciousness," as Mark Thompson asserts, then in a gendered society that identity and consciousness will be profoundly gender marked.[8] Denial of this reality by means of a generic "gay" is unavoidably sexist, reinforcing the invisibility of women.

As an example of the construction of interest and identity as monolithic and natural, we can use the best-selling book on gay politics *After the Ball*. This book was written by two white male Harvard graduates, Marshall Kirk and Hunter Madsen, currently working at high-prestige, high-income jobs. They propose a "marketing strategy" to overcome homophobia in the United States. This strategy includes advertisements that plant the idea that gays and lesbians are "just like everyone else." This is not just strategic; they believe that

> when treated with respect and friendship, we're as happy and psychologically well adjusted as they are. . . . We look, feel, and act just as they do; we're hard-working, conscientious Americans with love lives exactly like their own.[9]

This is a fascinating statement because it follows a hundred pages of castigation of gay male sexual, political, and personal behavior. Kirk and Madsen continually contrast the pathology of gay life to the nice, normal picture of heterosexuality. They manage this dissonance by separating the "bad gays" from the "good gays," claiming that "good gays" are just like heterosexuals. They experience themselves as just like their straight friends, and so they are embarrassed by the "deviants."

There is much to take exception with in this book, and much to think about. For one thing, these two men subsume lesbians into the category of "gay" with remarkable ease. Although they occasionally acknowledge that lesbians do not have the proclivity for casual sex that gay men do (a difference of which they approve) and that we face some problems as women, the bulk of the book makes no distinction between gays and lesbians. This erasure is not simply sexist but reflects these authors' ability to see gayness as a singular distinguishing mark in their lives. Were it not for their "sexual orientation," they would be just like their (white?) heterosexual friends and fellow Harvard graduates. Thus "gayness" appears to them as a discrete identifier, and the "gay" they are discussing emerges as male, white, and middle- (or upper-) class.

Because of this view, their aims are narrow. Kirk and Madsen seek simply to end antigay prejudice, to get equal rights (such as formal marriages) with heterosexuals, and, eventually, just to fit in like everyone else. They have no problem with any other structures of oppression in the United States, and so they urge "gays" not to distract themselves from the fight for gays by "admixture with superfluous issues that might further upset or distract ordinary Americans."[10] Included in the list of "superfluous" or "utterly extraneous" causes are racial justice, feminism, environmentalism, and others. They disdain the Rainbow Coalition concept as a distraction.

What is a lesbian to make of this? What is a Chicana (or Black, or Asian, or Native American, or poor, or . . .) lesbian to think? Kirk and Madsen are telling us not simply that feminism is not equivalent to lesbianism, but that feminism is dangerous to the cause of gay rights. Discussions of race or class are divisive.

Imagine the response of Audre Lorde. In *Zami: A New Spelling of My Name*, Lorde describes her position as a Black lesbian among lesbians in Greenwich Village:

> Being women together was not enough. We were different. Being gay-girls together was not enough. We were different. Being Black together was not enough. We were different. Being Black women together was not enough. We were different. Being Black dykes together was not enough. We were different. . . . It was a while before we came to realize

that our place was the very house of difference rather than any one particular difference.[11]

Within the "house of difference," Kirk and Madsen's advice is inadequate. And not only Black lesbians dwell in that house; the differences were differences among that progressively more narrowly defined group, inseparable from the individuality of its members. From this perspective, Kirk and Madsen's prescription is both politically naive and theoretically incoherent. It rests on the idea of gayness as a discrete identifier, in the manner of interest-group liberalism, and reduces that identifier to whom we have sex with. It then colonizes all those who have or would like to have sex with members of the same sex as "gays," and tells them to address that in isolation from the rest of their lives. Their aim is to "keep the message focused," but the effect is to isolate white bourgeois gay men from any potential allies other than straight white men. Just as the phrase "as a woman" has been discredited in feminism as "the Trojan horse of feminist ethnocentrism,"[12] we cannot rest with "as a gay" or "as a lesbian"; we need to produce public spaces to discuss what these words can mean, and we need to recognize their insufficiency in fully capturing the nature of our sexualities.

Kirk and Madsen provide us with an example of how a simple white identity politics can fail. Although they have many good suggestions for media campaigns to convince heterosexuals that we are "just like them," they fail to provide any reason for the majority of lesbians or queers of color to work with them. Theirs is a pre-Stonewall, prefeminism politics. (They state that "the gay revolution has failed," that post-Stonewall gay activism has been a "disaster," though the legal and social advances of lesbians and gays in the last two decades, when compared with the advances under homophile organizations, are staggering.)

The narrowness of this prescription rests on the assumption of a clear "gay interest." As we saw earlier, this is a problematic notion. Even if we could/can posit a discrete "gay interest," though, there is no entailment between such an interest and the rejection of coalition. One could assume such an interest and still advocate coalition politics. The motivation of such a politics would be a quid-pro-quo understanding: I'll protect you from "them" if you protect me. I'll support racial or class advances if you support feminism and lesbian rights.

Such conceptions of coalition have their basis in several assumptions of mainstream political science and white American life. First is the assumption of identifiable groups and corresponding interests, as discussed above. Next is the assumption of self-interest as the basis of political action, with its embedded assumptions about the nature of the self. These assumptions present persons as individualist satisfaction-maximizers, whose satisfaction may or may not arise from others' satisfaction or welfare. The language of individualism makes it difficult to discuss or conceive of rationales for coalition that are not essentialist, but the job is not impossible.[13]

The first break in the smooth surface of this presentation occurs with the recognition by early pluralists that persons possess (note the possessive) characteristics that will strongly influence their interests.[14] In pluralist theory, the "characteristics" of social actors are not simple possessions, but place them in social groups. Nonetheless, the interest paradigm remains, for these groups will have interests that are identifiable and separable; "blacks' interest" will be different from and unrelated to "lesbians' interest" and so forth.

This model collapses in the face of specific thinking about our lives. "Overlapping" memberships in various social groups may cause some people to hold "several agendas" for change at once: Black lesbians will have an agenda on the basis of race, on gender, and on sexuality. Thus for some, coalitions will be the only way to do justice to their concerns, their "interests." Even so, this argument still remains in the realm of essentialist thinking about social groups. It conceives of "Blacks" and "lesbians" as distinct and uniform groups; the anomaly of Black lesbians is precisely that they do not fit the modal version of either group. From an essentialist viewpoint, Black lesbians become "bridges" between groups that are otherwise coherent. But none of these groupings is "natural." *All* are the result of particular historical discourses about race, sexuality, and gender. The coherence and unity of the category of "Blacks," "whites," "lesbians," and so on is a politicohistorical event, not a logical or a natural one.[15]

Once we see that social formations and memberships are not naturally given but are invented or imagined, we can see the bonds between us. These bonds are not ones of mutual affection or concern, not ones of nature, but are the creation of systems of discursive power and hegemony that tell us who we are and where we fit. This recognition in turn forces us to rethink common action. If common action is not (or not exclusively) jostling for one's (pregiven) interest against others who would deny it, what is it? If our group memberships are provisional because those groups are provisional entities/concepts, how do we know whom to work with?

Local Politics

A lesbian politics that is not based on the authenticity of personal experience or subjectivity should not be confused with one that refuses consciousness or social location.[16] On the contrary, it has been part of the ideological function of the subject to remove people from their social locations and present them as equal, autonomous agents, when in fact they are unequal and usually dominated. And try as we might, we have not been able to provide a reformulation of the subject that would eliminate this ideological function and enable us to base claims on our actual, concrete, specific lives.

The answer to this difficulty is not to make the universal "truly" so, as has been the strategy of thinkers and activists for two centuries. Rather, it is to acknowledge that there is no true universal, that justice and freedom do not consist in inclusion per se, but require attention to the specific voice(s) or language(s) in which we speak and what we are saying. The association of justice with a metanarrative of universal principles and structures must give way to a more modest and contextual practice, though we need not be led to abandon "justice" entirely.

If we challenge the grand narratives of race, class, gender, and sexuality in favor of more local and specific analyses, we find that our allies are everywhere. Local politics, and the theories that sustain them, privilege no one axis of oppression. Instead, the space is opened simultaneously for a multiplicity of claims and struggles. Without a theory to tell us what and who belongs where, we have to begin to talk and listen, to endure conflict and welcome shared achievements.

The politics that I am calling for is "local" in two senses. In its first, "postmodern" sense, it is a politics that eschews universal narratives of oppression that base all oppressions on one "most basic" one, that posit the same mechanisms of oppression in all times and places, or that prescribe unitary or homogeneous ideals for all times and places. The rejection of these narratives has, as we have seen, engendered great anxiety on the part of those who see in these forms of narrative the only secure source of critique. The second sense in which my recommended politics is local deals with that issue. In this sense, local politics is a return to the original formulation of identity politics. As described by the Combahee River Collective, identity politics is a practice that resists political agendas given by others and works for those issues that stem from our own experiences and identities. Valuing local politics restores the theoretical priority of seeing the obvious, the injustice that is in front of our noses, rather than explaining or denying or postponing work on it. Local politics is identity politics, but a deessentialized identity politics. It is an identity politics in which we come to know, and come to fashion, the issues that are relevant to us. Such a politics does not require that we become provincial or self-centered. It does require us to notice and address the hunger and violence and exploitation at home as well as that faced far away by people who can never catch us in their eyes.

The privileging of experience in theory has been one of the central targets of feminist challenge and deconstruction. It might be feared that this local politics is a return to such a privilege. The politics I am proposing here is unlike that earlier theory in that the experience I am recommending as the basis for politics is the experience of a postmodern self. This self, aware of its own contradictory and ongoing construction, is a more humble self than that of modern theories. It is a self that knows itself to be product as well as initiator of local politics, and thus possessed of only incomplete knowledge. That we must act is certain; that we do so without full knowledge or understanding of our circumstances is equally so.

Beneath the fear of or skepticism about local politics lies the image of politics inherited from modern revolutions. In this image, real change is effected by massive popular uprising, seemingly as one, with one clear voice. The aim of the uprising is the seizure of power. This image haunts our discussions of "reform versus revolution," in which we have to choose between reform (when "they" retain power while "we" get some crumbs) and revolution (when "we" have power to realize "our" total goals of social reorganization). The statism of this model is obvious. The theoretical challenge to this model, launched perhaps most provocatively by Michel Foucault, broadens our vision beyond the state and its apparatuses to the more "social" minutiae in which power increasingly resides in the modern Western countries. This "micropower" requires not a totalizing theoretical umbrella to connect it to other micropowers and ultimately to the macropower of the state, but resistance. "Revolution" becomes the post-factum label by which we designate an enormity of confrontations, rearticulations, and reconfigurations of power, rather than the a priori designation of certain types of political action. On the other hand, Kirk and Madsen basically invite us to join dominant U.S. culture on its terms. Their "reformism" is the other side of the longing for revolution, daring nothing.

But we know of other possibilities. The work of thinkers such as Laclau and Mouffe converges (nonasymptotically) with that of multiculturalist writers and activists. The reminder that the social is an open field admitting of partial closures and linkages rather than a total system or structure can encourage us to envision new structures, new alliances and linkages. The work ahead of us is not simply public relations, overcoming "prejudice" so that we can be like "everyone else" (whoever they are), nor is it the institution of a comprehensive system of just relations. It is the patient simultaneous work of entry into and subversion of a social field that denies lesbian existence while presenting hypostatized images of "the lesbian." "Local" politics is participatory politics, perhaps modest in each particular location, but forming in the end a situation discretely different than the one(s) preceding it. Reforms become reformation, re-forming the sociopolitical terrain.

The most prominent recent example of the accumulation of reforms into revolution is the collapse of the Soviet Union. Until his ouster Mikhail Gorbachev oversaw the destruction of the Soviet empire and eventually of the USSR itself. Since Gorbachev's downfall Boris Yeltsin has aimed at the construction of a capitalist state, but the results of that plan are far from certain. Yet none of these changes was announced as such in 1985, and they are not the result of a blueprint hiding in the Kremlin. The shifts in Eastern Europe were unanticipated by those who focused their analysis on the structures labeled as central. The resurgence of nationalism and anti-Semitism and the decline in the moral authority of the churches confound most of the Western expectations for post-USSR Europe. The narrative of Marxism-Leninism assured us that nationalism and anti-Semitism would be erased (though there were always signs to the contrary), and the prominent adversarial role of the churches before the collapse led to beliefs that when they could, Eastern European Christians would flock to church and listen to their clergy. What is now evident is that Eastern Europe changed before "the collapse" in ways that fostered the destruction of Soviet hegemony but that do not lead it simply to capitalism or to harmony. The end of history is not yet upon us.

Another, more pertinent example is the long gradual growth of the structures needed before a "lesbian and gay movement" could develop. The Stonewall riots had a context in years of growing visibility and in the civil rights, feminist, and antiwar movements.[17] The work that made later events possible was "local politics": putting out newsletters, meeting to discuss issues of common concern, working to provide safe environments. These seemingly small acts provided the "free spaces" necessary for lesbians and gay men to learn the practices and the confidence necessary for effective political action.[18]

I thus agree with Kirk and Madsen that lesbians and gays must fight for basic civil rights and for the privileges currently reserved to heterosexuals, but I do not agree with their reassurances to heterosexuals about the limited impact of full equality. Marriage and military service are pedestrian, assimilationist goals, but their achievement would require a full-scale rethinking of these institutions. Citizenship for lesbians and gays would dislocate (which is not to say completely eliminate) the assumptions about heterosexual masculinity that currently drape the figure of the citizen. Domestic bliss would never be the same if lesbians were fully incorporated into the range of possible images. Would these changes be "revolutionary"? I think that is an inhibiting, constraining question. It amounts to checking our desires and our ability to struggle against an abstract list of possibilities. A better question to ask is, What would this change mean for the lives of those who want it and of those who care about them? This question will admit only of more modest, more specific answers, and that is its virtue.

Alliances beyond Identity

Lesbians engage in politics whenever they become visible as lesbians, as they challenge assumptions about heterosexuality. Visibility as lesbians serves to weaken charges of isolation from other politics. Active, visible participation in organizations that do not have lesbians as their main concern builds bridges with others who may not have been allies before. Work on "lesbian issues" is vital as well, but it need not be based on constructions of identity that isolate those issues from other causes. Refusing that isolation and the constructions that foster it provides the resiliency that is needed for continual struggle.

Lesbians are involved in every struggle, sometimes on sides I would not choose. Before it is an identity, lesbianism is a characteristic of many diverse people. Audre Lorde's powerful response to the charge that Black lesbians don't support Black struggle is a documentation of her presence, a Black lesbian presence, in all the struggles that supposedly did not involve gender or sexuality.[19] Lesbians active in antiracist work, in work against violence against women or U.S. imperialism or AIDS or for economic justice, all remain lesbian, as do their Republican, antifeminist, or militarist sisters. All belie a monolithic politics of unitary subjectivity.

This is not news, but this fact has historically been explained on the basis of oppressions that share the same root and the same oppressor—white, straight, bourgeois men versus everybody else—and the false consciousness of those who deny the connections. This line of argument is counterproductive, for it does not prepare us for the inevitable contradictions and conflicts among and within members of these various groups. A postmodern coalitional politics can avoid this by recognizing that such conflicts are inevitable, and that they are not cause for despair but grounds for continued rearticulation, new narratives of political structures and change. As a more modest politics, it reduces the invitation to despair and burnout that is such a chronic problem among opponents of the established order(s).

In this project, the issue is not whom to work with, but how to work with them; or it is both. If politics is a matter of negotiating identities and discourses as much as distribution of goods, then we cannot assume that the people we work with will remain the same (or that we will, for that matter). I do not mean by this that we will work with "different" people, but that identities will change as a result of our politics.

As an example, consider the status of mixed-blood Lakota Sioux before and after the events at Wounded Knee in 1973. Before the American Indian Movement challenged the power not only of the Bureau of Indian Affairs but also of the existing tribal leadership, mixed-bloods were not considered, and did not consider themselves, "really Sioux." In the wake of the siege at Wounded Knee, the turn toward indigenous spirituality to heal the community drew in many mixed-blood people, and now many identify themselves as Lakota rather than white or mixed.[20] Here, outsiders have become insiders.

On the other hand, sometimes insiders become outsiders. The construction of sexual categories in the nineteenth century formed whole groups of people who were no longer fully in their regional, political, social, or religious communities. There was now an "us," implicitly or explicitly heterosexual, and there were "homosexuals," who were no longer really "Americans" or "men" or "women" or "white" or "Black" or. . . . Suddenly, "homosexual men and women" were a group, and have been trying to act politically on the basis of that ascribed commonality for one hundred years. The great advantage of the lesbian feminist articulation of lesbians as women is that lesbians *like* women, and so are more likely to work well with women. Of course, not all lesbians like women, any more than all heterosexual women "like" men, but those lesbians who do not like women are, I suspect, even less likely to like gay men.

Lesbians have been divided between those who would or could work with men and those who would or could not, or between those who interpreted lesbianism as homosexuality and have based their political work on that interpretation and those who have treated it as feminism in practice, distinct from male love of men. I am strongly sympathetic to those who refuse common ground with gay men (especially white middle-class gay men); my own history of such work is disappointing and frustrating, fraught with sexism and misogyny. Nonetheless, lesbians do have a common cause with gay men, like it or not; however we interpret our lives, the hegemonic social and legal interpretation of lesbianism oppresses lesbians as "homosexuals," and thus provides a ground for common struggle.

We must recognize, though, and must keep reminding gay men, that the hegemonic interpretation is not necessarily everyone's. Kirk and Madsen are among the few gay writers to acknowledge the difficulties of this particular alliance:

> Indeed, all that gays and lesbians really share in common is their oppression at the hands of straights and their relative sexual indifference toward each other. Paradoxically, *gay men and women are forced into political intimacy with one another precisely because they don't wish to be sexually intimate*; and what situation could be more awkward than that?[21]

In working with gay men, feminist lesbians must not eschew feminism or tolerate misogyny. It does not serve any purpose to sacrifice central aspects of our selves. We cannot afford simply to leave, however. Bernice Johnson Reagon reminds us that, while we all like to build little "barred rooms" of sameness and comfort, we cannot remain within them all the time. At some point, "the door of the room will just be painted red and then when those who call the shots get ready to clean house, they have easy access to you."[22]

One way to avoid the "red door" problem is to engage in a diversionary "politics" that continually deconstructs or refuses the categories on which contemporary oppressions are based. This, indeed, is the strategy most commonly associated with postmodernism by both enemies and sympathizers. Though this deconstruction is crucial work for the long run, in the short run it is a mistake. It is a mistake first for the reasons Reagon describes. Voters in Colorado, or homophobes with baseball bats, will not be persuaded by discussions of gender ambiguity; such talk will exacerbate their anxiety. Telling them that I am not "really" a lesbian is different from saying it to readers of *Signs*; what the second audience can understand as deconstruction becomes before the first audience simply a return to the closet.

There is another way for postmodern lesbians to address the red door, however. It involves coalitions that are based not on stable identities, but on the recognition that some social signifiers presently embody and transmit relations of oppression. One's relationship to those signifiers need not be settled once and for all for them to be important constituents of one's life and politics. I may insist on my lesbian identity not because I believe myself to be "really" lesbian, but because my relationship to that category (whatever that relationship may be) importantly structures my life.

This brings us to the second mistake of a thoroughly deconstructed vision of politics. In writing about such a politics, it is easy to celebrate fractured identities and ambiguities. In doing the daily work of politics, these breaks and sutures are the source of deep pain and fear as well as joy. More "political" (or less privileged?) writers such as Anzaldúa and Alarcón describe this pain and fear vividly. The messiness so often cheered by contemporary theorists must be granted its due. The leap from theoretical understanding to visceral reaction is a huge one, fraught with danger and anxiety. If postmodern political theorists do not acknowledge this problem, we will be doomed to irrelevance. Becoming coalitional citizens is every bit as painful as becoming lesbians has been for most of us in (hetero)sexist societies. We need to continue to articulate a common political agenda that does not naturalize our alliance, that does not insist that gay men be feminist but that does ensure that our work together will not violate feminist commitments held by participants, and this continued articulation will be nothing short of infuriating.

Queer—A Coalitional Identity?

"Queer" politics is often presented as this articulation of a coalitional identity. Queer theory and politics are products of the 1980s. This new identity had several sources. First, the feminist sex wars exhausted many lesbians and led them to seek new locations. Second, the rising demands of bisexuals for inclusion in gay and lesbian communities and organizations invited a new analysis of the relationship between politics and sexuality. Third, AIDS introduced new patterns of relationships between men and women and provided a basis for alliances. Last, the ascendancy of poststructuralism provided a terrain for queer theory in the academy.

Arlene Stein has done a fine job of narrating the exhaustion of the sex wars.[23] In opposition to lesbian feminists who saw women as inherently life-affirming, gentle, and egalitarian, the prosex lesbians asserted the reality and the value of practices such as pornography, role playing (in and out of bed), and s/m. As a result of the split among lesbians, these "sex radicals" found themselves more often in alliance with nonlesbian "sexual minorities" than with lesbian feminists, and they developed analyses that articulated those alliances. This new articulation is most visible in Gayle Rubin's presentation at the 1982 Barnard conference. "Queer" has eventually become the umbrella that (sometimes) covers all of Rubin's dancing partners.

Inclusion of bisexuals forced another challenge to both gay and lesbian feminist constellations. The easy answer is simply to expand the shopping list—at my campus, the erstwhile Gay and Lesbian Student Union is now the Lesbian, Bisexual, and Gay Alliance—but this doesn't really appreciate the challenge of bisexuality. Bisexuals challenge both the popular view of heterosexuality/homosexuality—that everyone is one or the other—and the lesbian feminist portrayal of the tight linkage between sexuality and politics in which bisexual women are "unreliable" allies because they desire sex with men (whether they ever do it or not). More fundamentally, bisexuals have worked to challenge the automatic equivalence of desire and act, as women such as Robyn Ochs have insisted that they are bisexual even if they live their whole lives with women. By their insistence, they introduce another other, not at the margin but at the heart of lesbian theory.[24]

The third, and perhaps most important, shift was that produced by AIDS. The "crisis of AIDS" consists both in the devastation of the human immunodeficiency virus and in the renewed attacks from homophobes and bigots. Ironically, it may have been these attacks that led to an increased identification between lesbians and gay men, and mushrooming political power. While gay men were dying of AIDS, the sexism of popular discourse discussed "gays" without reference to sex, thereby leaving many heterosexuals equally afraid of lesbians and gay men. Forced again into a common defensive position, lesbians and gays rediscovered common cause in the 1980s. A more dubious foundation for this new alliance lay in the illness itself; the new position of white gay men as victims, as brothers needing help rather than oppressors, made them more appealing to many lesbians.

Finally, we should not overlook the importance in the academy of poststructuralist theories. Theories that focus on the role of language in the construction of the social, that emphasize the historical contingency of even those categories of identity that we consider most "personal," provided an opening for thinking about those who have been called lesbian and gay. Specifically, it allowed for new, postliberal arguments about our place in predominantly heterosexual societies. These arguments have not focused on our similarity to heterosexuals or our common humanity as a ground for rights, but have worked to displace certainty about the division between straight and queer and have thus called into question the very grounds of heterosexism. These theories carry a potential for social transformation that far exceeds the practice of liberal inclusion, but their esotericism also has limited their usefulness in practical battles for hegemony. Most of our political/legal successes have relied on liberal reasoning, and discussions about social constructionism have remained within the academy.

"Queers" are, by and large, younger than gays and lesbians. Many of them do not even know about the battles among lesbians or between gays and lesbians. They are on a path that follows a different geography than the route of their older sisters and brothers, a postmodern landscape sculpted by performance art, by punk rock and its descendants, by Madonna and multiculturalism, and by Reagan and Bush. They are unafraid of camp, or of "roles" that do not mean what they once did but do not mean nothing. They have a sense of humor unlike that of "gays" or "lesbians." The 1993 March on Washington exemplified much of this: although the march was organized along "political" lines, issues of justice and equity and inclusion and dignity, the marchers were much more diverse and hilarious. "We're here; we're gay; can Bill come out and play?" in front of the White House has a very different tone from "Hey, hey, ho, ho, homophobia's got to go!" I was raised on anger, but I was delighted in D.C.

In a deeper way, though, "queers" have not transcended any of the challenges facing "lesbians" or "gays." There are several angles to this. First, who is queer? To many, "queer" is simply a new label for "lesbian and gay." Among these, there is a split between those who use "queer" simply as a convenient shorthand and those who imply a nationalist politics. This second usage provides nothing new, and recycles much that is better left to decompose. Whereas the shorthand usage is a matter of claiming a word that was used against us, the nationalist version of "queer" reanimates the problems of lesbian feminism in its cultural feminist versions without resolving them.

For others, "queer" moves beyond "lesbian and gay" to encompass bisexuals, transgendered people, and other sexual minorities. This is the move toward a coalitional identity. In Lisa Duggan's words, this usage points toward a "new community" that is "unified only by a shared dissent from the dominant organization of sex and gender."[25] "Dissent from the dominant organization of sex and gender" does not, however, guarantee a feminist position. The feminist heritage of "lesbians" is crucial if queers are to avoid the pitfalls of "gay" (white male) politics. Though Queer Nation chapters worked consciously at being nonsexist and nonracist, the later battles within chapters dem-

onstrated that nirvana had not yet been achieved. All of these understandings of queer must be challenged to deny the colonization of lesbians and people of color that occurs within "gay" politics.

The tension between nationalism and its most thoroughgoing deconstruction lies latent in queerdom. Self-described queers include
both those who see queerness as a cross-cultural and transhistorical
"natural" identity or position and those who use "queer" to designate
a liminal position within the contingent sexual and gender frontiers of
contemporary capitalist societies. This tension is not to be resolved by
the ceding of one side to the other, but must remain a field of contestation. To the extent that queers become nationalist, they will ignore or
lose patience with those among them who do not fit their idea of the
nation. This dynamic in nationalism will always limit its political usefulness. The only fruitful nationalism is one that has at its heart the
idea of the nonnation—the nation of nonidentity, formed not by any
shared attribute but by a conscious weaving of threads between tat-
tered fabrics. And at that point, why speak of nations? Alliances are
not nations, and need not be to be strong.

"Queer" does not guarantee a better alliance politics than "gay" or
"lesbian" have. The larger notion of queer as encompassing all sexual
minorities does not eliminate this problem but reinscribes it in the
heart of the queer. The alliance with (heterosexual or homosexual)
sadomasochists, fetishists, and pedophiles that is adumbrated in this
usage does not enlarge the field of alliance but simply shifts the privilege within it. When others are faced with a "nation" that they do not
recognize or desire, they will simply leave. The hegemonic inscription
of the queer as *the* sexual minority will then amount to an exclusion-
ary colonization of those who refuse their membership.

Character and Coalition

In the end, identity politics will always be either a nationalist politics
or a "practical politics of the open end."[26] Doing a better identity politics does not mean finding the best definition of our identities so as to
eliminate problems of membership and goals; it means continual
shuffling between the need for categories and the recognition of their
incompleteness. No one can decide simply on the basis of identity—
any identity—whom any of us will be able to work with. Simple versions of identity politics, in which we know who and what we are and
we know by people's identifications whether they are trustworthy, are
inadequate. The contingency and multiplicity of agendas furthers this

indeterminacy. Because lesbians, gays, and queers differ in their political aims among themselves as well as between groups, the ground for common action cannot be "identity" but must be shared commitments; it must be sympathy and affinity rather than identity. Sympathy and affinity need not be total to be real and effective. They do, however, require a self-consciousness about one's actions and allegiances that is often taken for granted in identity politics. If identity is not sufficient ground for trust or political agreement, but abstract principles in the manner of liberalism or Marxism are not sufficient either, then we need to get specific with one another about what we value and what we will do to realize that value.

What does this specificity look like in action? When I, a white middle-class lesbian with a Jewish mother and Christian father, talk with my male, Jewish, straight, working-class friend, our conversations take time. They take time because we often need to stop and "mark," or note, where a gap between us is due to cultural differences. Sometimes it is relevant that my father was alcoholic, or that his grandparents were present in his life, or that he "is straight" or that I am not, or that he went to Yale and I to a state school. Knowing those things helps us to move through some sources of pain and fear to places where we can see some shared goals and struggles. Other times, however, these facts are less helpful. Even when we get through all the descriptors we can find—astrological, Jungian types, Greek versus Hebrew, as well as the aforementioned—we still find that we are not "just alike under the skin." Each of us is unique. Our friendship could not be transplanted onto our other family members, nor could our political goals or intellectual concerns. Only a very specific focus allows for this dual necessity, for the combination of structural analysis and stubborn individuality; not transcendence of our context, but forever living with the remainder, the unique, the unassimilable.

In a larger political framework, getting specific helps us to locate our allies at particular points, for particular struggles. Paying close attention to our particular social locations forces us to go beyond simple counting of the categories. Our lives are not lived as chunks; though we can certainly specify in some instances structural conditions and inequalities that produce results, most of the time we just live, all of our elements jostling together. Our identities are those jostling, shifting elements. Our politics must account for this complexity. I may work with gay men because we are both targets of a larger hegemonic culture. When I do such work, I do not experience the euphoria of community. I am often frustrated and disgusted. But it is necessary nonetheless, because heterosexism and homophobia structure my existence inescapably. When I work with women of other racial or ethnic identifications, I do so not out of "compassion" for them, or to assuage my guilt. I do so, first, because injustice is not segmentable, but spreads beyond garden borders laid down for it. I do so, second, because I value them in spite of my own racism. That value is not just the value of "difference," of the sort we see on the "ethnic days" in cities where groups gather to dance and sing and eat before returning to being Anglo. I value specific different voices because they intersect with my own, creating a world. There are other different voices that I do not value and do my best not to support: Nazis, white supremacists, antifeminists, corporate polluters, and many others. And then there are people in neither camp: those who, though racist, sexist, classist, or heterosexist, share concerns and try to overcome their pasts and presents as I try to overcome my own.

The question to ask about "allies," then, is not whether they are "really" allies, but how to *make* them allies. While narrow identity politics is framed in terms of the identity checklist for allies, a larger identity politics will ask instead about character. Identity politics, as a politics arising out of the specific oppressions faced by each of us, need not result in a politics shared only by others sharing those oppressions—indeed, it cannot, for that sharing will always be tested as we dwell together in the house of difference. The questions to ask are not whether we share a given position but whether we share a commitment to improve it, and whether we can commit to the pain of embarrassment and confrontation as we disagree. As Samuel Delany puts it,

> Gay men and gay women may well express solidarity with each other.
> But in the day to day working out of the reality of liberation, the
> biggest help we can give each other is a clear and active recognition of
> the extent and nature of the different contexts and a rich and working
> sympathy for the different priorities these contexts (for want of a bet-
> ter term) engender.[27]

The question is whether we can *decide* to be allies, and whether we have the strength to follow through on that decision. Unless these questions are addressed, no theory and no identity will provide a satisfactory result. With positive answers to them, we can forge the bonds between specificities to create a fence against oppression. These very local links can provide the ground for the strength needed to address structures that currently appear insurmountable.

Thus comes about the relevance to political theory both of ethics and of a certain aesthetics of the self. Ethics, treated not as simple rules but as guidelines and starting points for choice, and aesthetics, as the conscious fashioning of character, are both required if politics is to change and produce anything of lasting value. If we fail to address questions of character, formulations of identity will never produce change. Character is not a static entity on which we will be judged by some distant god; character is one name for the processes of the self. Those processes are inseparable from the processes of politics.

Let us say that a political group is "captured" by a driven, committed activist. This person may fight hard for lesbians and/or gays and/or queers, and so is deserving of some praise. While that person is working, she arrogates all power to herself, purports to speak for her organization, alienates other groups, and is unable to listen to criticism. After a while, she may find that she is alone: membership has dwindled, and no one seems to want to work with that group. She castigates the community for their apathy, further alienating everyone. Eventually, she is treated by heterosexuals as a brave fighter, a hero, while no lesbians will have anything to do with her and no real change has been made.

This is a failure of character, on the part of the activist and on the part of those around her. The activist has clearly destroyed that which she aimed to build. Those around her have failed as well, unless they have built an alternative organization that can do the work of the other. Allowing ourselves to abandon the field to the obnoxious activist makes us accomplices. These failures are not failures of theory or of ideology, of misplaced identity. They are failures of political process, and those failures are inseparable from arrogance, cowardice, denial, laziness. Better theory will not bring that organization, or that struggle, back to life. Political action will, and the success of that action relies on the ability of actors to act together. Character is not a "personal" issue, nor is it one to be reserved for right-wing Christians. It is not "the" most important issue, but it is a crucial one if any politics committed to justice is to move toward its professed goals.

Where will this character come from? Basically, from practice. Those looking for allies must begin by volunteering to become allies, developing a commitment to challenge oppression in ourselves and in others. Middle-class and wealthy lesbians must work to learn about and support working-class and poor people's lives and struggles. Men who want to be allies must become knowledgeable and become willing to learn from women. And so on. Alliances are not a matter of harmony and univocity. The distinction between coalitions and alliances is not one of unity or even of durability (though I think there are reasons to expect greater durability from alliances), but of motive and purpose. Recognition of the publicity, the "inter esse" of interest, requires the self-extension of each person toward others. While Nancy points out the incompleteness and instability of being-in-common, he also reminds us of its inevitability, of the necessity of such being-in-common for any individual being. This awareness must be developed into a conscious commitment to the welfare of others, both in general and in each person we meet. This is a form of love. It is a love of the world, a love of democracy, a love of others as inseparably part of the community within which we live. As an activity based on conscious commitment rather than a feeling, love can be chosen and it can be refused. Love need not entail self-negation, but it does require a willingness to "go under," to suffer the small deaths of humility and pain and self-examination. Just as love does not come from others unless we offer it to them, so allies will develop as we ally ourselves with their causes. And as we increasingly open our eyes and hearts, we will help to create those fences against oppression by modeling decency. Without decency and love, bringing us toward one another without requiring sameness, our rhetorical and heartfelt commitments to others will continually be frustrated in the face of ineluctable difference.

The "postmodern" awareness of the incompleteness of any narrative, of the instability of identities and of social topologies, is the opening from modern arrogance to such humility. It requires not only theoretical elegance and acuity but profound interrogation and transformation of oneself. Although not all arrogance is modern, surely the postmodern, "that which denies itself the solace of good forms, the consensus of a taste which would make it possible to share collectively the nostalgia for the unattainable,"[28] that which confronts the abyss of responsibility and choice, is inconsistent with arrogance of any sort. Faced with such an awareness, bereft of models that justify theoretical imperialism on anyone's part, we are forced to confront one another, to build a ground together instead of finding one and inviting others to sit on it.

Getting specific can help us to find the points of connection that enable us to talk to one another at all, as well as the points that keep us apart. If politics is about negotiation, I would rather negotiate with words than with bombs or guns. If democratic politics is about masses, about numbers and majorities, then all of us who share some fragmented parts of a common dream need to develop the ability to talk to each other. This cannot be done by ignoring differences; it must come by moving through and with them. Our politics, disappointingly enough, must consist of continued patient and impatient struggle with ourselves and those "within" and "without" our "communities" who seek to fix us (in the many senses of that term). We can afford neither simple assimilation into mainstream politics nor total withdrawal in search of the authentic community—or we must demand the right to both. We have to stand where we are, acknowledging the contradictions and forging the links between ourselves and other marginal citizens of the world, resisting the temptation to cloak crucial differences with the cloak of universality while also refusing to harden those differences into identities that cannot be crossed. The promise of getting specific is the promise of theorizing, which is to say discussing and working on, the possibility of such a politics.

Notes

Introduction

1. Biddy Martin, "Feminism, Criticism, and Foucault," *New German Critique* 27 (1982): 3–12.

2. Minnie Bruce Pratt, "Identity: Skin Blood Heart," in *Rebellion: Essays 1980–1991* (Ithaca, N.Y.: Firebrand, 1991), 27–81; Elizabeth V. Spelman, *Inessential Woman: Problems of Exclusion in Feminist Thought* (Boston: Beacon Press, 1988); Adrienne Rich, "Notes toward a Politics of Location," in *Blood, Bread, and Poetry: Selected Prose, 1979–1985* (New York: W. W. Norton, 1986), 210–31; Ruth Frankenberg, *White Women, Race Matters: The Social Construction of Whiteness* (Minneapolis: University of Minnesota Press, 1993).

3. Linda Alcoff, "Cultural Feminism versus Post-Structuralism: The Identity Crisis in Feminist Theory," *Signs: Journal of Women in Culture and Society* 13, no. 3 (Spring 1988): 420; Nancie Caraway, *Segregated Sisterhood: Racism and the Politics of American Feminism* (Knoxville: University of Tennessee Press, 1991).

4. Sidney Abbott and Barbara Love, *Sappho Was a Right-On Woman* (New York: Stein and Day, 1973), 136. For another, similar description, see Ti-Grace Atkinson, "Strategy and Tactics: A Presentation of Political Lesbianism," in her *Amazon Odyssey* (New York: Links Books, 1974), 135–89. However, Atkinson is very ambivalent about the actual political significance of lesbianism; see "Lesbianism and Feminism" in *Amazon Odyssey*, 83–88. See also Radicalesbians, "The Woman-Identified Woman," in *Radical Feminism*, ed. Anne Koedt, Ellen Levine, and Anita Rapone (New York: Times Books, 1973), 240–45; Adrienne Rich, "Compulsory Heterosexuality and Lesbian Existence," *Signs: Journal of Women in Culture and Society* 5, no. 4 (1980): 631–60.

5. For the most recent version of this notion, see Marilyn Frye, "Willful Virgin; or, Do You Have to Be a Lesbian to Be a Feminist?" in *Willful Virgin: Essays in Feminism* (Freedom, Calif.: The Crossing Press, 1992), 124–37. Her answer to "Do you have to be a lesbian to be a feminist?" is ambiguous: "It's not my call" (136). She does, however, "think everything is against it" (ibid.).

6. See Shane Phelan, *Identity Politics: Lesbian Feminism and the Limits*

of Community (Philadelphia: Temple University Press, 1989), and Alice Echols, *Daring to Be Bad: Radical Feminism in America, 1967–1975* (Minneapolis: University of Minnesota Press, 1989).

7. Gloria Anzaldúa, *Borderlands / La frontera: The New Mestiza* (San Francisco: Spinsters / Aunt Lute, 1987), and "Bridge, Drawbridge, Sandbar or Island: Lesbians-of-Color *Hacienda Alianzas,*" in *Bridges of Power: Women's Multicultural Alliances,* ed. Lisa Albrecht and Rose M. Brewer (Philadelphia: New Society Publishers, 1990, 216–31.

8. Diana Fuss, *Essentially Speaking: Feminism, Nature, and Difference* (New York: Routledge, 1989), 103.

9. Judith Butler, *Gender Trouble: Feminism and the Subversion of Identity* (New York: Routledge, 1989), 147.

10. Teresa de Lauretis, "Eccentric Subjects: Feminist Theory and Historical Consciousness," *Feminist Studies* 16, no. 1 (1990): 139.

11. Nancy Miller, *Reading Feminist Writing* (New York: Columbia University Press, 1988), 112.

12. Barbara Christian, "The Race for Theory," *Feminist Studies* 14, no. 1 (Spring 1988): 71.

13. Ibid., 68.

14. See the collection *Feminists Theorize the Political,* ed. Judith Butler and Joan W. Scott (New York: Routledge, 1992), especially Bonnie Honig, "Toward an Agonistic Feminism: Hannah Arendt and the Politics of Identity" (215–35) and Chantal Mouffe, "Feminism, Citizenship, and Radical Democratic Politics" (369–84).

1. Specificity

1. Friedrich Nietzsche, *The Portable Nietzsche,* ed. Walter Kaufmann (New York: Viking Press, 1954), 164.

2. I am indebted to Elizabeth Spelman for this point.

3. See Nancy Myron and Charlotte Bunch, *Lesbianism and the Women's Movement* (Baltimore: Diana Press, 1975); Bunch and Myron, *Class and Feminism* (Baltimore: Diana Press, 1974); Angela Y. Davis, *Women, Race, and Class* (New York: Random House, 1981); and bell hooks, *Ain't I a Woman?* (Boston: South End Press, 1981). For discussions of white women's racism in earlier feminist movements, see, for example, Kathleen M. Blee, *Women of the Klan* (Berkeley and Los Angeles: University of California Press, 1991); Davis; and hooks, *Ain't I a Woman?*

4. See hooks, *Ain't I a Woman?,* Davis, *Women, Race, and Class*; Paula Giddings, *When and Where I Enter: The Impact of Black Women on Race and Sex in America* (New York: William Morrow Books, 1984); Myron and Bunch, *Lesbianism and the Women's Movement;* and Bunch and Myron, *Class and Feminism.*

5. See Maria C. Lugones and Elizabeth V. Spelman, "Have We Got a The-

ory for You! Feminist Theory, Cultural Imperialism and the Demand for 'the Woman's Voice,' " *Women's Studies International Forum* 6 (1983): 573–81; Audre Lorde, *Sister/Outsider* (Trumansburg, N.Y.: The Crossing Press, 1984); and bell hooks, *Feminist Theory: From Margin to Center* (Boston: South End Press, 1984).

6. But see Cherríe Moraga's discussion of the way color hierarchy and male privilege operated in her family, in *Loving in the War Years: Lo que nunca pasó por sus labios* (Boston: South End Press, 1983).

7. Minnie Bruce Pratt, "Identity: Blood Skin Heart," in Elly Bulkin, Minnie Bruce Pratt, and Barbara Smith, *Yours in Struggle: Three Feminist Perspectives on Anti-Semitism and Racism* (Brooklyn: Long Haul Press, 1984); Adrienne Rich, "Notes toward a Politics of Location," in *Blood, Bread, and Poetry: Selected Prose, 1979–1985* (New York: W. W. Norton, 1986).

8. Elizabeth V. Spelman, *Inessential Woman: Problems of Exclusion in Feminist Thought* (Boston: Beacon Press, 1988), 66.

9. bell hooks asks this question: "Since men are not equals in white supremacist, capitalist, patriarchal class structure, which men do women want to be equal to?" (*Feminist Theory*, 18).

10. Spelman, *Inessential Woman*, 158.

11. Ibid., 159.

12. Ibid., 167.

13. Ibid., 172.

14. Sheldon Wolin, "On the Theory and Practice of Power," in *After Foucault: Humanistic Knowledge, Postmodern Challenges*, ed. Jonathan Arac (New Brunswick, N.J.: Rutgers University Press, 1988), 196.

15. Writers such as Kathleen Barry, Andrea Dworkin, and Catharine MacKinnon explicitly argue for the need for a unified analysis that "exempts" no man. Laura Lederer's collection, *Take Back the Night: Women on Pornography* (New York: Bantam Books, 1980), is another strong example of this viewpoint.

16. This declaration is disturbingly reminiscent of earlier assertions by Marxist men about the foundational priority of class struggle, assertions rejected by socialist feminists. See Lydia Sargent, ed., *Women and Revolution* (Boston: South End Press, 1981); Zillah Eisenstein, ed., *Capitalist Patriarchy and the Case for Socialist Feminism* (New York: Monthly Review Press, 1979); Alison Jaggar, *Feminist Politics and Human Nature* (Totowa, N.J.: Rowman and Allenheld, 1983); and Nancy C. M. Hartsock, *Money, Sex, and Power: Toward a Feminist Historical Materialism* (Boston: Northeastern University Press, 1984).

17. We see this aim in Adrienne Rich's landmark paper "Compulsory Heterosexuality and Lesbian Existence" (*Signs: Journal of Women in Culture and Society* 5, no. 4 [1980]: 531–60) and in much of the work based on Nancy Chodorow's *Reproduction of Mothering* (Berkeley and Los Angeles: University of California Press, 1978) and Carol Gilligan's *In a Different Voice* (Cambridge: Harvard University Press, 1982). For an extended discussion of this

point see my *Identity Politics: Lesbian Feminism and the Limits of Community* (Philadelphia: Temple University Press, 1989), chap. 4.

18. Spelman, *Inessential Woman*, 174.

19. Ibid., 70.

20. Literally, fear of the body. White women live with the Platonic/Christian message that bodies in general are dangerous and more specifically that women, being assigned the place of "body" in that culture, are dangerous, disgusting, less than human. In such a culture, the way to validate oneself is to be as bodiless as possible. For one discussion of the impact of this somatophobia on Sartre, see Margery Collins and Christine Pierce, "Holes and Slime: Sexism in Sartre's Psychoanalysis," in *Women and Philosophy: Toward a Theory of Liberation*, ed. Carol C. Gould and Max W. Wartofsky (New York: G. P. Putnam's Sons, 1976), 112–27. This position is shared by de Beauvoir, with disastrous results.

21. Adrienne Rich, *On Lies, Secrets, and Silence: Selected Prose, 1966–1978* (New York: W. W. Norton, 1979), 300.

22. "Postmodern" feminists are by no means exempt from this failure to recognize differences. Toril Moi argues that "so far, lesbian and/or black feminist criticism have presented exactly the same *methodological* and *theoretical* problems as the rest of Anglo-American feminist criticism" (*Sexual/Textual Politics: Feminist Literary Theory* [New York: Methuen, 1985], 86). She follows with a discussion of how this is so for lesbians, but ignores the issue of race, implying that all these distinctions are equivalent.

23. Rich, "Notes," 221.

24. Ibid., 212.

25. For examples see the collection of essays in Linda J. Nicholson, ed., *Feminism/Postmodernism* (New York: Routledge, 1990); Jane Flax, *Thinking Fragments: Psychoanalysis, Feminism, and Postmodernism in the Contemporary West* (Berkeley and Los Angeles: University of California Press, 1990); and Denise Riley, *Am I That Name? Feminism and the Category of "Women" in History* (Minneapolis: University of Minnesota Press, 1988).

26. Biddy Martin, "Feminism, Criticism, and Foucault," *New German Critique* 27 (1982): 15.

27. Chris Weedon, *Feminist Practice and Poststructuralist Theory* (Oxford: Blackwell, 1987), 157.

28. Sandra Harding, *The Science Question in Feminism* (Ithaca, N.Y.: Cornell University Press, 1986), and "Feminism, Science, and the Anti-Enlightenment Critiques," in *Feminism/Postmodernism*, ed. Nicholson, 83–106.

29. See Irene Diamond and Lee Quinby, eds., *Feminism and Foucault: Reflections on Resistance* (Boston: Northeastern University Press, 1988), and Weedon, *Feminist Practice*. This is one of the more curious phenomena in modernist readings of postmodernism: modernists continually assume the result of a postmodern analysis is a crippling despair at the totality of "language" or "discourses" or "power/knowledge," when in fact work such as Foucault's is aimed at suggesting strategic interventions and interruptions of

hegemonic structures and processes. The fact that he denies the possibility of "total liberation" should be cause for despair only for those who think the possibilities they can imagine are in fact the only ones, and those who think that any power is bad. The dream of total revolution should no longer be comforting to most of us; it is time to imagine other sorts.

30. The question of the uses of theory, and the forms that theory should take, is an important and exciting debate among women of color. See the essays in Gloria Anzaldúa, ed., *Making Face, Making Soul / Haciendo caras* (San Francisco: Aunt Lute, 1990), sec. 7, and bell hooks's response to Barbara Christian in *Talking Back: Thinking Feminist, Thinking Black* (Boston: South End Press, 1989), chap. 6.

31. Michel Foucault, *Power/Knowledge: Selected Interviews and Other Writings, 1972–1977*, ed. Colin Gordon (New York: Pantheon Books, 1980), 81.

32. Ibid., 83; emphasis in original.

33. Martin, "Feminism, Criticism, and Foucault," 9.

34. Ibid.

35. Midrash, the interpretation of Torah, is similarly contextual and open. Midrash is an activity that has meaning only within a community and for that community. It is guided by implicit and explicit ideas of the good and of justice, but its full meaning can be discovered and articulated only in particular contexts. Here, as in common law, political judgment is inseparable from history, from time and place. See Dennis Fischman, *Political Discourse in Exile: Karl Marx and the Jewish Question* (Amherst: University of Massachusetts Press, 1991).

The universal, categorical ideal of the modern white West is intimately bound to the rise of bureaucratic state power. Actual achievement of justice requires close attention to legal and political processes; though it is an "abstract" term, justice in practice requires careful attention to the categories upon which social inequalities have been based, not a legal "colorblindness."

36. See Patricia Williams, *The Alchemy of Race and Rights* (Cambridge: Harvard University Press, 1991); and Martha Minow, *Making All the Difference: Inclusion, Exclusion, and American Law* (Cambridge: Harvard University Press, 1990).

37. Kathy E. Ferguson, *The Feminist Case against Bureaucracy* (Philadelphia: Temple University Press, 1984), 4.

38. Ibid.

39. Ibid., 193.

2. Building a Specific Theory

1. For an extended critique of this belief, see Kirstie McClure, "The Issue of Foundations: Scientized Politics, Politicized Science, and Feminist Critical

Practice," in *Feminists Theorize the Political*, ed. Judith P. Butler and Joan W. Scott (New York and London: Routledge, 1992), 341–68.

2. Michel Foucault, "Critical Theory / Intellectual History," in *Politics, Philosophy, Culture: Interviews and Other Writings, 1977–1984*, ed. Lawrence D. Kritzman (New York and London: Routledge, 1988), 26.

3. Ibid., 27; emphasis in original.

4. It is crucial to our understanding of Foucault's work that we heed his words in volume 2 of *The History of Sexuality*: "After all, what would be the value of the passion for knowledge if it resulted only in a certain amount of knowledgeableness and not, in one way or another and to the extent possible, in the knower's straying afield of himself?" (New York: Pantheon Books, 1985; 8). Another paper deserves to be written on the importance of the disagreement between Habermas and Foucault on this point. For the theorists whom Adorno would label "identitarian," among whom I include Habermas, the point of knowledge is the *return* to self, not straying.

5. Theodor W. Adorno, *Minima Moralia*, trans. E. F. N. Jephcott (London: Unwin Brothers Ltd., 1978), 18.

6. Foucault, "Critical Theory," 10.

7. Michel Foucault, *The Archaeology of Knowledge* (New York: Harper and Row, 1972), 191.

8. Ibid.

9. Michel Foucault, "Politics and the Study of Discourse," *Ideology and Consciousness* 3 (1978): 10; emphasis in original.

10. Ibid., emphasis in original.

11. Ibid., 11.

12. Hubert L. Dreyfus and Paul Rabinow, eds., *Michel Foucault: Beyond Structuralism and Hermeneutics*, 2d ed. (Chicago: University of Chicago Press, 1983).

13. Michel Foucault, *Power/Knowledge: Selected Interviews and Other Writings, 1972–1977*, ed. Colin Gordon (New York: Pantheon Books, 1980), 117. For another useful description of genealogy, see Kathy E. Ferguson, *The Man Question: Visions of Subjectivity in Feminist Theory* (Berkeley and Los Angeles: University of California Press, 1992), especially chap. 1.

14. Michel Foucault, "The Subject and Power," in Dreyfus and Rabinow, eds., *Michel Foucault*, 109.

15. See, for example, Joan Cocks, *The Oppositional Imagination: Feminism, Critique, and Political Theory* (New York: Routledge, 1989), 48.

16. Edward Said, "Traveling Theory," in *The World, the Text, and the Critic* (Cambridge: Harvard University Press, 1983), 244.

17. Foucault, *Power/Knowledge*, 92. Foucault's 1973 remarks that the political is "everything that has to do with class struggle" and the social "everything that derives from and is a consequence of the class struggle" suggest that his aim is not to erase Marxism but to extend it. See "An Historian of Culture," in *Foucault Live*, ed. Sylvère Lotringer (New York: Semiotext(e), 1989), 87.

18. On this point see Biddy Martin, "Feminism, Criticism, and Foucault," *New German Critique* 27 (1982): 3–30; and Shane Phelan, "Foucault and Feminism," *American Journal of Political Science* 34, no. 2 (1990): 421–40.

19. Ernesto Laclau and Chantal Mouffe, *Hegemony and Socialist Strategy: Towards a Radical Democratic Politics* (London: Verso, 1985), 95. See also Ernesto Laclau, "The Impossibility of Society," in *New Reflections on the Revolution of Our Time* (London: Verso, 1990), 89–92.

20. Laclau and Mouffe, *Hegemony and Socialist Strategy*, 113, 105.

21. Laclau, *New Reflections*, 233.

22. Adrienne Rich, "Compulsory Heterosexuality and Lesbian Existence," *Signs: Journal of Women in Culture and Society* 5, no. 4 (1980): 531–60. For more discussion of this articulation, see Shane Phelan, *Identity Politics: Lesbian Feminism and the Limits of Community* (Philadelphia: Temple University Press, 1989), chaps. 3–5.

23. Laclau and Mouffe, *Hegemony and Socialist Strategy*, 105, 109, 108.

24. Nancy Fraser, *Unruly Practices: Power, Discourse, and Gender in Contemporary Social Theory* (Minneapolis: University of Minnesota Press, 1989), 162.

25. Ibid., 164.

26. See, however, Randy Shilts, *And the Band Played On: Politics, People, and the AIDS Epidemic* (New York: St. Martin's Press, 1987), for the argument that "official" gay male activists had a strong role and shared responsibility for interpretations and policy about AIDS. Shilts's history suggests that we cannot speak of "the" gay community as a unity in this case, and that doing so is a hegemonic move, inseparable from political aims.

27. Fraser, *Unruly Practices*, 166.

28. Ibid., 175.

29. Ibid., 176.

30. Gayatri Spivak, *The Post-Colonial Critic*, ed. Sara Harasym (New York: Routledge, 1990), 139.

31. Spivak, of course, does in fact privilege Marxism in its relation to deconstruction, but the privilege is not simple authority. Her insistence that deconstruction is "a corrective and a critical movement" is balanced by the insight that this correction points out that *no* movement or theory is fully self-grounded or foundational. She argues strongly against trying to found a political project on deconstruction, seeing "wishy-washy pluralism on the one hand, or a kind of irresponsible hedonism on the other" as the results (*The Post-Colonial Critic*, 104). This sort of political deconstruction, or deconstructed politics, is described by Nancy Fraser in her article "The French Derrideans" in *Unruly Practices*. A related example is Richard Rorty's work, which urges the abandonment of theory altogether in favor of a pragmatic "bourgeois liberalism."

32. Toni Cade, ed., *The Black Woman: An Anthology* (New York: New American Library, 1970).

33. Pauli Murray, "The Liberation of Black Women," in *Women: A Feminist Perspective*, ed. Jo Freeman (Palo Alto, Calif.: Mayfield, 1975), 351.

34. See, for example, Mae C. King, "Oppression and Power: The Unique Status of the Black Woman in the American Political System," *Social Science Quarterly* 56, no. 1 (1975): 116–28.

35. Frances Beale, "Double Jeopardy: To Be Black and Female," in Cade, ed., *The Black Woman*, 90–100.

36. See Alison Jaggar, *Feminist Politics and Human Nature* (Totowa N.J.: Rowman and Allenheld, 1983); Zillah Eisenstein, ed., *Capitalist Patriarchy and the Case for Socialist Feminism* (New York: Monthly Review Press, 1979); and Lydia Sargent, ed., *Women and Revolution* (Boston: South End Press, 1981).

37. Gloria Joseph, "The Incompatible Ménage à Trois: Marxism, Feminism, and Racism," in *Women and Revolution*, ed. Sargent, 95, 94.

38. See Patricia Hill Collins, *Black Feminist Thought: Knowledge, Consciousness, and the Politics of Empowerment* (Boston: Unwin Hyman, 1990), chap. 1.

39. See Cherríe Moraga, "La güera" (50–59) and "A Long Line of Vendidas" (90–144), in *Loving in the War Years: Lo que nunca pasó por sus labios* (Boston: South End Press, 1983); Alma Garcia, "The Development of Chicana Feminist Discourse," in *The Social Construction of Gender*, ed. Judith Lorber and Susan A. Farrell (Newbury Park, Calif., and London: Sage Publications, 1991), 369–87; and Aida Hurtado, "Relating to Privilege: Seduction and Rejection in the Subordination of White Women and Women of Color," *Signs: Journal of Women in Culture and Society* 14, no. 4 (1989): 833–55.

40. Denise Segura, "Chicanas and Triple Oppression in the Work Force," in *Chicana Voices: Intersections of Class, Race, and Gender*, ed. Teresa Cordova et al. (Austin: Center for Mexican American Studies, 1986), 147–65.

41. Hurtado, "Relating to Privilege," 842–43.

42. Pauli Murray, "The Liberation of Black Women," 352–53.

43. It is perhaps not irrelevant that Elizabeth Spelman's book *Inessential Woman: Problems of Exclusion in Feminist Thought* (Boston: Beacon Press, 1988), which details the position of nonhegemonic women as "not quite women," was heralded as providing "new insight" into areas that women of color have been describing for over a century.

44. Pauli Murray, "The Liberation of Black Women," 362; emphasis in original.

45. Ibid.

46. See Paula Giddings, *When and Where I Enter: The Impact of Black Women on Race and Sex in America* (New York: William Morrow Books, 1984).

47. McClure, "The Issue of Foundations," 365.

48. Barbara Christian, "The Race for Theory," *Feminist Studies* 14, no. 1 (1988): 68.

49. Iris Young, *Justice and the Politics of Difference* (Princeton, N.J.: Princeton University Press, 1990), 102–3.

3. (Be)Coming Out

1. As examples of this early theory, see Radicalesbians, "The Woman-Identified Woman," in *Radical Feminism*, ed. Anne Koedt, Ellen Levine, and Anita Rapone (New York: Times Books, 1973), 240–45; and Charlotte Bunch, "Lesbians in Revolt," in *Passionate Politics: Feminist Theory in Action* (New York: St. Martin's Press, 1987), 161–67.

2. Jean-François Lyotard, *The Postmodern Condition: A Report on Knowledge* (Minnneapolis: University of Minnesota Press, 1984), 8.

3. Sandra Harding, "Feminism, Science, and the Anti-Enlightenment Critiques," in *Feminism/Postmodernism*, ed. Linda J. Nicholson (New York: Routledge, 1990), 87.

4. See Michel Foucault, *Discipline and Punish: The Birth of the Prison* (New York: Vintage Books, 1979) and Thomas L. Dumm, *Democracy and Punishment: Disciplinary Origins of the United States* (Madison: University of Wisconsin Press, 1987).

5. Kathy E. Ferguson, "Interpretation and Genealogy in Feminism," *Signs: Journal of Women in Culture and Society* 16, no. 2 (1990): 324.

6. Lyotard, *The Postmodern Condition*, xxv.

7. See, for example, Michel Foucault, "What Is Enlightenment?" in *The Foucault Reader*, ed. Paul Rabinow (New York: Pantheon Books, 1984), 32–50; David Couzens Hoy, "Foucault: Modern or Postmodern?" in *After Foucault*, ed. Jonathan Arac (New Brunswick, N.J.: Rutgers University Press, 1988), 12–41; and Andreas Huyssen, "Mapping the Postmodern," in *Feminism/Postmodernism*, ed. Nicholson, 234–77.

8. See Jacques Derrida, "Cogito and the History of Madness," in *Writing and Difference*, trans. Alan Bass (Chicago: University of Chicago Press, 1978), 31–63, for Derrida's critique of Foucault. For more general descriptions of Derrida's project see "Structure, Sign, and Play in the Discourse of the Human Sciences," ibid., 278–93, as well as "Différance" (1–27) and "White Mythology: Metaphor in the Text of Philosophy" (207–71) in Jacques Derrida, *Margins of Philosophy*, trans. Alan Bass (Chicago: University of Chicago Press, 1982). See also Jean-François Lyotard, *Discours, figure* (Paris: Klincksieck, 1971), and *The Differend: Phrases in Dispute*, trans. G. Van den Abbeele (Minneapolis: University of Minnesota Press, 1983); and Jean-François Lyotard and Jean-Loup Thebaud, *Just Gaming*, trans. Wlad Godzich (Minneapolis: University of Minnesota Press, 1985).

9. Gayatri Spivak argues that the conflation between the two is the result of U.S. academics' dual fear that postmodernism is insufficiently "political," leading to inactivity, and that "a coherent discourse about political commitment" is inevitably repressive; see Gayatri Chakravorty Spivak, *The Post-*

Colonial Critic: Interviews, Strategies, Dialogues, ed. Sarah Harasym (New York: Routledge, 1990), especially chaps. 2 and 12.

10. Spivak, "In a Word," *differences: A Journal of Feminist Cultural Studies* 1, no. 2 (1989): 124–56.

11. Linda Alcoff, "Cultural Feminism versus Post-Structuralism: The Identity Crisis in Feminist Theory," *Signs: Journal of Women in Culture and Society* 13, no. 3 (1988): 420. For similar expressions of concern see Seyla Benhabib, "Epistemologies of Postmodernism: A Rejoinder to Jean-François Lyotard," in *Feminism/Postmodernism*, ed. Nicholson, 107–30; Christine Di Stefano, "Dilemmas of Difference: Feminism, Modernity, and Postmodernism," in *Feminism/Postmodernism*, ed. Nicholson, 63–82; and Nancy Hartsock, "Rethinking Modernism: Minority vs. Majority Theories," *Cultural Critique* 7 (1987): 187–206.

12. Alcoff, "Cultural Feminism versus Post-Structuralism," 421.

13. Ibid.

14. Mary Poovey, "Feminism and Deconstruction," *Feminist Studies* 14, no. 1 (1988): 60.

15. Iris Marion Young, *Justice and the Politics of Difference* (Princeton, N.J.: Princeton University Press, 1990), 4. I will not here enter into the debate over whether there is a scientific knowledge that can make these claims; I am concerned to establish that such standards are not appropriate for ethical or political judgments.

16. See, for example, Genevieve Lloyd, *The Man of Reason: "Male" and "Female" in Western Philosophy* (Minneapolis: University of Minnesota Press, 1984).

17. See, for example, Christine Di Stefano, "Dilemmas of Difference"; Nancy Hartsock, "Foucault on Power: A Theory for Women?", also in *Feminism/Postmodernism*, ed. Nicholson, 157–75; and Isaac D. Balbus, "Disciplining Women: Michel Foucault and the Power of Feminist Discourse," in *Feminism as Critique*, ed. Seyla Benhabib and Drucilla Cornell (Minneapolis: University of Minnesota Press, 1987), 138–60.

18. Kaja Silverman, "White Skin, Brown Masks: The Double Mimesis; or, With Lawrence in Arabia," *differences: A Journal of Feminist Cultural Studies* 1, no. 3 (1989): 3.

19. The best discussion of this dynamic is still in G. W. F. Hegel, *The Phenomenology of Spirit*, trans. A. V. Miller (Oxford: Oxford University Press, 1977), 119–38. For another perspective that highlights the powerlessness involved in the genesis of subjectivity, see Friedrich Nietzsche, *The Genealogy of Morals*, in *The Birth of Tragedy and The Genealogy of Morals*, trans. Francis Golffing (Garden City, N.Y.: Doubleday, 1956).

20. See Theodor W. Adorno, "Subject and Object," in *The Essential Frankfurt School Reader*, ed. Andrew Arato and Eike Gebhardt (New York: Urizen, 1978), 497–511; and Sandra Harding, *The Science Question in Feminism* (Ithaca, N.Y.: Cornell University Press, 1986).

21. I am referring here to the cluster of theories known as "standpoint the-

ories" of knowledge. For examples see Nancy C. M. Hartsock, "The Feminist Standpoint: Developing the Grounds for a Specifically Feminist Historical Materialism," in *Discovering Reality: Feminist Perspectives on Epistemology, Metaphysics, Methodology, and Philosophy of Science*, ed. Sandra Harding and Merrill Hintikka (Dordrecht, The Netherlands: D. Reidel, 1983), 283–310; and Patricia Hill Collins, *Black Feminist Thought: Knowledge, Consciousness, and the Politics of Empowerment* (Boston: Unwin Hyman, 1990). For a critique of standpoint theories, see Harding, "Feminism, Science, and the Anti-Enlightenment Critiques" and *The Science Question in Feminism*.

22. See, for example, Monique Wittig, "One Is Not Born a Woman," in *The Straight Mind and Other Essays* (Boston: Beacon Press, 1992), 9–20.

23. See Poovey, "Feminism and Deconstruction," 60–61; and Leslie Wahl Rabine, "A Feminist Politics of Non-Identity," *Feminist Studies* 14, no. 1 (1988): 28.

24. For a classic "nature" argument, see James Weinrich, "Reality or Social Construction?" in *Forms of Desire: Sexual Orientation and the Social Constructionist Controversy*, ed. Edward Stein (New York: Garland, 1990), chap. 8. For a discussion of the strategic role of nature, see Steven Epstein, "Gay Politics, Ethnic Identity: The Limits of Social Constructionism," also in *Forms of Desire*, ed. Stein, 239–93.

25. On the role of nature in political argument, see Shane Phelan, "Intimate Distance: The Dislocation of Nature in Modernity," *Western Political Quarterly* 45, no. 2 (1992): 385–402; and Jane Flax, "Postmodernism and Gender Relations in Feminist Theory," in *Feminism/Postmodern*, ed. Nicholson, 39–62.

26. See Luce Irigaray, *Speculum of the Other Woman*, trans. Gillian C. Gill (Ithaca, N.Y.: Cornell University Press, 1985); and *This Sex Which Is Not One*, trans. Catherine Porter (Ithaca, N.Y.: Cornell University Press, 1985).

27. Radicalesbians, "The Woman-Identified Woman," in *Radical Feminism*, ed. Anne Koedt, Ellen Levine, and Anita Rapone (New York: Times Books, 1973), 240.

28. See Rich, "Compulsory Heterosexuality and Lesbian Existence," *Signs: Journal of Women in Culture and Society* 5, no. 4 (1980): 631–60; Nancy Sahli, "Smashing: Women's Relationships Before the Fall," *Chrysalis* 8 (1979): 17–28; Blanche Wiesen Cook, "Female Support Networks and Political Activism," *Chrysalis* 3 (1977): 43–61; Lillian Faderman, *Surpassing the Love of Men* (New York: William Morrow Books, 1981); Ann Ferguson, Kathryn Pyne Addelson, and Jacquelyn N. Zita, "On 'Compulsory Heterosexuality and Lesbian Existence': Defining the Issues," in *Feminist Theory: A Critique of Ideology*, ed. Nannerl O. Keohane, Michelle Z. Rosaldo, and Barbara C. Gelpi (Chicago: University of Chicago Press, 1982), 147–88; and Shane Phelan, *Identity Politics: Lesbian Feminism and the Limits of Community* (Philadelphia: Temple University Press, 1989), chap. 4.

29. Diana Fuss, *Essentially Speaking: Feminism, Nature, and Difference* (New York: Routledge, 1989), 100.

30. Jeffner Allen, *Lesbian Philosophy: Explorations* (Palo Alto, Calif.: Institute of Lesbian Studies, 1986), 90; emphasis in original.

31. Sandra Harding notes the similarities between the descriptions of "women's ethics" and epistemology and those of non-European peoples—a relation that supports the possibility that this ethic is not due to an innate something in women but is the result of structural position. See Harding, *The Science Question in Feminism*, chap. 6.

32. In fact, as Ruth Salvaggio has noted (personal communication, 7 January 1991), many lesbians and other women have a strong capacity for abstraction. The universalization of ethics of care and metaphysics of touch serves to render those women invisible.

33. Barbara Ponse, *Identities in the Lesbian World: The Social Construction of Self* (Westport, Conn.: Greenwood Press, 1978), 208.

34. Mark Blasius, "An Ethos of Lesbian and Gay Existence," *Political Theory* 20, no. 4 (1992): 655.

35. Ponse, *Identities in the Lesbian World*, 23–28.

36. See Linda Silber, "Negotiating Sexual Identity: Non-Lesbians in a Lesbian-Feminist Community," *The Journal of Sex Research* 27, no. 1 (1990): 131–40.

37. "A materialist feminist approach shows that what we take for the cause or origin of oppression is in fact only the mark imposed by the oppressor: the 'myth of woman,' plus its material effects and manifestations in the appropriated consciousness and bodies of women" (Wittig, "One Is Not Born a Woman," 11). I borrow this for lesbians: the "cause" of lesbian oppression is the mark "lesbian," a mark internal to the structure of oppression. Focus on that mark restricts me to the terrain of heterosexual society as normative.

38. Biddy Martin and Chandra Talpade Mohanty, "Feminist Politics: What's Home Got to Do with It?" in *Feminist Studies / Critical Studies*, ed. Teresa de Lauretis (Bloomington: Indiana University Press, 1986), 203.

39. Teresa de Lauretis, "Eccentric Subjects: Feminist Theory and Historical Consciousness," *Feminist Studies* 16 no. 1 (1990): 136.

40. For these debates, see Carole Vance, *Pleasure and Danger: Exploring Female Sexuality* (Boston: Routledge and Kegan Paul, 1984); Joan Nestle, *A Restricted Country* (Ithaca, N.Y.: Firebrand, 1987); Joan Nestle, ed., *The Persistent Desire: A Femme-Butch Reader* (Boston: Alyson, 1992); Madeline D. Davis and Elizabeth Lapovsky Kennedy, "Oral History and the Study of Sexuality in the Lesbian Community: Buffalo, New York, 1940–1960," in *Unequal Sisters: A Multi-Cultural Reader in U.S. Women's History*, ed. Ellen Carol DuBois and Vicki L. Ruiz (New York: Routledge, 1990), 387–99.

41. Ann Ferguson, "Is There a Lesbian Culture?" in *Lesbian Philosophies and Cultures*, ed. Jeffner Allen (Albany: State University of New York Press, 1990), 84; my emphasis.

42. In a related vein, bell hooks argues that the postmodern critique of essentialism allows African-Americans to challenge "a narrow, constricting notion of blackness" that has been enforced from "both the outside and the in-

side." Though sensitive to the dangers and critiques of "postmodern think-ing," she nonetheless sees the challenge to essentialism as empowering for the expression of the diversity of African-American experience (*Yearning: Race, Gender, and Cultural Politics* [Boston: South End Press, 1990], 28–29).

43. For the debates over racial identities, see Mario Barrera, "Chicano Class Structure" (130–38), and Vine Deloria Jr., "Identity and Culture" (94–103), in *From Different Shores: Perspectives on Race and Ethnicity in America*, ed. Ronald Takaki (New York: Oxford University Press, 1987); and Michael Omi and Howard Winant, *Racial Formation in the United States from the 1960s to the 1980s* (New York: Routledge and Kegan Paul, 1986).

44. De Lauretis, "Eccentric Subjects," 144.

4. Lesbians and Mestizas

1. Combahee River Collective, "A Black Feminist Statement," in *All the Women Are White, All the Blacks Are Men, but Some of Us Are Brave: Black Women's Studies*, ed. Gloria T. Hull, Patricia Bell Scott, and Barbara Smith (New York: The Feminist Press, 1982), 13.

2. See Trinh T. Minh-ha, ed., *She, The Inappropriate/d Other* (single topic volume, *Discourse* 8 [1986/87]).

3. Michael Omi and Howard Winant, *Racial Formation in the United States from the 1960s to the 1980s* (New York: Routledge and Kegan Paul, 1986), 15.

4. Daniel Bell, "Ethnicity and Social Change," in *Ethnicity: Theory and Experience*, ed. Nathan Glazer and Daniel Patrick Moynihan (Cambridge: Harvard University Press, 1975), 169.

5. Omi and Winant, *Racial Formation in the United States*, 52.

6. Vine Deloria Jr., "Identity and Culture," in *From Different Shores: Per-spectives on Race and Ethnicity in America*, ed. Ronald Takaki (New York: Oxford University Press, 1987), 97.

7. Mario Barrera, "Chicano Class Structure," in Takaki, ed., *From Dif-ferent Shores*, 130–38.

8. Omi and Winant, *Racial Formation in the United States*, 33.

9. Deloria, "Identity and Culture," 100.

10. I exclude Jews here: Jews are not all European, and even Ashkenazim (European Jews) do not agree on whether they are "white" or not. The status of Jews is a wonderful example of the instability of racial articulations, as well as the extreme discomfort that such instability causes many (that is, anti-Semitism).

11. I do not want to equate ethnicity and race here. As Omi and Winant make clear, the ethnicity paradigm for understanding race has been liberal at best and reactionary at worst in its implications. For more discussion see Omi and Winant, *Racial Formation in the United States*. For a sweeping discussion of the sexuality-as-ethnicity debates, see Steven Epstein, "Gay Politics, Ethnic

Identity: The Limits of Social Constructionism," in *Forms of Desire: Sexual Orientation and the Social Constructionist Controversy*, ed. Edward Stein (New York: Garland, 1990), 239–93.

12. Kobena Mercer, " '1968': Periodizing Politics and Identity," in *Cultural Studies*, ed. Lawrence Grossberg, Cary Nelson, and Paula Treichler (New York: Routledge, 1992), 434.

13. See Epstein, "Gay Politics, Ethnic Identity," 244–51.

14. This phrase is that of Harold Isaacs in "Basic Group Identity: The Idols of the Tribe," in *Ethnicity*, ed. Glazer and Moynihan, 30.

15. Barbara Ponse, *Identities in the Lesbian World* (Westport, Conn.: Greenwood Press, 1978), 24–29.

16. Ibid., 124–133.

17. Omi and Winant, *Racial Formation in the United States*, 60.

18. For examples, see Celia Kitzinger, *The Social Construction of Lesbianism* (London [England] and Newbury Park, Calif.: Sage Publications, 1987).

19. I have in mind here especially the work of Mary Daly, and also Adrienne Rich's 1980 argument. See Mary Daly, *Gyn/Ecology* (Boston: Beacon Press, 1978) and *Pure Lust* (Boston: Beacon Press, 1982); and Adrienne Rich, "Compulsory Heterosexuality and Lesbian Existence," *Signs: Journal of Women in Culture and Society* 5, no. 4 (Summer 1980): 631–60.

20. Judy Grahn, *Another Mother Tongue: Gay Words, Gay Worlds* (Boston: Beacon Press, 1984), xiii–xiv.

21. See, for example, *Another Mother Tongue*, 139–44, where Grahn derives the epithet "bulldyke" from the name of the Celtic queen Boudica without any evidence that Boudica slept with or desired women; Boudica's claim to ancestral status is her independence and strength rather than her sexuality.

22. Scott Bravmann, "Invented Traditions: Take One on the Lesbian and Gay Past," *NWSA Journal* 3, no. 1 (Winter 1991): 86.

23. Matters are no less complex when the subjects of appropriation are modern whites who did not choose the identity of lesbians. Adopting independent women as heroes or inspirations is not problematic; adopting them as ancestors is. Each adoption amounts to a retrospective redefinition of these people into terms that were not available to them, or that were available and were rejected.

24. Grahn, *Another Mother Tongue*, xiv.

25. See, for example, Kathleen M. Blee, *Women of the Klan: Racism and Gender in the 1920s* (Berkeley and Los Angeles: University of California Press, 1991); Claudia Koonz, *Mothers in the Fatherland* (New York: St. Martin's Press, 1987); and Randy Shilts, *Conduct Unbecoming: Gays and Lesbians in the U.S. Military* (New York: St. Martin's, 1993). Although Shilts does not document active racism among gays and lesbians, his subjects almost uniformly desire to serve in the U.S. military, finding no difficulty with its mission as a colonizing force.

26. Peter K. Eisinger, "Ethnicity as a Strategic Option: An Emerging View," *Public Administration Review* 38, no. 1 (January-February 1978): 90.

27. See Donald L. Horowitz, "Ethnic Identity," in Glazer and Moynihan, *Ethnicity*, ed. Glazer and Moynihan, 114.

28. Ernesto Laclau and Chantal Mouffe, *Hegemony and Socialist Strategy: Towards a Radical Democratic Politics* (London and New York: Verso, 1985), 95.

29. Ibid., 113.

30. Gloria Anzaldúa, *Borderlands / La frontera: The New Mestiza* (San Francisco: Spinsters / Aunt Lute, 1987).

31. John A. Garcia, "Yo Soy Mexicano . . . : Self-Identity and Sociodemographic Correlates," *Social Science Quarterly* 62, no. 1 (1981): 89.

32. Garcia found that "Chicano" was generally used by younger respondents and those with higher education levels than other groups, and was virtually absent among those born in Mexico.

33. Anzaldúa, *Borderlands / La frontera*, 80.

34. Anzaldúa, "Bridge, Drawbridge, Sandbar or Island: Lesbians-of-Color *Hacienda Alianzas*," in *Bridges of Power: Women's Multicultural Alliances*, ed. Lisa Albrecht and Rose M. Brewer (Philadelphia: New Society Publishers, 1990), 216–31.

35. Ibid., p. 223.

36. Ontological separatism is often espoused in writing by women who do not publicly identify as separatists, such as Mary Daly and Sonia Johnson. For descriptions of and arguments for what I am calling political separatism, see K. Hess, Jean Langford, and Kathy Ross, "Comparative Separatism," in *For Lesbians Only: A Separatist Anthology*, ed. Sarah Lucia Hoaglund and Julia Penelope (London: Only Women Press, 1988), 125–32; Bette S. Tallen, "Lesbian Separatism: A Historical and Comparative Perspective," in *For Lesbians Only*, ed. Hoagland and Penelope, 132–45; and Sarah Lucia Hoagland, *Lesbian Ethics: Toward New Value* (Palo Alto, Calif.: Institute of Lesbian Studies, 1988).

37. See Norma Alarcón, "The Theoretical Subject(s) of *This Bridge Called My Back* and Anglo-American Feminism," in *Making Face, Making Soul / Haciendo caras*, ed. Gloria Anzaldúa (San Francisco: Aunt Lute Foundation, 1990), 356–69; and Cherríe Moraga, "A Long Line of Vendidas," in *Loving in the War Years: Lo que nunca pasó por sus labios* (Boston: South End Press, 1983), 90–144.

38. Laclau and Mouffe, *Hegemony and Socialist Strategy*, 138.

39. Jacquelyn N. Zita, "Lesbian Body Journeys: Desire Making Difference," in *Lesbian Philosophies and Cultures*, ed. Jeffner Allen (Albany: State University of New York Press, 1990), 342.

40. Anzaldúa, *Borderlands / La frontera*, 79.

41. See Nancy Fraser, *Unruly Practices: Power, Discourse, and Gender in Contemporary Social Theory* (Minneapolis: University of Minnesota Press, 1989), chap. 4; and Gayatri Chakravorty Spivak, *The Post-Colonial Critic: Interviews, Strategies, Dialogues*, ed. Sarah Harasym (New York: Routledge, 1990), 13.

42. Spivak, *The Post-Colonial Critic*, 18.

43. Iris Marion Young, *Justice and the Politics of Difference* (Princeton, N.J.: Princeton University Press, 1990), 98.

44. "There are at least two ways in which lesbianism has been isolated in feminist discourse: the homophobic oversight and relegation of it to the margins, and the lesbian-feminist centering of it, which has had at times the paradoxical effect of removing lesbianism and sexuality from their embeddedness in social relations" (Biddy Martin and Chandra Tolpade Mohanty, "Feminist Politics: What's Home Got to Do with It?" in *Feminist Studies / Critical Studies*, ed. Teresa de Lauretis [Bloomington: Indiana University Press, 1986], 203).

45. Ann Ferguson makes a similar argument about the conditions of existence for lesbians in her response to Adrienne Rich, "Patriarchy, Sexual Identity, and the Sexual Revolution," in *Feminist Theory: A Critique of Ideology*, ed. Nannerl O. Keohane, Michelle Z. Rosaldo, and Barbara C. Gelpi (Chicago: University of Chicago Press, 1982), 147–61. See also Ann Ferguson, "Is There a Lesbian Culture?", in *Lesbian Philosophies and Cultures*, ed. Allen, 82.

46. Gloria Anzaldúa, "Bridge, Drawbridge, Sandbar or Island."

47. In these cases, the question is not whether it is fair to the cited source to use the source's ideas, but whether such use does not constitute co-optation or colonization by privileging the work of such an author.

48. See Nancy Caraway, *Segregated Sisterhood* (Knoxville: University of Tennessee Press, 1991).

49. I am extending this charge only to white women because middle-class members of other racial groups are often extremely conscious of where their class locates them in their communities; middle-classness may be unremarkable in white communities, but not among people of color.

50. Mercer, " '1968,' " 434. On this problem, see also Catharine Stimpson, " 'Thy Neighbor's Wife, Thy Neighbor's Servants': Women's Liberation and Black Civil Rights," in *Woman in Sexist Society: Studies in Power and Powerlessness*, ed. Vivian Gornick and Barbara K. Moran (New York: Basic Books, 1971), 622–57.

51. Trinh T. Minh-ha, "Not You / Like You: Post-Colonial Women and the Interlocking Questions of Identity and Difference," in *Making Face, Making Soul / Haciendo caras*, ed. Anzaldúa, 372.

52. Ibid., 375.

53. Ibid.

54. Although *différance* is not so absolute as "difference" in its closures or oppositions, *différance* suffers from the temptation to evade location rather than specify it, producing an "antiessentialism" that is politically anemic. For the concept of "identity points," see Teresa de Lauretis, "Feminist Studies / Critical Studies: Issues, Terms, and Contexts," in *Feminist Studies / Critical Studies*, ed. de Lauretis, 9.

55. I thank Iris Young for this question.

56. Anzaldúa, "Bridge, Drawbridge, Sandbar or Island," 218; emphasis in original.

57. For the notion of "world traveling," see Maria Lugones, "Playfulness, 'World'-Travelling, and Loving Perception," in *Making Face, Making Soul / Haciendo caras*, ed. Anzaldúa, 390–402.

58. Anzaldúa, *Borderlands / La frontera*, 79.

59. Thanks to Nancy Love for pointing out this distinction to me.

60. Nancy C. M. Hartsock, *Money, Sex and Power: Toward a Feminist Historical Materialism* (Boston: Northeastern University Press, 1983).

61. Cherríe Moraga and Gloria Anzaldúa, *This Bridge Called My Back: Writings by Radical Women of Color*, 2d ed. (New York: Kitchen Table, Women of Color Press, 1983).

62. Norma Alarcón, "The Theoretical Subject(s) of *This Bridge Called My Back* and Anglo-American Feminism," in *Making Face, Making Soul / Haciendo caras*, ed. Anzaldúa, 364.

63. Ibid.

64. Ibid., 365.

65. Bernice Johnson Reagon, "Coalition Politics: Turning the Century," in *Home Girls: A Black Feminist Anthology*, ed. Barbara Smith (New York: Kitchen Table, Women of Color Press, 1983), 356–68.

66. See Omi and Winant, *Racial Formation in the United States*; Adolph L. Reed Jr., "Black Particularity Reconsidered," *Telos* 39 (Spring 1979): 71–93.

67. Zita, "Lesbian Body Journeys," 329.

5. Getting Specific about Community

1. George Hillery, "Definitions of Community: Areas of Agreement," *Rural Sociology* 20 (1955): 114.

2. Ibid., 117.

3. Thomas Bender, *Community and Social Change in America* (New Brunswick, N.J.: Rutgers University Press, 1978), 8.

4. R. M. MacIver and Charles Page, *Society* (New York: Macmillan, 1962), 8–9; emphasis in original.

5. Anthony Black, *State, Community, and Human Desire: A Group-Centred Account of Political Values* (New York: St. Martin's Press, 1988), 87.

6. Judy Grahn, *Another Mother Tongue: Gay Words, Gay Worlds* (Boston: Beacon Press, 1985). Note that for Grahn "lesbian" fits into the larger rubric of "gay," though she acknowledges certain differences. This subsumption is as problematic as the general ascription of sexual identities across times and cultures.

7. Julia Stanley, "Lesbian Relationships and the Vision of Community," *Feminary* 9, no. 1 (1978): 6.

8. Ibid., 6–7.

9. Sheldon Wolin, *Politics and Vision: Continuity and Innovation in Western Political Thought* (Boston: Little, Brown, 1960), 97.

10. Iris Marion Young, *Justice and the Politics of Difference* (Princeton, N.J.: Princeton University Press, 1991), 235.

11. Jean-Luc Nancy, *The Inoperative Community* (Minneapolis: University of Minnesota Press, 1991), 152.

12. Ibid., 2.

13. Ibid., xxxviii.

14. For a lucid discussion that links identity as sameness with personal identity see Ed Cohen, "Who Are 'We'? Gay 'Identity' as Political (E)motion (A Theoretical Rumination)," in *Inside/Out: Lesbian Theories, Gay Theories*, ed. Diana Fuss (New York: Routledge, 1991), 71–92.

15. Nancy, *The Inoperative Community*, xxxviii; emphasis in original.

16. Robert Nisbet, *The Sociological Tradition* (New York: Basic Books, 1966), 48.

17. Jean-Luc Nancy, "Of Being-In-Common," in *Community at Loose Ends*, ed. Miami Theory Collective (Minneapolis: University of Minnesota Press, 1991), 9.

18. Nancy, *The Inoperative Community*, 29; emphasis in original.

19. Ibid., 24; emphasis in original.

20. Sarah Lucia Hoagland, *Lesbian Ethics: Toward New Value* (Palo Alto, Calif.: Institute of Lesbian Studies, 1988), 3.

21. See Stanley, "Lesbian Relationships and the Vision of Community," 5; and Hoagland, *Lesbian Ethics*, 9.

22. Teresa de Lauretis, "Eccentric Subjects: Feminist Theory and Historical Consciousness," *Feminist Studies* 16, no. 1 (1990): 138.

23. Denyse Lockard, "The Lesbian Community: An Anthropological Approach," in *Anthropology and Homosexual Behavior*, ed. Evelyn Blackwood (Binghamton, N.Y.: The Haworth Press, 1986), 90.

24. See Mary P. Follett, "Community Is a Process," *The Philosophical Review* 28, no. 6 (1920): 576–88.

25. Ibid., 580–81.

26. See John D'Emilio, *Sexual Politics, Sexual Communities: The Making of a Homosexual Minority in the United States, 1940–1970* (Chicago: University of Chicago Press, 1983); and Toby Marotta, *The Politics of Homosexuality* (Boston: Houghton Mifflin Company, 1981).

27. Objectives quoted in Barry D. Adam, *The Rise of a Gay and Lesbian Movement* (Boston: Twayne, 1987), 64. Note that these discussions, framed as they were within the hegemonic views on lesbianism, broke invisibility without necessarily providing insulation from hostility. Members often sat and listened to "professional" speakers lecture on the sickness and pathetic nature of the homosexual. While (perhaps) better than public attack, it is a far cry from that to true insulation.

28. Barbara Ponse, *Identities in the Lesbian World* (Westport, Conn.: Greenwood Press, 1978); Joan Nestle, *A Restricted Country* (Ithaca, N.Y.:

Firebrand Books, 1987); and Audre Lorde, *Zami: A New Spelling of My Name* (Trumansburg, N.Y.: The Crossing Press, 1983).

29. See Alice Echols, *Daring to Be Bad: Radical Feminism in America, 1967–1975* (Minneapolis: University of Minnesota Press, 1989).

30. See Sara M. Evans and Harry C. Boyte, *Free Spaces: The Sources of Democratic Change in America*, 2d ed. (Chicago: University of Chicago Press, 1992).

31. Cynthia Ozick, quoted in Letty Cottin Pogrebin, *Deborah, Golda, and Me: Being Female and Jewish in America* (New York: Crown Publishers, 1991), 50.

32. Susan Moller Okin, *Justice, Gender, and the Family* (New York: Basic Books, 1989).

33. See Allan Bloom, *The Closing of the American Mind* (New York: Simon and Schuster, 1987), 379; Nancy Hartsock, "Foucault on Power: A Theory for Women?" in *Feminism/Postmodernism*, ed. Linda J. Nicholson (New York: Routledge, 1990), 157–75; Christine Di Stefano, "Dilemmas of Difference: Feminism, Modernity, and Postmodernism," also in *Feminism/Postmodernism*, ed. Nicholson, 63–82; and Barbara Christian, "The Race for Theory," *Feminist Studies* 14, no. 1 (1988): 68.

34. M. Jacqui Alexander, "Redrafting Morality: The Postcolonial State and the Sexual Offences Bill of Trinidad and Tobago," in *Third World Women and the Politics of Feminism*, ed. Chandra Talpade Mohanty, Ann Russo, and Lourdes Torres (Bloomington: Indiana University Press, 1991), 133–52.

35. Lesbians of Color, "Loving and Struggling," in *Piece of My Heart: A Lesbian of Colour Anthology*, anthologized by Makeda Silvera (Toronto: Sister Vision Press, 1991), 163.

36. Ibid.

37. Ibid., 164.

38. bell hooks, *Feminist Theory: From Margin to Center* (Boston: South End Press, 1984), chap. 2.

6. The Space of Justice

1. Stuart Hall has commented on the problem of AIDS for cultural studies. He asks: "Against the urgency of people dying in the streets, what in God's name is the point of cultural studies? . . . On the other hand, in the end, I don't agree with the way in which this dilemma is often posed for us, for it is indeed a more complex and displaced question than just people dying out there. The question of AIDS is an extremely important terrain of struggle and contestation. . . . AIDS is the site at which the advance of sexual politics is being rolled back. It's a site at which not only people will die, but desire and pleasure will also die if certain metaphors do not survive, or survive in the wrong way" (Stuart Hall, "Cultural Studies and Its Theoretical Legacies," in

Cultural Studies, ed. Lawrence Grossberg, Cary Nelson, and Paula Treichler [New York: Routledge, 1992], 284–85).

2. Diana Fuss, *Essentially Speaking: Feminism, Nature, and Difference* (New York: Routledge, 1989), 105.

3. Judith Butler, *Gender Trouble: Feminism and the Subversion of Identity* (New York: Routledge, 1989), 14.

4. There is great ideological disparity even in these words. The "preference" language is liberal, implying a purely private desire along the lines of consumer choice. The "orientation" discourse is denser, aiming at suggesting an enduring, probably innate, facet of one's identity. I include both terms here because both have been used in lesbian identity politics, and the oscillation from one to the other continues even as "orientation" becomes the legal term of choice.

5. Murray Edelman, "The Gay Vote, 1990: Preliminary Findings," paper presented at the annual meeting of the American Political Science Association, Washington, D.C., August-September 1991. Approval ratings of George Bush were most striking: when asked "Do you approve or disapprove of the way George Bush is handling his job as President?" the total ratio was 57 approve / 40 disapprove, the ratio for "all women" was 54/42, that for gay men was 45/53, and that for lesbians was 32/60. When asked whether they considered themselves liberal, moderate, or conservative, the total was 18/46/33; gay men, 47/41/9; lesbians, 48/38/13.

6. Ruthann Robson, *Lesbian (Out)law: Survival under the Rule of Law* (Ithaca, N.Y.: Firebrand Books, 1992), 19. It should be noted that the division between outlaw and solid citizen here is not the same as the "good girl / bad girl" split of the 1980s "sex wars." There, many of those who would be "outlaws" in Robson's sense because of their feminist agenda were "good girls" in their critique and/or rejection of sadomasochism and butch/femme For a review of those debates, see Shane Phelan, *Identity Politics: Lesbian Feminism and the Limits of Community* (Philadelphia: Temple University Press, 1989), chap. 6; and Carole Vance, "Pleasure and Danger: Toward a Politics of Sexuality," in *Pleasure and Danger: Exploring Female Sexuality*, ed. Carol Vance (Boston and London: Routledge and Kegan Paul, 1984), 1–27.

7. See Martha Minow, *Making All The Difference: Inclusion, Exclusion, and American Law* (Cambridge: Harvard University Press, 1990), passim.

8. Ibid.

9. Ibid., 134.

10. Theodore Lowi, *The End of Liberalism: The Second Republic of the United States*, 2d ed. (New York: W. W. Norton, 1979), 51.

11. Albert O. Hirschman, *The Passions and the Interests: Political Arguments for Capitalism before Its Triumph* (Princeton, N.J.: Princeton University Press, 1977), 32.

12. Ibid., 54.

13. James Madison, No. 10, in *The Federalist Papers* (New York: New American Library, 1961), 79.

14. Anna G. Jonasdottir, "On the Concept of Interest, Women's Interests, and the Limitations of Interest Theory," in *The Political Interests of Gender*, ed. Kathleen B. Jones and Anna G. Jonasdottir (London [England] and Newbury Park, Calif.: Sage Publications, 1988), 39–40. See also Isaac Balbus, "The Concept of Interest in Pluralist and Marxian Analysis," *Politics and Society* 1, no. 2 (1971): 151–77; William E. Connolly, "On 'Interests' in Politics," *Politics and Society* 2, no. 4 (1972): 459–77; and Irene Diamond and Nancy Hartsock, "Beyond Interests in Politics: A Comment on Virginia Sapiro's 'When Are Interests Interesting? The Problem of Political Representation of Women,'" *American Political Science Review* 75, no. 3 (1981): 717–23.

15. Martha Ackelsberg, "Communities, Resistance, and Women's Activism," in *Women and the Politics of Empowerment*, ed. Ann Bookman and Sandra Morgen (Philadelphia: Temple University Press, 1988), 298.

16. If the farmer does make such a decision, all hell will break loose in American politics. For the behavior of the national and state governments makes clear that they expect their citizens to construe their interest as narrowly as possible.

17. Michael Walzer, *Spheres of Justice: A Defense of Pluralism and Equality* (New York: Basic Books, 1983), 62.

18. Anne Phillips makes this point about women's participation when she says that "the crucial requirement is for women's political presence: which is not to say that only women can speak on 'women's' issues, that women must speak only as a sex" (Anne Phillips, *Engendering Democracy* [University Park, Pa.: The Pennsylvania State University Press, 1991], 167).

19. For discussion of the interpenetration of sexism and homophobia in the U.S. military see Randy Shilts, *Conduct Unbecoming: Gays and Lesbians in the U.S. Military* (New York: St. Martin's Press, 1993).

7. Oppression, Liberation, and Power

1. Iris Marion Young, *Justice and the Politics of Difference* (Princeton, N.J.: Princeton University Press, 1990), 37.

2. Ibid., 22; quoted from Michael Walzer, *Spheres of Justice: A Defense of Pluralism and Equality* (New York: Basic Books, 1983), 7. Nancy Fraser, *Unruly Practices: Power, Discourse and Gender in Contemporary Social Theory* (Minneapolis: University of Minnesota Press, 1989), 162.

3. Young, *Justice and the Politics of Difference*, 49.

4. Ibid., 53.

5. Ibid., 56.

6. Ibid., 59.

7. For the extensive debates among feminists about the use of the Marxist model, see, for example, Lydia Sargent, ed., *Women and Revolution* (Boston: South End, 1981); Zillah Eisenstein, *Capitalist Patriarchy and the Case for*

Socialist Feminism (New York: Monthly Review Press, 1979); Alison Jaggar, *Feminist Politics and Human Nature* (Totowa, N.J.: Rowman and Allenheld, 1983); and Ann Ferguson, *Blood at the Root* (London: Pandora, 1989) and *Sexual Democracy* (Boulder, Colo.: Westview Press, 1991).

8. Aida Hurtado, "Relating to Privilege: Seduction and Rejection in the Subordination of White Women and Women of Color," *Signs: Journal of Women in Culture and Society* 14, no. 4 (Summer 1989): 843.

9. See Shilts, *Conduct Unbecoming: Gays and Lesbians in the U.S. Military* (New York: St. Martin's Press, 1993), bk. 5, especially chap. 52.

10. Donna Haraway discusses this problem in relation to fetuses and jaguars: the issue is, Who speaks for the jaguar? She describes the ways in which the "liberal logic of representation" works by distancing: "the power of life and death must be delegated to the epistemologically most disinterested ventriloquist," a delegation that works to "disempower precisely those—in our case, the pregnant woman and the peoples of the forest—who are 'close' to the now-represented 'natural' object," making the represented the object rather than the initiator or partner in action" (Donna Haraway, "The Promises of Monsters: A Regenerative Politics for Inappropriate/d Others," in *Cultural Studies*, ed. Lawrence Grossberg, Cary Nelson, and Paula Treichler [New York and London: Routledge, 1992], 312).

11. Indeed, it should be acknowledged that the word "oppression" as a description of the problem carries this sense of power as weight with it. It may be that abandoning the liberation model will require abandoning the metaphor of oppression as well.

12. For classic examples, see John Locke, *Two Treatises of Government*, and John Stuart Mill, *On Liberty*.

13. For a classic exposition, see V. I. Lenin, *The State and Revolution* (New York: International Publishers, 1969).

14. Dennis Fischman, *Political Discourse in Exile* (Amherst: University of Massachusetts Press, 1991), 112.

15. This makes clear what was wrong with Senator Sam Nunn's proposed "compromise" on "gays" in the military. His suggestion—"(We) don't ask, (you) don't tell"—allowed for continued invisibility of gays and lesbians. While the end of witch-hunts would be progress, this proposal didn't begin to allow lesbians and gays to serve. What if I do tell? What if I don't say "lesbian," but I mention my partner and bring her to events? If that's not acceptable, how many heterosexuals would tolerate such restrictions?

16. Jean Baker Miller, "Women and Power," in *Rethinking Power*, ed. Thomas Wartenburg (Albany: State University of New York Press, 1992), 247.

17. Ernesto Laclau, *New Reflections on the Revolution of Our Time* (London: Verso, 1990), 33.

18. William E. Connolly, *The Terms of Political Discourse*, 2d ed. (Princeton, N.J.: Princeton University Press, 1983), chap. 1.

19. Hannah Arendt, "Communicative Power," in *Power*, ed. Steven Lukes (New York: New York University Press, 1986), 64.

20. Nancy Hartsock, *Money, Sex, and Power: Toward a Feminist Historical Materialism* (Boston: Northeastern University Press, 1983), 218.

21. Arendt, "Communicative Power," 71.

22. Hannah Arendt, *On Violence* (New York: Harcourt, Brace, and World, 1969), 44; cited in Hartsock, *Money, Sex, and Power*, 218.

23. Ernesto Laclau and Chantal Mouffe, *Hegemony and Socialist Strategy: Towards a Radical Democracy* (London: Verso, 1985), 189.

24. For a more extended discussion of the relation of lesbians to medical discourse, see Shane Phelan, *Identity Politics: Lesbian Feminism and the Limits of Community* (Philadelphia: Temple University Press, 1989), chap. 2.

25. Even as I write this I am cognizant of the usefulness of the medical model. William F. Buckley, long a foe of homosexuals, wrote a column in which he asserted that homosexuality appears to be a fixed feature, "genetic," in his terms. On this basis, he challenges the "compromise" whereby gays could serve in the military if they had no sex, on or off base: "to demand of gays that they have no sexual life in the military, even off base, is to impose upon a class the requirements of celibate life. And the question arises whether that is a sacrifice that is simply unreasonable." He does not move to say that the ban must fall, but his argument manifests the progressive force in the biological determinist argument (William F. Buckley, "Gays in Military Issue Far from Settled," *Albuquerque Journal*, 27 May 1993).

26. See Ian Shapiro, *The Evolution of Rights in Liberal Ideology* (Cambridge: Cambridge University Press, 1986), chap. 1.

27. See Peter Bachrach and Morton Baratz, "Two Faces of Power," *American Political Science Review* 56, no. 4 (1962): 947–52.

28. Patricia Williams, *The Alchemy of Race and Rights* (Cambridge: Harvard University Press, 1991), 152; emphasis in original.

29. Mark Blasius, "An Ethical Basis for Lesbian and Gay Politics in the Relational Right," paper presented at the Seventh International Conference on Social Philosophy, Colorado College, August 1991, 24–25.

30. Ibid., 15.

31. Thomas B. Stoddard, "Why Gay People Should Seek the Right to Marry," *Out/Look: National Lesbian and Gay Quarterly*, no. 6 (1989): 9–13; and Paula L. Ettelbrick, "Since When Is Marriage a Path to Liberation?" *Out/Look: National Lesbian and Gay Quarterly*, no. 6 (1989): 9, 14–17.

32. On the need for such a specific universalism, see Ernesto Laclau, "Community and Its Paradoxes: Richard Rorty's 'Liberal Utopia,' " in *Community at Loose Ends*, ed. Miami Theory Collective (Minneapolis: University of Minnesota Press, 1991), 97; and Chantal Mouffe, "Radical Democracy: Modern or Postmodern?", in *Universal Abandon: The Politics of Postmodernism*, ed. Andrew Ross (Minneapolis: University of Minnesota Press, 1988), 36.

33. Karl Marx, "On the Jewish Question," in *Karl Marx: Selected Writings*, ed. David McLellan (Oxford: Oxford University Press, 1977), 39–62.

34. As of this writing, the Hawaii Supreme Court has issued a ruling that, while not providing for same-sex marriage, has opened the door. In *Baehr* v. *Lewin* (1993 WL 14262 [Hawaii], the court ruled that restrictions on the basis of sex are subject to "strict scrutiny" and that therefore the Hawaii marriage statute (HRS 572–1 [1985]) "is presumed to be unconstitutional unless it can be shown that the statute's sex-based classification is justified by compelling state interests and that it is narrowly drawn to avoid unnecessary abridgements of constitutional rights." Because "it does not appear beyond doubt" that the restrictions are unconstitutional, the Hawaii Supreme Court remanded the case to the circuit court. A bill specifically banning same-sex marriages has since been introduced in the Hawaii legislature.

35. See Kathy E. Ferguson, *The Feminist Case against Bureaucracy* (Philadelphia: Temple University Press, 1984).

36. For San Francisco, see Randy Shilts, *The Mayor of Castro Street: The Life and Times of Harvey Milk* (New York: St. Martin's Press, 1982); for the military, see Shilts, *Conduct Unbecoming.*

Interlude II

1. Neil Miller, *In Search of Gay America: Women and Men in a Time of Change* (New York: Atlantic Monthly Press, 1989).

2. Marilyn Frye, *The Politics of Reality: Essays in Feminist Theory* (Trumansburg, N.Y.: The Crossing Press, 1983).

3. *Albuquerque Tribune,* 29 March 1993, 1.

4. Richard Mohr develops the analogy to religion more extensively in *Gays/Justice* (New York: Columbia University Press, 1988).

8. Alliances and Coalitions

1. Gayatri Spivak, *In Other Worlds: Essays in Cultural Politics* (New York: Routledge, 1988), 103.

2. Sandra Harding, *Whose Science? Whose Knowledge? Thinking From Women's Lives* (Ithaca, N.Y.: Cornell University Press, 1991), 252.

3. On justice as distributive, see Iris Marion Young, *Justice and the Politics of Difference* (Princeton, N.J.: Princeton University Press, 1990).

4. Michel Foucault, "Friendship as a Way of Life," in *Foucault Live,* trans. John Johnston, ed. Sylvère Lotringer (New York: Semiotext(e), 1989), 203–9.

5. Donna Haraway, "A Manifesto for Cyborgs," in *Feminism/Postmodernism,* ed. Linda J. Nicholson (New York and London: Routledge, 1990), 197.

6. This is the point of the title of the landmark text in Black women's studies, *All the Women Are White, All the Blacks Are Men, but Some of Us*

Are Brave, ed. Gloria T. Hull, Patricia Bell Scott, and Barbara Smith (New York: The Feminist Press, 1982). For an extensive discussion of this point, see Kimberle Crenshaw, "Demarginalizing the Intersection of Race and Sex: A Black Feminist Critique of Antidiscrimination Doctrine, Feminist Theory and Antiracist Politics," in *Feminist Legal Theory: Foundations*, ed. D. Kelly Weisberg (Philadelphia: Temple University Press, 1993), 383–95.

7. See Ozick's comment in chap. 5.

8. Mark Thompson, introduction to *Gay Spirit: Myth and Meaning*, ed. Mark Thompson (New York: St. Martin's Press, 1987), xi.

9. Marshall Kirk and Hunter Madsen, *After the Ball: How America Will Conquer Its Fear and Hatred of Gays in the 90's* (New York: Penguin Books, 1989), 379.

10. Ibid., 180.

11. Audre Lorde, *Zami: A New Spelling of My Name (A Biomythography)* (Trumansburg, N.Y.: The Crossing Press, 1982), 226.

12. Elizabeth V. Spelman, *Inessential Woman: Problems of Exclusion in Feminist Thought* (Boston: Beacon Press, 1988), 13.

13. On individualism as a language that inhibits public discourse among white U.S. citizens, see Robert Bellah et al., *Habits of the Heart* (Berkeley and Los Angeles: University of California Press, 1985).

14. See Kirstie McClure, "Postmodernity and the Subject of Rights," paper delivered at the meetings of the Western Political Science Association, Newport Beach, California, March 1990.

15. For a discussion of social formations as historically specific and "imagined," see Benedict Anderson, *Imagined Communities: Reflections on the Origins and Spread of Nationalism* (London: Verso, 1983). The most impressive example of personal recognition and exploration of these bonds by a white person remains Minnie Bruce Pratt's essay "Identity: Blood Skin Heart," in Minnie Bruce Pratt, Barbara Smith, and Elly Bulkin, *Yours in Struggle: Three Feminist Perspectives on Anti-Semitism and Racism* (Brooklyn, N.Y.: Long Haul Press, 1984). Rather than discuss that work here, I recommend that every reader of this book drop everything and read it!

16. See Joan W. Scott, "Experience," in *Feminists Theorize the Political*, ed. Judith Butler and Joan W. Scott (New York: Routledge, 1992), 22–40.

17. See John D'Emilio, *Sexual Politics, Sexual Communities: The Making of a Homosexual Minority in the United States, 1940–1970* (Chicago: University of Chicago Press, 1983).

18. See Sara M. Evans and Harry C. Boyte, *Free Spaces: The Sources of Democratic Change in America*, 2d ed. (Chicago: University of Chicago Press, 1992).

19. Audre Lorde, "I Am Your Sister: Black Women Organizing across Sexualities," in *A Burst of Light* (Ithaca, N.Y.: Firebrand Books, 1988), 19–26.

20. This description relies on Milo Yellow Hair's documentary, *In the Spirit of Crazy Horse*, which describes the struggles of the Sioux from the 1860s to the present.

21. Kirk and Madsen, *After the Ball*, 257; emphasis in original.

22. Bernice Johnson Reagon, "Coalition Politics: Turning the Century" in *Home Girls: A Black Feminist Anthology*, ed. Barbara Smith (New York: Kitchen Table, Women of Color Press, 1983), 358.

23. Arlene Stein, "Sisters and Queers: The Decentering of Lesbian Feminism," *Socialist Review* 22, no. 1 (1992): 33–55.

24. See Stacey Young, "Bisexual Theory and the Postmodern Dilemma; or, What's in a Name?", paper presented at the fifth annual Lesbian and Gay Studies Conference, Rutgers University, November 1991.

25. Lisa Duggan, "Making It Perfectly Queer," *Socialist Review* 22, no. 1 (January-March 1992): 20.

26. See Gayatri Chakravorty Spivak, "The Practical Politics of the Open End," in *The Post-Colonial Critic: Interviews, Strategies, Dialogues* (New York and London: Routledge, 1990), 95–112.

27. Samuel Delany, introduction to *Uranian Worlds: A Reader's Guide to Alternative Sexuality in Science Fiction and Fantasy*, ed. Eric Garber and Lyn Paleo, 2d ed. (Boston: Hall, 1990), xix.

28. Jean-François Lyotard, *The Postmodern Condition: A Report on Knowledge* (Minneapolis: University of Minnesota Press, 1984), 81.

Index

Shane Phelan is associate professor of political science at the University of New Mexico. She is the author of *Identity Politics: Lesbian Feminism and the Limits of Community* (1989) and has written articles on feminism, lesbian theory, Foucault, Adorno, and other topics.